D0078261

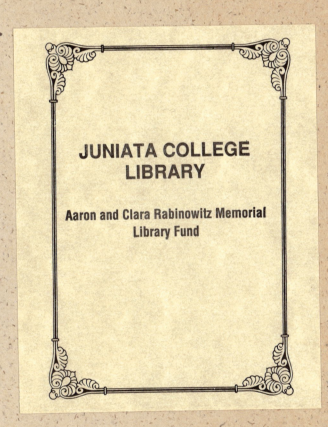

JUNIATA COLLEGE
LIBRARY

Aaron and Clara Rabinowitz Memorial
Library Fund

HILL
COUNTRY
TEACHER

Oral Histories from the
One-Room School and Beyond

TWAYNE'S
ORAL HISTORY SERIES

Donald A. Ritchie, Series Editor

PREVIOUSLY PUBLISHED

Rosie the Riveter Revisited: Women, The War, and Social Change
Sherna Berger Gluck

Witnesses to the Holocaust: An Oral History
Rhoda Lewin

FORTHCOMING TITLES

The Unknown Internment:
An Oral History of the Relocation of Italian Americans during World War II
Stephen C. Fox

Life on the Homestead: Interviews with Women of Northwestern Colorado, 1890–1950
Julie Jones-Eddy

Peacework: Life Stories of Women Peace Activists
Judy Adams

Between Management and Labor: Oral Histories of Arbitration
Clara H. Friedman

Grandmothers, Mothers, and Daughters: An Intergenerational Oral History
Corinne A. Krause

LA

DIANE MANNING

HILL
COUNTRY
TEACHER

*Oral Histories from the
One-Room School and Beyond*

TWAYNE PUBLISHERS · BOSTON
A Division of G. K. Hall & Co.

Twayne's Oral History Series No. 3

Copyright 1990 by G. K. Hall & Co.
All rights reserved.

Published by Twayne Publishers
A division of G. K. Hall & Co.
70 Lincoln Street, Boston, Massachusetts 02111

Copyediting supervised by Barbara Sutton.
Book design and production by Janet Z. Reynolds.
Typset by Huron Valley Graphics, Ann Arbor, Michigan.

Cover photo is the Divide Common School, 1936. Sibyl Bennet,
teacher, is in the back row, third from left.

Printed on permanent/durable acid-free paper
and bound in the United States of America.

First printing 1990.
10 9 8 7 6 5 4 3 2 1

Library of Congress Cataloging-in-Publication Data

Manning, Diane.
    Hill country teacher : oral histories from the one-room school and beyond
beyond / Diane Manning.
        p.   cm. — (Twayne's oral history series ; no. 3)
    Includes bibliographical references (p.   ).
    ISBN 0-8057-9102-7
    1. Women teachers—Texas—Texas Hill Country—Interviews.
    2. Retired teachers—Texas—Texas Hill Country—Interviews.
    3. Rural schools—Texas—Texas Hill Country—History.   4. Texas Hill
Country (Tex.)—Biography.   I. Title.   II. Series.
LA2315.T4M36   1990
370.19′346′097648840922—dc20   89-48349
                                                                              CIP

LA
2315
.T4
M36
1990

To Paul Balson
and
Edward H. Knight and Vann Spruiell

SERIES EDITOR'S NOTE

Historians since Herodotus have interviewed eyewitnesses to great events, but twentieth-century technology provides the opportunity for more widespread and systematic collection of oral history. First on wax cylinders, then with wire-recorders, reel-to-reel and cassette tape recorders, and video cameras, modern interviewers have captured an enormous quantity of reminiscences, from presidents to pioneers, literati to laborers.

Oral history may well be the twentieth century's substitute for the written memoir. In exchange for the immediacy of diaries or correspondence, the retrospective interview offers a dialogue between the participant and the informed interviewer. Having prepared sufficient preliminary research, interviewers can direct the discussion into areas long since "forgotten," or no longer considered of consequence. "I haven't thought about that in years," is a common response, uttered just before an interviewee commences with a surprisingly detailed description of some past incident. The quality of the interview, its candidness and depth, generally will depend as much upon the interviewer as the interviewee, and the confidence and rapport between the two adds a special dimension to the spoken memoir.

Interviewers represent a variety of disciplines, and work either as part of a collective effort or an individual enterprise. Regardless of their different interests or the variety of their subjects, all interviewers share a common imperative: to collect memories while they are still available. Most oral historians feel an additional responsibility to make their interviews accessible for use beyond their own research needs. Still, important collections of vital, vibrant interviews lie scattered in archives throughout every state, undiscovered or underutilized.

Twayne's Oral History Series seeks to identify those resources and to publish selections of the best materials. The series lets people speak for themselves, from their own unique perspectives on people, places, and events. But to be more than a babble of voices, each volume will organize its interviews around particular situations and events and tie them together with interpretive essays that place individuals into the larger historical context. The styles and format of individual volumes will vary with the material from which they are drawn, demonstrating again the diversity of oral history and its methodology.

Whenever oral historians gather in conference they enjoy retelling experiences about inspiring individuals they met, unexpected information they elicited, and unforgetable reminiscences that would otherwise have never been recorded. The result invariably reminds listeners of others who deserve to be interviewed, provides them with models of interviewing techniques, and inspires them to make their own contribution to the field. I trust that the oral historians in this series, as interviewers, editors, and interpreters, will have a similar effect upon their readers.

Donald A. Ritchie, Series Editor
Senate Historical Office

CONTENTS

ACKNOWLEDGMENTS

The insightful and unfailing sensitivity of Howard J. Osofsy and the thoughtful comments and support of Edward F. Foulks, Susan Tucker, Beth Willinger, Bill C. Malone, and Joan Seabright contributed greatly to an improved final version of this book. The generous assistance of Irma J. Bland, Clifford T. Hall, and Denise Dorsey fostered my ability to interpret the material presented by the interviewees. Suzanne Dickey, Janice Sayas, and Donna Franco provided careful help with the transcriptions and production of the manuscript. Ruth Andrews, Marian Chambliss, Arthur M. "Pat" Folks, Ginny and Robert H. Hughes, Cordelia A. Klein, Helen Hall Moffett, Willie Lee and Read S. Morgan, Zona Bell and A. H. "Bob" Pritchard, Marie Schwarz, Betty Strohacker, Constance White, Sister Rose of Lima, Sister Suzanne Marie, Henry F. Wilson, Miss Charles Wilson, and Joe Z. Haynes added immeasurably to the richness of the background chapters. The inspiration for this book belongs to Effie and Carole Green and Marguerite Bondy Bougere, Philo T. Pritzkau, Reginald Hannaford, Carl E. Nimitz, Grace E. King, Ruth Steinkraus, James F. Kilroy, and my first teacher and mother, Eva R. Daniels.

INTRODUCTION

Students in a class at the university where I teach recently refused to believe my graduate assistant's statement that before World War II women teachers often were forbidden to marry. Even the professor seemed skeptical, and my graduate assistant used the oral histories in this book as proof of her claims. The incident is a reminder that few people today know what being a teacher was once like and demonstrates the need to preserve the firsthand experiences of retired teachers.

Women teachers are familiar figures in literature, but given their literate status, there is a remarkable paucity of memoirs and autobiographies in which the subjects speak for themselves.[1] Interesting exceptions are Nancy Hoffman's *Women's "True" Profession: Voices from the History of Teaching*[2] and Frances R. Donovan's *The Schoolma'am*.[3] Those who taught before World War I can no longer share their experiences firsthand, but teachers who taught from the Roaring Twenties through the 1960s can explain personally how they viewed themselves and their profession. As the first generation of the first profession where large numbers of women were able to combine careers and family life, they hold a unique place in the history of both education and working women. For those reasons, I became an oral historian and interviewed some of them to preserve their stories for successive generations of teachers.

Some oral historians work with a research team and are granted funds to support their projects. My work was done alone and at my own expense. I began somewhat naively by looking for one or two retired teachers who would allow me to record experiences that I could share with my education classes. The best place to find suitable subjects would be in a community with many retirees, I decided, and I asked friends of my parents who lived in Kerrville, Texas, sixty-five miles northwest of San Antonio, whether they knew any retired teachers who might let me interview them. Through "a friend of a friend" I was put in touch with

Mrs. Elizabeth Shelton, who was then president of the Hill Country Retired Teachers Association (HCRTA), a local unit of the Texas Retired Teachers Association. To my surprise, HCRTA had 150 active members, and the energetic Mrs. Shelton, without whose generous help this book never would have come to fruition, requested volunteer interviewees from this group.

From the first call for volunteers, it was apparent that there were many more retired teachers than I alone could interview in depth. With Mrs. Shelton's and the other teachers' help I located potential interviewees who had once taught in one-room schools. Of the approximately fifty HCRTA members whom I eventually met, only one said she "hadn't done anything special" and refused to participate. It was a real loss to the project that no one was able to persuade this vibrant and generous lady otherwise, even though we spent many enjoyable hours together. Several teachers were tape-recorded who were not members of the HCRTA but were identified by members for possible inclusion.

Over a fifteen-month period, I interviewed approximately twenty teachers at least twice for three hours or more. I tape-recorded the interviewees until subsequent retellings of past teaching experiences began to reproduce previously reported material, but I continued to meet informally with them. I did not have one set of questions to ask everyone, but I did interject questions and comments to clarify or stimulate responses. After knowing these teachers over a two-year period in a variety of informal settings, almost without exception no real new material about their professional experiences emerged after the formal taped interviews were completed. This may have been because the interviews were untimed and anamnestic rather than ones following a formal schedule, or perhaps because the interviewees had shared all they wished to in this context.

I conducted and recorded all of the interviews, which were transcribed by me or graduate students in education under my direct supervision and then edited for ease of reading. For clarification, I occasionally changed the order in which the material was presented. When it became apparent that I would have enough material from interviewees who began their careers in one-room schools to comprise an entire book, the selection of which testimonials to include was made almost by default. The six white women who were included began their careers in one-room schools in rural Texas during the 1920s and 1930s and continued to teach until after the desegregation of the public schools in the 1960s. The married black couple included began teaching in Texas rural schools in 1931 and were greatly responsible for the peaceful integration of the Kerrville public schools during the years 1963 to 1966.

The interviewees' initial teaching experiences spanned fourteen years from 1921 to 1935. Although four of them began during a time when the rest of the country was experiencing the Roaring Twenties and four began during the Great Depression, their early teaching experiences were virtually indistinguishable because all began in small rural country schools where money was never plentiful. Thus, the book describes the experiences of a particular generation of teachers. Some of the women interrupted their teaching careers for marriages or children, but all continued to teach during their adult lives and most retired at the mandatory age of sixty-five. Their careers spanned a time of major changes in the American educational scene, including public school desegregation, compensatory programs such as Head Start, mandated special education, consolidation of schools, standardization of education (including IQ and achievement testing), and the end of school prayer. The last interviewee to retire did so in 1975.

My intention was not to focus on only one locale when I first went to Kerrville, but including teachers who taught in a relatively defined geographic area in the same time frame enabled me to trace common threads of their experiences. An emotion or event recalled by one interviewee can be validated by reference to the essentially similar memories of others. Reports that otherwise might seem highly personal or idiosyncratic can be evaluated properly as a trend shared by others in similar situations. Thus, the validity and reliability of the data, often cited as shortcomings of qualitative methods, were improved by the geographical and historical parameters of the study. Although limiting the interviewing to one locale makes generalizing difficult, the detail provided may facilitate other researchers' comparisons and contrasts with other settings by heightening similarities and differences.

SPECIFIC PURPOSES

These oral histories of retired teachers preserve the unique experiences and contributions of a generation of teachers who pioneered in combining professional and family life. As the interviewing process progressed, I grew increasingly interested in understanding the social and personal meanings of a number of humiliating intrusions into teachers' personal lives not extracted from women in other jobs. The most costly aspect of these intrusions was the prohibition against marriage for female teachers that was widely practiced throughout the United States, particularly wherever and whenever jobs were scarce, until World War II. By written contract, single female teachers (but not male) were forced to choose between marriage and career. A wedding ceremony meant the termination of a woman's paycheck, the independence it brought, and the opportunity to pursue the other gratifications of practicing one's profession.

I also was intrigued by the personal characteristics that enabled these teachers to overcome socioeconomic obstacles, including the special restrictions imposed on women teachers, that defeated most of their generation. Those character traits that enabled them to challenge the obstacles of poverty, gender, and race and to clear new paths for professional women appear to differ from the strengths typically associated with men. Although their stories as told here do not describe all facets of this strength, their words reveal common coping styles and defense mechanisms that might elucidate it.

It should be emphasized that no attempt was made to draw a complete portrait of any particular teacher. Descriptions typify the group and not the person chosen to illustrate a particular characteristic.

ENVIRONMENTAL IMPACT

Character is shaped by environment, and the environment the interviewees shared—the often lonely, sometimes challenging vastness that is rural Texas—intrudes on the teachers' oral histories as much as any human character does.

Texas provided a particularly appropriate setting for an oral history of teaching experiences because it was settled and urbanized later than other parts of the country. Rural electrification, for example, did not reach Texas until the 1950s. Although the stories told here should not be used to derive conclusions about people and events in other states during the 1920s and 1930s, readers can use them to project across time and imagine what earlier teachers elsewhere may have experienced.

The "Hill Country" referred to in the title of this book is the region of Texas where most of the interviewees spent the greater part of their teaching careers. It is hilly, rural, agrarian, and dotted with rivers—not unlike certain parts of Germany from which many of its settlers came. It is a harsh environment, often blazing hot in the summer and frigid cold in the winter. A good physical description of this land, which spawned the thirty-sixth president of the United States, and of its impact on the people who lived there prior to World War II is given in Robert Caro's *The Years of Lyndon Johnson: The Path to Power.*[4]

Of interest here is the region's geography and its influence on and meaning to the teachers interviewed for this book. The teachers share a pride in their citizenship in Texas in general and in Kerrville in particular. More than one teacher tells of her efforts to get a teaching job "back in town" from where she had come or aspired to live. This reflects a clear hierarchy in which jobs in a big school in a large community were perceived as superior to and were paid better than jobs in small rural schools. The tale heard throughout the book of moving from one-room rural schools to large, in-town schools is the story of upward mobility.

The land is characterized by flat, unbroken miles of fields and grazing land but also by tree-studded hills laden with fragrant spring peach blossoms, and these contrasts are reflected in the spirit of the people. The untamed rawness of the "wild west" is experienced in the premeditated murder of a sheriff and his deputy after a school play, but the generosity of a close-knit community is displayed when a timid young woman is offered her first teaching job because she needs one. Despite verbal adherence to principles of democracy, social prejudices are widespread. The Germans of Fredricksburg, the poor whites of Medina Lake, and the blacks and Mexicans in Kerrville have definite places in the social hierarchy described by the teachers, and the speaker is quite likely to express a particular pride in his or her own ancestors.

The isolation and boredom of life in rural communities can scarcely be imagined in an age of telecommunications. As one teacher said, "There wasn't any picture show. Wasn't anything." Several interviewees describe the importance of Christmas and end-of-year school programs. These events could make or break a young teacher, who could be accepted or rejected by the community on the basis of this twice-a-year ceremony attended by parents and relatives and by ranchers and cowboys for miles around. Of equal importance was church life, and the young female teacher who failed to meet community religious standards lost her contract. In such a setting, then, imagine the excitement generated by dressing up in hat and gloves to ride a horse-drawn buggy twenty miles across hot, plowed fields to high tea at an English neighbor's, as one teacher describes.

Several teachers mention climbing down from buggies and opening the gates so that the horses could pass through. Even today one can drive for miles and miles in a car and still see nothing but prairie and fences, interrupted only by the gate that the party's lowliest person, usually the teacher, would have to jump down to open.

"Being a lady" is important to the women in this book and is a paramount reason given for choosing teaching as a career: it was a *lady's* only choice. In a land of grueling poverty, the vagaries of nature and the U.S. economy of the twenties and thirties must have made achieving or maintaining status as a lady precarious indeed. Most interviewees mentioned the "unladylike" jobs they had as schoolteacher—chopping wood for the school fire, hauling water, scrubbing the school floor. This was the kind of back-breaking work that the schoolchildren's mothers did day in and day out, in broiling heat or finger-numbing cold, and it is not hard to imagine that the desire to escape this grinding toil motivated some young women to enter teaching. The physical work teachers were called on to do reflected local standards for other rural women as well as the poverty of the community and not community insensitivity to the ladylike aspirations of the schoolmarm. Education was valued, but so were other considerations—namely, survival.

From this environment and the people who were shaped by it emerged the one-room school. Often little more than a shanty, some schools could be mistaken for shelters for animals by modern viewers. The remnants of one I saw never had more than a dirt floor, and cracks of daylight showed between the round, thin trunks of bushes or small trees used to form the walls. These schools were built by the fathers of the children who attended them, and their styles matched the families' own resources of time and money. Sometimes the schools were temporary shelters used for only a year or two while there were enough school-aged children in the families of a rancher and his employees to justify their own teacher and school. The school year was short, sometimes only seven months, and its duration was determined by the weather, the seasonal jobs that children were needed to perform, and the amount of money the families could raise to pay the teacher.

Having a school that served only one or two families had practical benefits. Because travel was difficult and uncertain (if not outright dangerous) and took time away from home chores, parents did not want their children to venture far away from home. Feuds between families and entire communities to maintain their small schools and avoid consolidation continued into the 1960s, and today the only one-room school in the hill country—the one on the Divide—faces some of the same problems as those in the past.

EMERGENT THEMES

These teachers lived and worked in a common place and time, and the close-knit agrarian life they shared fostered a degree of intimacy between teachers and community that is unparalleled today. Rules about teachers' personal behavior are just one manifestation of this phenomenon, but the closeness was widespread and reciprocal. Today it is unusual for a school superintendent to give an unmarried teacher fatherly advice about dating or for teachers to make the kind of effort to know intimate details about their students' personal and family lives that yesterday's teachers did. Sometimes the links between teachers and community became bonds that chafed, but often those links nurtured a mutuality and caring that seems lost. For example, many teachers deeply mourned the deaths of the young World War II soldiers who recently had been their pupils. One teacher in this book even wrote a poem commemorating her feelings.

In many communities the teacher's role was almost that of a family member—that of mother to her flock of pupils. Although scarcely more than a child herself, the young teacher was given parental authority and served as surrogate mother in ways unheard of today. She scraped mud, brought in the wood, made fires, and swept the floor. She brought food from home and purchased new clothes for needy students out of her own meager paycheck. Physical punishment in school was seen as an extension of parental responsibilities; children knew that "a spanking at school meant a spanking at home."

Teachers often taught in their home communities and were known from childhood by the families, and when teachers came from a distant community, they were encouraged to board with a school trustee who would act in locus parentis for them just as they did, in turn, for the schoolchildren. The boarding arrangement allowed the young teacher to absorb local standards and customs and complete her moral education, and she, in turn, played a major role in transmitting spiritual and cultural values to her pupils. "Preachers and teachers" is a phrase used by several interviewees, who note a history of both careers in their families. As the husband of one teacher says, he learned more from his teachers than any preacher, and he, his parents, and his teachers felt that was appropriate. Within this context, the bitterness that many of the teachers express about the banning of school prayer takes on a special meaning. Banning school prayer was a professional issue as much as a religious one and, as such, attacked one of a teacher's most important duties—the improvement of her pupils' morals, character, and spirit.

HISTORICAL CONTEXT

The personal experiences of the teachers in the book take place within historical events that had major implications for the teaching profession. The taming of the "wild west" spurred the building of one-room schools, and fledgling teachers, barely more than children themselves, found a way to support themselves when virtually no other professional opportunities were available. As one hopeful young teacher stomped her foot and demanded to know, "How will I get experience if no one will give it to me?" She and many forgotten others found their answer in the one-room school.

The Great Depression brought a reverse of fortune for the nation and for women teachers, particularly if they were married. Countless women teachers were denied contracts so that men could have their jobs. Even dedicated career teachers tolerated the idea that it was "unfair" for two members of the same family to hold jobs while another man's family went hungry.

World War II is often credited with bringing the United States out of the depression, and it certainly marked the end of the prohibition against marriage for women teachers. Jobs for married teachers were not offered to provide equality of opportunity for men and women, however, but because of a pragmatic need for teachers to lead classrooms. Even when neither husband nor wife was particularly anxious for the woman to teach, pressure for her to return to the classroom was as pronounced as it was for other women to join the war effort in factories. One interviewee reports that her gate was practically "worn off its hinges" by school trustees entreating her to return to the classroom.

The increased opportunities for women in teaching were slower to affect black teachers and their pupils. In 1940 the principal of the all-black school in Kerrville was paid less than the town garbage man, and his teacher-wife was paid even less. Both earned less than their white peers. Not until two decades later was racial desegregation implemented, and with it some barriers were lifted for blacks in the classroom. (This process began somewhat earlier for Mexican-Americans, at least in this part of Texas, but it was still in transition when black schools were desegregated.) Although the desegregation experience of this group of Texas teachers was not marked by the violence that occurred in other parts of the country, it was a difficult time for both the black and the white communities. The black teachers' regret at the closing of their school is a reminder that ultimately the individual man or woman who stands in front of the children makes the real difference in the quality of the education they receive.

In addition to the historical events occurring nationwide, education itself was changing during this period. Both racial segregation and the "separate but equal" doctrine were eliminated during the interviewees' careers. Surprisingly, white interviewees make little mention of either. Only one white teacher says that "It was one of the most exciting things that happened to me because I believed in it." For the black interviewees, desegregation brought many professional and personal changes, not all of them positive.

Little information was elicited from interviewees about the experience of Mexican-American students and their teachers. One interviewee accepted a position as a teacher in the school for Mexican students as a means of getting a job "in town," but she later switched positions with another teacher who was assigned to the white high school but who had difficulty maintaining discipline there. Placing an inferior teacher in the school for Mexican-American students evidently was seen as a good solution to a disciplinary problem in the school for whites. Other interviewees recalled that Mexican-American students were integrated into white schools earlier than black students, but no one was able to recall any details of the integration process. Other than the one intervieweee mentioned, no one was able to identify any other teacher who had taught in the segregated Mexican-American schools.

Another group of previously "invisible" students, those who were physically or emotionally handicapped, also made its appearance during the 1960s as the interviewees approached the end of their teaching careers. Two of them—a black woman just entering the integrated system and a white woman forced to retire at age sixty-five—began second careers as special education teachers when no other teachers knew how to teach these youngsters or wanted to learn. Characteristically, both became certified and earned master's degrees in special education even though they were already credentialed teachers and did not need to do so.

By the end of the interviewees' teaching careers most one-room and small rural schools in Texas were closed. The move toward consolidation and standardization affected American education as well as industry, and by the late 1940s the "bigger is better" philosophy reached rural Texas. Testing for achievement and IQ was begun during this time, and two interviewees raised the same questions good teachers ask today about the limitations of paper-and-pencil measures of children.

Consenting to be interviewed and then identified for publication in a book is an act of courage not immediately perceived as so by someone not faced with that choice. An oral history exposes an important part of a person to the scrutiny of others, and interviewees have no guarantees about what their neighbors' reactions may be. The specialness of the interviewees' lives and the importance of their contributions may not be as obvious to them as to others, and it is part of their exceptional characters that they are willing to share themselves in this book despite their sometimes considerable trepidations.

A friend and published oral historian who disguises the identities of her subjects said after reading a draft of this book, "You make your work sound easy. You should say how hard it is." Doing oral history is a lot of work, but the hard part is seeing to it that the trust these contributors have placed in me is not tarnished, even inadvertently. If any statements attributed to them or made by me offend or suggest that the individuals in this book are less than worthy of deep respect and gratitude, the fault is entirely mine.

Finally, I want to express my regret that not every story that was told to me appears in this volume. Be assured that all who shared their life stories with me contributed to my better understanding of the lives and times of earlier teachers.

Notes

1. Donald Roden, "From 'Old Miss' to New Professional: A Portrait of Women Educators under the American Occupation of Japan, 1945–52," *History of Education Quarterly* (Winter 1983):469–89.

2. Nancy Hoffman, *Women's "True Professions": Voices from the History of Teaching* (Old Westbury, N.Y.: Feminist Press, 1981).

3. Frances R. Donovan, *The Schoolma'am* (New York: Frederick A. Stokes, 1938).

4. Robert Caro, "The Side Irons," chapter 27 in *The Years of Lyndon Johnson: The Path to Power* (New York: Knopf, 1982), 502–15.

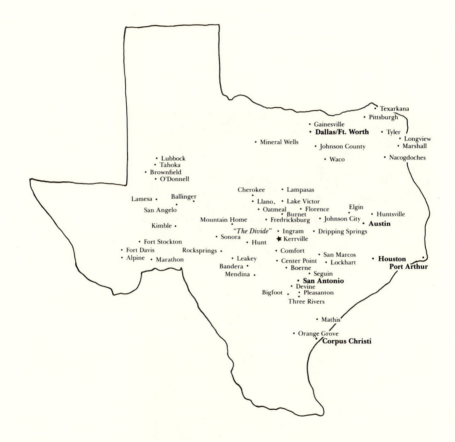

ONE

Sibyl Sutherland

Sibyl Sutherland and family ca. 1980.

I signed a contract out on the Divide that I wouldn't marry during the year. And that I wouldn't wear nail polish or startling makeup. Can you imagine? I look back and think, "Why did I sign it? Why didn't I say, 'I refuse to sign this thing?' "

SIBYL BENNET SUTHERLAND began teaching in 1935 at the age of nineteen out on the Divide between Kerrville and Rocksprings near where the only one-room schoolhouse in Texas today remains in operation near the Y.O. Ranch. She interrupted her career to be a wife and mother but returned to the classroom when the school trustees "started wearing the hinges off my gate" during the teacher shortage created by World War II. She continued to teach until 1982, when she retired from the Kerrville schools at the mandatory age of sixty-five.

Sibyl's life holds strong images: fainting from hunger after walking ten miles through the snow to college; sitting in a treehouse with her pupils throwing crumbs from homemade bread down to the wild turkeys below; writing poetry in the cemetery by moonlight as a young country wife and mother, a stone's throw from the derelict poles that would bring electricity, radio, and washing machine only when men returned home from war to put them into the ground; the jeers of "Old Lady Sutherland" hurled by defiant students at the end of a career. From these images emerges a personality that was often challenged by life's circumstances but ultimately triumphed over them.

Unlike most of her contemporaries, Sibyl was the child of divorced parents. Her father was a newspaper man, and her mother ran a boarding house. Perhaps because of her own experiences, Sibyl's mother encouraged her only child to obtain a college degree and be self-supporting. Sibyl washed dishes and won a work-study scholarship and eventually earned a bachelor's degree.

Sibyl displayed some individual characteristics that helped her meet life's personal and professional challenges. As the child of divorced parents, she must have experienced financial and other hardships, but she minimized problems. Similarly, in later life, the "lower community" of her one-room schoolhouse frowned on dancing and good times, but she had fun and attended her first dance with a school trustee from the more open-minded "upper community."

Sibyl had an ability to make others want to help her. The pull of her personality was apparent from the inception of her career, although she often underestimated it. She won her first teaching job in the depression over thirty-one other candidates but claims that "I always accused my mother of bribing them." She was warmly welcomed by the family with whom she boarded and by the community where she taught. Later, in one of the unhappiest periods of her life, she "fell into a situation" where a woman prepared her meals in exchange for her doing the dishes and was "adopted" by a family who thought she resembled a daughter who had recently died. Still later, the president of Schreiner College gave her a full work-scholarship and after learning she had fainted from hunger during an exam, declared she was eligible to eat free in the faculty dining hall.

Although Sibyl often elicited help in her career from significant life figures (precursors of the mentors sought by today's career women), an important side of her character is reclusive and introspective—dreamy, creative, self-sufficient. She is a woman who once wrote poetry by moonlight. Unique among the teachers interviewed, Sybil never expresses an ambition to have a career. Some of the women wanted to be teachers; others began with a different ambition but transferred it to teaching instead. With her opening words, Sibyl says she was content living as a trapper until her mother forced her to get a teaching job. Her only other stated goal came recently in retirement when she asked to have time to be alone and read.

Just as Sibyl underestimates the attractiveness of her personality to others, she also externalizes credit for her considerable abilities. She attributes her career success to higher forces: "All my life long, I guess the Lord must have been with me. Nearly everybody came looking for me and said, 'Will you teach for us?' "

In spite of her initial indifference to a career, many episodes in her life attest to considerable effort exerted, first to attain credentials and then to exercise her craft with distinction. In fact, once established in her career, she remained in it for many years "until I got it out of my system." The humor in this remark was given a practical and reality-oriented twist by the young teacher when she taught some recalcitrant students a lesson by stranding them on the schoolhouse roof where they had climbed despite repeated warnings. The altruism that is evident in other teachers also was displayed by Sibyl, who clothed a poor girl in her class every year.

In addition to the idiosyncratic features of Sibyl's life, the story she tells illuminates certain historical conditions. First, Sibyl observes that teaching was a good opportunity for women who did not want to marry and have children. Perhaps this possibility occurred to her more than others because of her similarity to a friend's sister who had died in childbirth. She tells the reader to read the tombstones in the cemetery to learn how often young women died in childbirth in those days.

Second, Sibyl's vignette about how the school trustees "started wearing the hinges off my gate at Center Point wanting me to come back and teach" personalizes how World War II opened up teaching to married women universally for the first time. Only a shortage of men allowed women equal opportunity as teachers.

Third, in spite of the cruelty and chauvinism of some men (such as the professors who deliberately embarrassed her in class), there were incidences of remarkable kindness by other men who supported the education and professionalism of women. Notable in Sibyl's life were Dr. James Delaney of Schreiner College in Kerrville, Texas, and several of her principals.

When we try to understand why the teachers tolerated certain conditions modern women reject, it helps to remember that the world then was vastly different. In one anecdote Sibyl and a friend were driving through Odessa, Texas, on their way to college in Alpine, and the waitress overheard them saying they were going to continue driving to Fort Stockton since a cattlemen's convention had booked all the hotel rooms in Odessa. The waitress refused to let the two girls continue on the road at night and found them a place to stay overnight. As Sibyl herself says, "You wouldn't do anything like that today—go into a stranger's home!"

In retirement, Sibyl enjoys the pleasures of the reclusive side of her personality. She is the only interviewee in this book who is not active in the Retired Teachers organization and says she had enough of joining as a teacher to last a lifetime. Instead, she enjoys the solitary delights of reading and shares the love of her growing family of grandchildren.

♾

Divide Common School, 1936. *Front row,* second- and third-grade students; *back row,* seventh- and eighth-grade students. Sibyl Bennet, teacher, is third from left.

I didn't want to teach. My mother practically drove me into it. I'd been to Schreiner College for two years, and then I stayed home a year. I'd finished high school at sixteen because I started school when I was five, and we didn't have but ten grades at that time. After college, I just stayed home and trapped. I caught fox and ring tails and so forth.

Then one day Mother said, "You can't sit around here. You need to get out!"

She told me later she was just like a mother bird shoving her little one out of the nest. She said she could just see me staying at home 'til I was an old lady.

I always accused her of paying them to hire me. She went out with me to the interview. I didn't want to go talk to them. I was very shy. So she went out and just flat talked for me. They said they wanted someone who had a car and did I know how to drive? I didn't, but my mother assured me that I could get a car and that I could learn to drive.

So out of thirty-two applicants, I never did know why they chose me. That's why I told her, "I'm sure you slipped them something on the side to take me!"

But anyway, we came back and bought a Model A Ford. I paid six hundred dollars for it. It wasn't new, but it wasn't old. It was a good car, and I got eight hundred dollars for it when I sold it—more than I paid for it.

My stepfather taught me to drive. I went out from driving on paved roads to the Rocksprings Road, which was like nothing that you've ever been over in your life. You literally lurched off of one embankment down to another one just off of ledges! One ledge to another—bouncing.

I've often reminded my mother of the day when she hauled me out there and put me down. I cried all the way out, saying, "You know I don't want to do this. You're just doing this to get rid of me."

"Nonsense!" she said. "You'll get used to it. You might even come to like it."

When I was arguing I didn't want to teach, I said, "I don't like kids." She said, "You don't know. You've never been around any."

We argued like that the whole way to Rocksprings.

She took me to Mr. Auld, where I was supposed to stay and share a room with his seven-year-old daughter. That was really an eye opener.

That night it rained fifteen inches. You couldn't think of going to school the next day. I sat around the house and stared out the windows and wondered, "What have I gotten into?"

The next day I started out for school in the car with the Auld girl. The reason for the car was I was supposed to take some of the children to school with me.

When I stopped to pick up the little Snodgrass girl, I got stuck in the mud. Her daddy came and got a chain out of his car and helped me get mine started and on my way again.

I got down to about the third gate, and then the motor died. I couldn't start the car again. So I walked to Mr. Thurmond's where I was supposed to pick up another child and told him I couldn't start the car. He came out and shook my car. He got hold of the top of it and just shook it like this. Something popped out, and we went on.

When I finally got to school, there were all these fathers and mothers and their children sitting around waiting. They'd been there since eight-thirty A.M., and here was the new teacher arriving an hour late!

I hadn't had any training about how to issue a book or anything. I hadn't had any practice teaching, and I was just literally beside myself. But I managed to get out the books and register them just by looking in the register itself and finding out what I had to have. I gave them a list of supplies I wanted them to get and somehow got through that first day.

On the way home that afternoon—I had just one little one with me by that time—I ran a stick through the rear tire, and it blew out. I climbed out of that car, walked to the house, threw my books on the front porch, burst into tears, and cried, "I want to go home!"

Mr. Auld just said, "Oh, stay with us a litttle while. You'll come to like it."

It was depression times. That's why there were thirty-two applicants for that one teaching job. They didn't have the standards then that they have now. You could go to college for a year and go out there and teach.

I was about twenty years old . . . not quite. Nineteen. I made twenty during the year. After I'd taught just a month or so, I came to love those children. We had such a good time together, and I felt I started some things with them. For instance, they drank out of an old dipper and bucket, and I told them that wasn't good for their health. So every morning I hauled a little small barrel, put it on the front bumper of that car, and went down with Mr. Hughes and filled that barrel with water. I made each one bring a wash pan and towel, and they all had them on a shelf with their names over them. Each one brought a tin cup, and we dipped from the barrel. We used that water to wash our hands before we ate. They thought that was so great.

I tried to teach things that the whole class—from the first through the sixth or seventh—could understand. Except for their reading, math, and spelling, we'd have this sort of general class. There wasn't any special curriculum you had to follow. You got your books from the county superintendent, who was Judge Atkins here at that time.

We built rock walks. All those years they'd had school out there, and the path struggled through the mud to get to the two out-houses the boys and girls used.

I said, "This is foolish. Let's lay us a walk."

A creek was fairly close by, and those boys just hauled big rocks one at a time out of that creek. We fit them together, turned them around until they fit well, and built those walks. We spent a couple of months. We carried sand in from the creek bed to fill in the cracks all in between so they could walk down there without getting mud all over their shoes.

I don't know if the walks are still there.

I guess the little old schoolhouse is. We used to hold some wild dances in it. Some of the church members out there in what they called the "lower community" were very much churchgoers. But the "upper community" wasn't so much that way, and they loved to dance. Well, when they moved the new school out, the powers that be just decreed there weren't going to be any dances. It was going to be used as a church and as a school and as nothing else. But there was a little old school further up the road where they still held the dances.

When Mr. Auld first talked to me, he said, "Do you dance?"

I said, "Well, yes, I dance, but it's not necessary. I can keep from it if you'd rather."

"Oh, we like for our teachers to dance. Sure."

In fact, I went to my first dance out there with him. The other trustees didn't much like it, though. They were always fuming and fussing.

They had what they called the upper community and the lower community. A certain bunch of ranchers lived above Garvin's store, and that was the upper community. The lower community was below Garvin's store. I knew the lower community better because I lived in with them. I met the others at dances, and knew of them, but didn't know them that well. They were fine people, and I always had happy memories of the time I spent out there.

Church was right in the school building, but everybody did strictly as they pleased about going. It was a community thing. One month the Baptist minister came out, and the next month the Presbyterian. They just divided them up. People went. Those of a particular congregation usually just went to one meeting a month. I occasionally went. I didn't pay any attention to which one.

The next year when I went back, they increased the school year by a month and added the eighth grade because one child wanted to add the eighth grade. They asked me if I'd be willing to teach it, and I told 'em, "Yes."

I had seventy-five dollars a month. What was funny at that time, you never could get it. They paid you in scrip, so I'd have to borrow from the bank. Some time that month the money would come in to pay off that note. But I constantly had a note in the bank. With the interest on the note, I was really getting less than seventy-five dollars a month, when you get down to it. But it went just as far as what I was making at the end. I paid twenty dollars a month board, and I paid twenty dollars a month car payment. My gasoline was cheap at that time because it was about twelve cents a gallon. So the rest of it was mine to gloriously spend on beauty shop appointments and whatever my little heart desired, and my clothes looked better than they do now.

That year I had an experience. Some of the boys got to climbing up on the roof. They laid a board from the tree to the corner of the house and would climb up there. I told them repeatedly not to go out. Next time I looked, they'd be up there. So one day I just went out and took their board down. I went back into the building. I could hear them calling and shouting. I rang the bell for them to come in and, of course, they didn't come. They were up on that roof.

I could hear them shouting. So I went out, and they said, "We're ready to come down now."

And I said, "Well, I'm not ready for you to come down. I told you to stay off, and twice you've ignored that and gone right on and climbed up. So I'm going to leave you up there until you've had all the roof-sitting that you want. Then I'll let you down."

Then I put that board in the fire and burned it.

One of them said, "I'm going to jump off here, and if I get hurt, it'll be your fault."

I said, "No it won't be, either. Because I told you not to get up there."

"I'm going to tell my father," he said.

"Good," I said. "I'm going to tell him, too."

Anyway, I finally got them down after they'd been up there about an hour longer than they wanted to be. That did put a stop to it.

One particular day Judge Atkins came in. It was May Day, and the kids had woven up a little crown out of buttercups and bluebonnets and crowned me Queen of the May. It was noon, and we had just finished eating. I was sitting with this crown of flowers on my head when Judge Atkins drove in. I went out to greet him and invited him in. He said he had come to visit and would like to spend the afternoon with us. So I rang the bell, and all the kids came in.

I just talked my heart out. Here this was my one visit of the year!

When he left, we told him goodbye and that we'd appreciated his visit to us.

He looked down at one of the kids and said, "Gee, Miss Bennet, you sure look funny with those little flowers on your head."

And there I'd been teaching all afternoon with that thing sitting on top of my head! I never had made an explanation to him of why I had it. I'd just forgotten about it. I was so embarrassed.

I thought, "I wonder what he thinks?" But he got out of there and went, and I never knew.

When I was staying at the second place out on the Divide, where this lake was, one day I washed my underwear and put it out on the line to dry. And here came the lady of the house all out of breath, "Barney's coming! I know you'll want to take your things in so he won't see them. You won't want him to see your underwear. Run get it off the line real quick."

I blinked and said more or less, "I don't mind it being out there."

She said, "I've lived with Mr. Klein all these years, and he never saw my underwear." Six or seven children, I'm sure he saw her underwear sometime, somewhere in there. I thought that was just hilarious. I guess it's just the way people are brought up.

My mother never went to that extreme. She had three lines, and she would hang sheets on the outer ones and then put our personal clothes down through the middle. Maybe that was out of a sense of modesty, I don't know. She never did say.

But I ran out and got them off the line so Barney wouldn't see them. It was just four or five panties and a couple of bras, and maybe a few hose.

I paid room and board at both places I stayed on the Divide. At the first place, they really were fairly well-to-do. They had good meals, and they really used imagination fixing our lunches. Of course, the little girl's had to be fixed, and mine too, and they fixed the same ones. You really never knew what you were going to have. There would be some delicious sandwich, or maybe a little jar of stew, or fried chicken. Just something really nice. Always such a neat dessert, and something different.

When I got to the second place, I got where I couldn't even eat lunch because I had a bologna sandwich and an apple every single day from the time I went there until I left. And a thermos of milk. They didn't have refrigeration, and that milk! I just got where I couldn't even drink it. It had an odor or a taste that I couldn't stand.

I signed a contract out on the Divide that I wouldn't marry during the year. And that I wouldn't wear nail polish or startling makeup. Can you imagine? I look back and think, "Why did I sign it? Why didn't I say, 'I refuse to sign this thing?' "

11

I also signed at O'Donnell that I wouldn't marry during the school year.

You had to wear a certain type of stockings. They had to be that lisle. It's that cotton stuff, that creepy crawly stuff. And you had to wear brogan-type shoes. But when I taught on the Divide in '35 and '36, I taught in boots and britches.

That first school where I taught is the only one-room school that still exists in Texas. Today it's on the Y. O. Ranch—between Kerrville and Rocksprings, below Mountain Home—though it wasn't on the Y. O. at that time. Back then it was down on the Dee Hughes Ranch. It was a little seven-month school. That first year I had three first-graders, three second-graders, a fifth-grader, a sixth-grader, and a seventh-grader— nine students in all.

It was about 1935. The ranchers were afraid that Hunt was going to close down their school so they moved it off the Dee Hughes Ranch and across the highway onto another ranch. They were afraid they'd have to consolidate—make their children come into Hunt.

Hunt wasn't very big—not even a town. I guess fifty people lived there. But their school served a pretty big community. They had quite a good school for it to be such a small little place.

The ranchers built a little rock school, which served as school, church, and community center. When they built the new building, they didn't get around to building any outdoor privies. This was very worrisome in that year because the boys just went in one direction, and the girls in another. All there was out there was a shin oak, which is a low, shrubby brush about waist to chest high. I'd wait until they all got back, and then I'd depart in another direction away from all of them. You can see over a lot of it, but we just assumed distance was decency. After you went a certain distance out there you hoped nobody could see. This was miserable to me 'cause I went still a further way away from the children, but I always had the feeling, you know, I don't know whether I'm far enough away or not. I was always uncomfortable all year because I never knew whether I was further enough away. Just distance was decency. That was about it. I never knew, and I was just miserable over there. But that was the only thing I didn't like about it.

The state tried to shut down the Divide school last year, the last ranch school in Texas. Charles Schreiner the Third went over to the legislature and fought for it. Where they live, they're fifty miles away from every-thing, and he convinced them the children would have to wait too long for a bus.

Today the school still serves the ranches around there. It has five to fifteen students at a time depending on how many ranch workers there are and how many children they have. The ranch workers' children and the ranchers' children still go to school together—just like always. Some of the better-known families out there have been ranchers for generations, and their hired workers were there for years the same way. They were lovely people, wonderful to me, and I guess that's what made me decide to launch out on a career in teaching.

When I taught out on the Divide, most children came into Kerrville for high school. Some of the parents moved to Kerrville and sent their children. Some of the children moved by themselves or with their mothers alone and had room and board with a family. Most of the kids who came from the country were honor students.

In the Divide school, they learned from each other. They shared in whatever area of study the grades above them or below them had.

I believe it's still the same today.

After two years teaching on the Divide, I decided to go back to school and get my degree. Mr. Klein, one of the trustees, came to me and asked me if I planned to come back. Cordelia, a sister-in-law of his, wanted the place. I told him I had been thinking about going and getting my degree.

He said, "We can't hire her if I'm a trustee. I'll resign and give her a chance at it if you don't plan to come back. But if you want the school, it's yours, and I'll continue to be a trustee."

I told him, "Well, suppose I just burn my bridges right here. You just go ahead and resign and hire her because I'm going to school."

So I sold that car but not right then. I went on out and went to summer school. A girl from Center Point went with me. We went clear to Alpine—here with San Marcos close to us. But I had heard it was cool and pretty out there, so I talked her into going out with me.

That was quite a trip out there. I'd never been hardly out of the county. I'd lived in San Antonio as a child, and Birmingham, Alabama, for a couple of years when I was a child. The rest of the time had been spent in this county. So we gypsied out. I ordered two tires from Sears Roebuck, and they came in at four o'clock one evening. We put 'em on, and I told Mother we were going to leave out. Well, she just had a fit.

"Four in the evening! Why don't you wait and go in the morning?"

"No, I'm ready to go. We're packed, and we're going," I said.

We drove that night and got to Odessa. They were having a cattlemen's convention, and all of the hotel rooms had been taken. We were sitting, eating a hamburger, deciding what we were going to do.

I said, "Well, there isn't anything we can do. We'll just have to drive on."

The lady that was serving us said, "You girls aren't planning to drive on towards Fort Stockton?"

I said, "Yes."

She said, "You can't do that. I won't allow it." She just threw a fit.

She said, "Let me call a friend of mine," and she did.

Her friend said that her son was out of town, and we could have his room. When we went over, she changed the sheets. You wouldn't do anything like that today—go into a stranger's home. But she was so nice, and so sweet to us. We had a bath and went to bed.

And then the son came home after all! We offered to get up and to leave, but he said, "No," he'd sleep on the couch that night. It wouldn't matter to him.

The next morning there was a lovely breakfast fixed for us when we got up. She wouldn't take any money for it. We kept saying, "Of course, we've got to pay you. Just to take two people out of the blue that you've never have heard of before in your life and to go to all this trouble?"

We insisted, and she finally said, "All right. Five dollars."

When we got to Fort Stockton I understood why they didn't want us to go on. It was a hundred miles with nothing but a filling station at Sheffield where you could get gas. The rest was just sage and lizards. Not another thing. Not even a buzzard in the sky. No wonder they didn't want us to go. My mother would have dropped dead to think I was starting out into something like that about eleven o'clock at night.

At the end of that summer, I just decided that I would go on to school. I sold my car for tuition and went back to Alpine. On my own. Out into the blue.

I needed money for room and board, and I didn't have a job. I called the dean of women and told her.

She said, "Well, come and stay at my house. Tomorrow we'll start looking for something."

I thought maybe I could get a job in the cafeteria, but she said, "No, the boys have that all tied up."

The dean finally called me and told me there was a lady who ran a boarding house, but she'd always had boys to help her. My mother had run a boarding house, and I said I understood a little about it. My teen years were spent helping my mother. The woman agreed to try me, to give me room and board for helping her. Her son and two of his friends lived out in the garage, and she'd turned the rest of her house over. She had about ten girls that stayed with her all the time, and then forty kids ate their meals with her. It was right at the foot of a hill.

I had an aunt who lived in Alpine, and when I first wrote and told her that I was going to Alpine for school I interpreted her letters as being a little snippy. Mother said it wasn't, that was just Aunt Annie. Anyway, when I went out there, I was determined I wasn't going to contact her, wasn't going to have anything to do with her, so I just went on. We drove in, found a place to stay, and I'd been there about two weeks when I ran into her in a grocery store. She said, "Sibyl, what are you doing here?" And I said, "I told you I was coming out to school."

"Well, my goodness, I thought you would contact us as soon as you got here," she said. "You'll have to come up and eat with us."

So my roommate and I went and ate with them several times during the year, but I wasn't around there a great deal. But she insisted, was really insistent, that we come and use her washing machine. So about once every two weeks I gathered up all the towels and sheets and went over there and washed that kind of stuff, but the rest of the time I just kept our clothes clean.

I suppose there was some place where the wealthier kids had their laundry done by somebody. There were always people around who did it, but we just did our own. I always thought it was strange.

I didn't stay in a dorm, I never stayed in one in my life. I stayed at boarding houses where the ladies had rooms—like seven or eight rooms. They would keep maybe fourteen girls, or boys, as the case may be—but never mixed. It was cheaper to stay in a boarding house than a dorm. We had four together in a room with two double beds. It was cheaper for there to be four in the room than for two in the room. I know our big bedroom had two double beds in it.

Here again I slept with someone and found it difficult. As long as I was there in the summer, I went with a girl from Center Point that I grew up with. She didn't smoke so we got along great. But several of the girls I stayed with did smoke and that did bother me because I never did get used to the smell of smoke.

I was a little unhappy that year because one of the girls was a communist. She got up every morning saying, "Hail to the Red Flag of Liberty!"

I got to where I'd leave at seven and not come back 'til ten at night. I just didn't want to hear her philosophy and her theorizing. She was very excited. That was the year they had a kind of a communistic uprising in San Antonio. You remember—they were a bunch of pecan shellers. She took part in that and some strikes and one thing or another that they had. It was a time when they said America was closer to turning communistic than it ever had been before because there were literally thousands of people who belonged to the Communist Party. This was in about 1936. Depression times—that's what brought it on.

Anyway, this communist group had a big meeting in the Municipal

Auditorium in San Antonio, and the veterans went down there and broke all the windows out of the Municipal Auditorium because the communists were holding this meeting there. She was there, and she thought it was so wonderful.

She'd come from up North somewhere, and she said, "You all do not know."

I had asked her what she was doing down here. She said, "Well, it's warmer. It's cheaper to live here. Up North it gets very cold."

She was just going to school on a wing and a prayer. She didn't have any money. She washed clothes for some of the other kids in order to even eat. She worried about food constantly. Maybe she'd had a bad time. We'd set up a card table and fix our meals. If you had a peach in the bowl, you would be halfway through your meal, and she'd start in, "Aren't you going to eat your peach?"

I'd say, "Yes, when I get through eating. I eat it like a dessert." Of course if you didn't eat it, well, then she did. She was always hounding. The other girls felt the same as I did, except they continued to be civil and nice to her. I just got to where I'd leave and wouldn't come back 'til night so I wouldn't have to listen to her. She was always telling me that I was naive, and I was this, and I was that. Which was probably true. But that's all part of growing up—people that you meet.

Alpine didn't have too many people. Alpine had possibly twelve hundred. That's what I liked about it. It was a small town, and I always felt at home and at ease in a small town. I do not like cities to this day. I'm miserable in San Antonio. People here shop down there, and I say, "What can you find down there you can't find here?"

I can remember going to San Antonio to buy shoes in my younger days, but this! There's so many people and everybody going in a different direction. They even smell to me. They even have a certain odor to them, cities do. You go in a place like Kresge's or Woolworth's. I don't know what it is. It's a combination of people I guess.

I can remember as a kid only having oranges at Christmas time. Apples we got more often. Oranges were always a part of Christmas. It was always an apple and an orange in your stocking at Christmas and a few nuts. Walnuts and yellow nuts which we called nigger toes. Do you know why we called them that? I don't know. And hazelnuts. My granddad would buy a box of oranges right before Christmas and bring them home. That's the only time I ever saw oranges up here. For years we didn't have bananas too often. Once in a while we'd go into a grocery store and see them. I thought they all grew on stalks. Like this on the stalk and hanging upside down. Chop a certain number off the bunch, and that was it.

Sul Ross College in Alpine had been founded in 1928, and I was going in about 1935. It was a four-year college, but there weren't too many students. I would say there weren't but about four hundred going there.

The president of the college was so involved in getting land set aside for Big Bend National Park that he spent all his time riding around doing that. He hardly functioned as far as school president was concerned. We saw him twice all year. Every time we saw him he was talking about this international park. Mexico was supposed to donate a certain amount of land, and we would donate a certain amount of land. Ours mostly. So the Big Bend should be named for Professor Morlock. By the way, he taught in Kerrville in his earlier years.

I think all those early teachers' colleges were called *normal* at one time. I know San Marcos was. I don't know what that meant—*normal.* Later on, they gave them the name of *teachers' colleges.* Normal schools were only two years. Then when they went to a four-year bachelor degree, they became a college.

I don't know why those eight were called teachers' colleges except I know you had practice teaching. You were taught how to make lesson plans. You were actually taught how to teach, and those were the only colleges that did that at that time. There was one at Commerce, Sam Houston Teachers' College, San Marcos, Sul Ross. There were eight of them.

So I went on and got my degree. It took me all that year and the next to get it.

In April I had written all kinds of letters looking for a teaching job, and I'd given them to a friend of mine to mail. Two months later he found them still in the pocket of his suitcase. He'd forgotten to mail them, and that alarmed him so that he stopped in every town he went through and gave them one of those letters with my picture and application. It didn't make any difference who it was written to—just gave them one!

Suddenly one day—it was about four days 'til graduation—I got a phone call from O'Donnell, Texas, asking me if I'd be interested in teaching the first grade. It was strange circumstances. The superintendent said, "The first-grade teacher here that we're very fond of's father has cancer, and she wants to spend this remaining year with him. She will have her job back just as soon as he passes away. But if you want it under those circumstances, we'll try to help you if we have another opening. And if we don't, we'll try to help you find one."

I said, "Sure."

He said, "Well, could you come up for an interview?"

I rode all night, walked out in fields and talked to guys on tractors. They said, "Yes," I could have it.

All my life long, I guess the Lord must have been with me. Nearly everybody came looking for me and said, "Will you teach for us?"

So I came back to Alpine, graduated, went home, packed my things, and went back to O'Donnell.

Well, O'Donnell was an eye opener, too. It lies between Lubbock and Lamesa—on the high plains. Lamesa's the next large town above San Angelo. There were no trees, no water, no hills—on the high plains. I thought, "If I could get back to where there are some trees and water, I'll never leave again."

Even Alpine, as far west as it is, is like a little Switzerland minus the snow. There are lots of hills and trees. Alpine's hills are higher and more closed than here. You can't look any direction without seeing more hills. It's a strange kind of mixture. Some of it's like our hills with timber on it, and some of it is those strange-looking hills like they have way out West— like Monument Valley. Fort Davis is nearby and it's heavily timbered. It's five hundred miles from here. It's just in a little pocket of timbered land. All the rest is flat and level. Just sage.

I don't know why I was so homesick there. Every day I'd go to get the mail, the tumbleweed would be stacked up against the door until you'd have to claw it out of the way. Then I'd get the mail, go home, and lie on my bed and cry a while.

I found a place to live with a lady and her husband and her elderly father. I had a room there. They were nice to me, and people asked me out. I did nothing to try to make friends with those people. I just laid at home and cried a lot. I never have known why I acted like that. I just felt so far away and so cut off from everybody in the world.

I wasn't pining away for anyone. In fact, I started going with one that I had gone to school with. He had two sisters. He always thought I looked so much like his sister, and he told his father and mother that he'd met a girl that was just like his sister that had died the year before. She died in childbirth.

When they saw me, they hugged me—the father and mother—and they said, "You look just like Charlotte. Exactly like her."

They asked me out very often, and I got where I went pretty frequently to their home. I went with this boy to shows and things together, but we didn't have a great thing going. The times I wasn't over at their house I was just miserable.

One of the teachers that taught there, the second-grade teacher, would worry about me. I had kitchen privileges at the place I was staying. I had stocked a neat little pantry, but it just stayed there, and I never did cook anything. I ate peanut butter and crackers, and cheese and fruit, and cereal, whatever I could eat that I didn't have to cook.

And yet I drifted into a nice relationship there. This lady did not like to wash dishes. She was very neat. She washed out all the plates, stacked them, and everything. They didn't have dishwashers, and she just loathed washing dishes. She had really pretty nails, and she always wore rubber gloves. She would sit there and go like this, and I thought, "My goodness! Here I'd washed for forty people and could sling them out faster than you could think of."

So I just got in there. It took two minutes to wash them. She would just die over that, "Oh, you are so nice! I saved you a dessert."

She got to saving me a whole meal so I got more home-cooked food than you might think. I wasn't doing it for that. I had just started doing them 'cause they were there, and I didn't like the looks of them. She would never wash them more than once a day and sometimes once every two days. But they were stacked, and she'd put a cloth over them. I thought, "Why does she hate to do that so? What does it take? Five minutes?" She liked to play bridge, and she liked to keep her hands nice-looking.

This second-grade teacher would worry, too, and say, "You need to come over. You need some vegetables. Come over to my house tonight. I'm going to cook you a meal."

She, too, hated washing dishes. So the trade was made. She'd cook for me, and we shared expenses on the groceries. We'd buy them, and I'd go over to her house. We'd broil steaks or pork chops, something like this, and she'd cook spinach or corn and these kinds of things. We'd sit and eat and talk and laugh and visit with each other. Then I'd get up and wash the dishes and clean up the kitchen and go home. We did that any number of times.

I also traded labor with a girl when I was up in school. She absolutely loathed washing clothes. My mother taught me when I was growing up to wash my hose, panties, and bra every night when I took them off and hang them up. She said you constantly had a clean supply, and there's no smelly, dirty clothes lying around in a closet somewhere. So I just automatically did this every night. Well, I got to taking my roommate's, Dorothy's, and washing hers at the same time. She said, "Well, you wash for me, I'll iron for you."

I thought I had the best of the trade 'cause I didn't like to iron. She ironed all my blouses and skirts and did a beautiful job of it. So I washed for her, and she ironed for me.

My friend's sister had died in childbirth. That happened pretty often in those times. In fact, if you go out in the cemeteries and look at those dates that are on graves, a great many children died with diphtheria and whooping cough. So there are all sorts of children's names there, and many women did die in childbirth.

I remember a lady in Center Point. Everybody was so upset over her. She had six little boys. Everybody had their babies at home in those days, and some neighbor lady or relative would come stay. With her last baby, she started hemorrhaging after the doctor left, and by the time he got back to her, she had died and left those six little boys. Her husband, his name was Wharton, reared those boys. Never did marry again. And if you go to her cemetery today in Center Point it has, "Ruth Wharton, mother. Love."

Teaching probably was a good opportunity for women who maybe didn't want to get married and have children. A good many taught. Short of nursing or working in a beauty parlor, about the only opportunity a woman had to get out and do anything was teaching. I guess there were secretaries, too, but that never occurred to any of us. I never had a friend who became a secretary. The ones I know of were all men.

I think of Miss Minnie Irving. I can't imagine her ever even going with a man. She was head postmistress. She was a teacher a long time, and then she became the town postmistress for about twenty years. She was so exacting about how things were to be done in the post office. If you brought in a package, if it wasn't tied up or taped the way she thought it ought to be, she'd tell you to take it home and do it over. She drove people nutty like that. Precise. Every penny accounted for. Everything done the way it should be done. I'm sure it's the only time in the history of that town that the post office was run the way it should have been run.

Another one of my teachers was a stickler for convention. I can't see her going with any man. Just like two teachers there in our retired teachers' group. They have never been married. I bet one of them never even looked at a man other than her brother-in-law.

One of the kids came in one day and asked me, "Who is that teacher that looks like George Washington?"

I all but died laughing because I knew that it was Minnie. She wore her hair parted in the middle. It came down and made two kind of rolls here over her ears. Mostly white, some of it was grey. It was white on each roll. She had that austere mouth held a certain way. You knew instantly who George Washington was.

Yet I was very fond of her. I found out some things about her when I taught next to her. She clothed a child every year. She picked a child in her room who she felt was in real need and bought her a dress. Always a girl, never a boy. She bought dresses and shoes. I thought that was so neat and so good of her that I started doing it, too. It really was a rewarding thing.

I would contact a little child first and ask if she could go shopping with me some afternoon. I would usually go down to J. C. Penney or some place like this. I couldn't afford something vastly expensive. I would tell her, "Now I want you to pick out some underwear, two dresses, a sweater, and a pair of shoes." And oh, she would be just beside herself, trying on styles!

I never did a boy either. I was strictly girls.

Once I found a little girl whose mother was dead. She was living with her father and older siblings. Her hair always looked so stringy, simply horrible and unwashed. So I asked her if she would like to have a permanent? She stayed after school one evening, and we washed her hair down at the place where the kids washed their hands, and I gave her a home permanent, cut her hair and bought her some hair ribbons. I showed her how to tie bows. Oh, she was just delighted. Thrilled to death!

When I took that child home, my heart just bled for her. They didn't even have an outdoor privy, somewhere out there in Oak Park, way to the end of nowhere. She kept saying she could walk from Oak Park. She didn't want me to go home with her, but I took her all the way there. There was an old board laid across a muddy ditch that they walked over. Their house was real tiny and terrible.

I thought, "Well, it's a wonder that that kid was as clean as she was." She wore the same old clothes, kind of grubby, and then I found out her mother was gone.

I taught another one how to braid her hair. It was growing so limp and terrible. When I had the children, I used to have them write something like, "I wish . . . " and they could write about what they wish, and "I'm afraid when . . . " She was forever saying something about her house. She was ashamed of her house. She wished she had a bigger house. She wished she had a nice house. If she had six thousand dollars, she'd spend it on a house. This went on constantly with her. I taught her how to braid her hair. It was long. She insisted on it being long. So I taught her how to both French-braid and how to just regularly braid her hair. It looked a lot nicer after that.

I taught a little girl one time that I and the other teachers had got to noticing. We thought she dressed funny. Her clothes were a lot longer than other kids' were. She'd come to school with a thing tied under her chin and gloves and galoshes when nobody else in the whole wide world was wearing them, and we got to thinking, "What kind of people must she have?"

We found out she was an only child, and she was reared by this rather older father and mother. The child was very talented and musical, but she just didn't act like other kids. She sat in the library and read when other kids were out playing on the playground. Her parents seemed so concerned about her health. If it rained or if it was cold, she didn't come to school.

I would see them eating in places round town. The child had perfect manners. Everything was "Please" and "No, thank you." But I thought, "What have they been preparing her for? She isn't ever going to fit in with her bunch."

I don't know what finally ever happened to her. She had a beautiful complexion. I just wonder if she ever got away from them—became a different person.

Some of the retired teachers here married late in life. One was married in her forties. She went socially with a lot of people and seemed to have a good time. In fact, she used to pain me 'cause she would always try to act younger than she was. She'd come down the hall skipping in the morning, like a child would, and here she was in her forties. But she met her husband, and they seemed to hit it off okay, and as far as I know they still do.

The one I told you about before, the postmistress? She was rather tall and thin and somewhat masculine-looking in all her ways. I remember her being so austere—never a frill, never a lace. She wore a bar pin and a white blouse and a black skirt, and that was practically her uniform. Back when I was a student myself, and she was a teacher, someone told me one day, "Miss Minnie wants you." I just turned into a state, a mass of jello. What could Miss Minnie possibly want with me? She didn't teach me, but she did keep a study hall that I was in.

So I went up and said, "Miss Minnie, did you want me?" She said, "Yes, come with me."

So I went with her. We went into this study hall, and we walked down the aisle and stopped at the desk that I sat in. She said, "Did you do this?"

Well, I had to squint to see what she was pointing to, and here was a little "SB"—probably scratched with a pen. I probably did do it, but I had no memory of it. Those were my initials. I had no memory whatever of scratching it on there with a pen, but I supposed I must have 'cause it was on there.

I just said, "Yes." There it was—*SB*.

She said, "Well, just a moment."

She went up to her desk, took out a can of varnish, a piece of sandpaper, and a brush and said, "Sand that off, and paint this desk."

So I did.

When I returned them to her, she said just as calm, not at all unkind, "We mustn't scratch on desks."

I said, "Yes, ma'am," and made my escape. But I always remembered that 'til the end of time.

The whole town called her Miss Minnie. Even when she was postmistress, she was Miss Minnie to everybody. A lady lived with her. They lived out on the edge of town, and Miss Minnie did all the outside work. She milked the cow. She gardened. They say she wore pants and put on boots and did all this outside work. Her friend kept the house and cooked. They were together for years—were buried together in the cemetery. Nobody ever questioned their being together. You never heard any unkind word about them. In fact, I can't conceive of Miss Minnie being anything other than Miss Minnie. That was her life.

Everyone in O'Donnell was very nice and sweet to me, but I was so glad when that year in O'Donnell was over. The superintendent kept his word to me because he took me to Brownfield. I got a place there. He took me to Tahoka. I got a place there. But I kept writing letters of application back closer to home and finally to Kerrville itself. All summer long I'd take one job and then resign to move to another one closer to home. When I had a chance at Kerrville, I took it.

I taught there a year, and then I got married in 1941 and resigned. I didn't have to quit, I just decided I was through with teaching. I was going to stay home and have a family.

Of course, Pearl Harbor was a year later. War broke out, and that's why my career didn't end at all. They started wearing the hinges off my gate at Center Point wanting me to come back and teach, but I said no.

I stayed home two years and had quite an experience with my husband. We couldn't get any help. We got out and cut a hundred acres of corn, chopped the fodder, and tied it with strings because there wasn't any wire. We couldn't get anybody to help us. The government had started rural electrification, but there wasn't any wire obtainable. Here were all the holes dug, the poles lying on the ground, and no wire. And no help at all. We had to do everything ourselves.

Sometimes I'd go out at night and sit on one of those posts that were lying on the ground. There wasn't any light you could see by. At home, we'd always had electricity in town. I reared my children without electricity. The only one I ever had any electricity with was the last one. 1951 was when it finally got to us. We used lamps and old kerosene stoves.

Other times when I got angry at my husband, I'd wander off into the cemetery. He'd come looking for me, and I'd be sitting on a tombstone writing poetry.

Poems about life, and love, and death, and all sorts of things. I have some of them still. Funny, I've never written any since.

Between the time I finished high school and when I went to teach in the Divide, I went to school at Schreiner College. It was during the 30s— '32, '33, and '34—and they just started to let girls go there. We had six girls and all those boys. You would have thought that would have been hog heaven for us, but I can remember being so embarrassed so many times. For instance, I was in chemistry class with thirty boys, and I the only girl in it. The teacher would start to tell a kinda off-color joke, and then he'd remember I was present. So he'd just break off and the boys'd go, "Ooooh," and that would embarrass me.

Then I was in a psychology class with a whole bunch of boys and invariably the instructor would say, "Well, let's get the female point of view," and he'd read mine out loud to all of them. He was always giving us subjects like, "How I'd act if I were a member of the opposite sex." Mine would be the only one in there that'd be an opposing view.

A lot of those boys were from families who were traveling, or they were foreign students. Some of them were children with problems.

I had a ride to school in the morning, but I did not have a way home in the afternoon and I walked. It was ten miles. So when you talk about walking through the snow, I did literally. I was dying to go to school.

I always wanted to go to college. When I finished school, it was the depression. I thought college was just as far away as the moon.

After graduation, I went up to the high school and asked if they'd allow me to arrange the library Dewey Decimal System. They had just stacked the books alphabetically. I made out all those cards and started rearranging the library.

My mother came in one day. She said she'd been talking to my father, and he'd agreed to pay half my college tuition, and she would pay half. How would I like to go to Schreiner? Well, of course, they could have sent me just as easily to San Marcos cheaper because books, room, board, and tuition would all have been less than the tuition at Schreiner. It was probably thirty or forty dollars the semester hour then—way up there.

By Christmas, my father decided he couldn't do it, and he sent me a letter and said he could no longer do it. My father and mother were separated. Divorced. So Dr. Delaney called me in, and he said, "You must really want to go to school because I know you walk home in the afternoons."

I said, "Oh, I do want to go to school." I wanted to do just about anything—decent that is—to continue going to college.

So Dr. Delaney got me the NYA—the National Youth Administration— where they paid me twenty dollars a month. He said, "I know you make high grades in English and that you're good in literature. So I want you to write book reviews for our school paper, and I'll pay you so much for that." Then he asked me to tutor some high school boys in English. So three times during the day I taught grammar to high school boys while I went to college.

I got twenty dollars on the NYA, and the rest of it amounted to about thirty dollars. I just turned that in. I signed my check and gave it right back. Evidently they let it cover whatever I owed because they never did ask me for anything else.

I didn't know it at the time, but evidently I had hypoglycemia. I was one of those that got terribly weak and started feeling faint, and occasionally I did faint. It was because I hadn't eaten since morning. It was a matter of false pride because my mother would have gladly fixed lunch for me. She fussed at me all the the time about it, and I'd say, "I'll eat when I come in." But because I got out at different times every day, I'd give out on those long afternoons when I got out at four. My mother even took me to the doctor about it, but they hadn't heard of it back then.

I all but collapsed one day there at school, and they sent me over to the nurse. I was shaking all over. She asked me what the matter was, and I said, "I don't know. My knees got weak, and I feel like I'm gonna fall or something."

After that, Dr. Delaney called me in and said, "I want you to come over and eat in the faculty cafeteria"—being kind to me. He said since I was tutoring those boys, I was a faculty member, and he wanted me to eat in the cafeteria with the other teachers.

The next year Dr. Delaney said that I got a scholarship. That paid my tuition the second year. They did a lot for me. I was always grateful that I went to Schreiner.

After I taught in the rural school and before I went away to college, I went with this cousin to the church camp meetings. We'd stay overnight and camp out for two weeks. There were young people, oldsters, all kinds. Some of the girls chose to stay with their father and mother in their own tent. They have a place out there for mobile homes and campers, but very few go in campers.

The camp meetings are still going on now, and how many years is that? About fifty years and still going on. I think it started up in the thirties at the Fish Hatchery. Johnny Hill started it. They made the salad and the barbeque and the bread. A lot of people from here went just for all that food. This went on for two or three Sundays, just on Sundays. You'd go back home at night.

They'd have services in the open air building. The crying and carrying on some of them did at those meetings! It got to be kind of like homecoming.

By the way, we had a homecoming at Alison Hunt four years ago where all the stragglers came back. I had such a good time because the town was just like it used to be when I was little. All the Louis Park School people were there. The oldest graduate was from 1910. She was ninety-two. I never had so many stand up and hug me. And I hugged them, and we were so glad to see each other. Years ago, I had been homecoming queen, and my cousin was the graduation speaker.

I started school at Louis Park in the first grade, and I went back in the seventh grade as my father and mother broke up. I attended school there through the tenth grade, which was all they had. Then I came up here to high school in Kerrville one year, and then I went to Schreiner College two years.

There was a movie star from Louis Park. What was her name? They had a parade for her. It was hot, but they had a nice parade for it to be such a small town. The town was like it used to be. That's what I enjoyed. Every place that I was at, there was one that I knew. When I go down there now, I can't find five people that I know because all of north Dade County, Florida, has moved in, and the ranches have been broken up into little areas. Lots of mobile homes, this sort of thing, and you don't really know the people any more.

When I taught at Louis Park it was quite a bit different than when I was a student there. We no longer had the double desks. We had single desks that were screwed to the floor. Later on they put those desks on runners, three on a runner, and you could shift and move. I never did that 'cause the kids could move them around. They'd move their desks up close to each other and way far apart. They were always moving around, and I liked them when they were screwed down. They couldn't get out of place. That's just a notion I had about it.

Later on, when we had chairs, I put them in circles and all kinds of ways, and that was nice. You could put them in groups and do group work. But the trouble was you had to watch them half the time 'cause they'd switch them around to suit themselves and arrange themselves where they could have tea parties and such.

Yet I was never very strict about that sort of thing. I always let them chew gum from the beginning. I never could understand why teachers didn't do these sort of things in polite company. But I allowed the kids to. It seemed like after I announced to them that they could, they'd chew madly for a week or two and then give it up.

I used to tell the other teachers, "Some of you smoke, and I really don't like that. So I don't see why you object so to their chewing it if it helps them concentrate."

I had some rules about it. I said, "Chew gum as long as I don't see or hear it."

They'd say, "How can we do that?"

When I'd see it sticking out of their mouths or wound around their pencils, or pulled out to here, or in a big bubble, I'd say, "Ooooh, that looks like your liver or spleen!"

They'd all laugh about that.

26

Something else I tried one time, and it only worked in that grade. I could never figure that out. I had fifth grade, which is my favorite of all grades. I just love ten-year-olds. I got tired of this: "May I go to the restroom? May I go to the restroom?" No matter how much you cautioned them at recess to be sure they went, and set aside a time when they could go, there still would be somebody who had to go.

So I said, "Okay, just write your name on the board. When you come back, erase it. No one else may go as long as there's a name up there. If you abuse the privilege, we'll have to do away with it."

That worked fine. People seldom left—once in a great while.

I tried it in junior high, and it didn't work. They stayed out of the room all the time.

In the rural school where they had to go out in the brush, they would ask me permission to go, and I would say, "All right." I didn't have but eight or ten kids there so that wasn't so bothersome. When you've got thirty-two or -three, and they're ding-donging about it all the time, you find yourself spending more time.

They had a fit here in Kerrville when I let the kids just sign out. They wanted teachers to keep a record when kids left the room. I found I was spending more time writing down when they were going to the restroom than I was teaching. So I told the children when they had left the room three times, then they had to give me five minutes after school. Most of them didn't want to stay after school so that put a stop to that. But others, they'd just as soon stay their five minutes.

By 1942 I'd had my first child. I kept saying I couldn't teach because I had a baby, and they said, "Well, we have one teacher that has a baby just three weeks old. We're going to let her go home and nurse it at recess and whenever she needs to because she lives in the Baptist parsonage right across from the school."

"Well, I don't have anyone to leave my baby with," I said.

"Your mother can take care of your baby," they said. "It's patriotic duty. We need you." And they kept on.

Finally, my husband said, "Go ahead and do it."

So I taught two more years in Center Point.

Our principal that second year lost his mind. I think I decided when I met him that he didn't have one to begin with. He did such strange things. I mean at Christmas he left out and just never did come back. We heard he'd been put in a mental institution. He'd had a nervous breakdown.

He had installed some sort of system where he could speak to everybody in every classroom. We'd never had anything like it in any school. All day long these announcements would come over, "Attention all class-

27

rooms! Attention all classrooms! Who moved a chair out of the library?" It was just something like this all day long. And he did away with a lot of the things we'd worked so hard to get accredited at Center Point. It was just a little old, small-town school. And things like homemaking and the boys' agriculture he dismissed as nothing and put in commercial business type courses like typing and bookkeeping in place of them. I suppose the trustees allowed it. I don't even remember.

He was with us a half year. The principal, who later became the superintendent, felt just like I did about it. We talked about it any number of times. He said, "There's something weird about this person." The principal called me in after the Christmas holidays and showed me a letter the man had written in which he was applying for a position somewhere else. He said he was a small man, five feet and four inches tall, but he could lick his weight in wildcats. It was just a strange kind of letter to be a letter of application, you know. He signed it, "Yours truly and I hope we lick the Japs." And signed his name to it.

The principal said, "Doesn't that strike you as a strange letter of application?"

I said, "It certainly does."

Then he told me that he'd made superintendent, and he'd like for me to be his principal. He said there won't be anything other than if you'd consider it an honor because you won't have a raise in pay, and it's just a lot of hard work. You've got a bunch of monthly reports to get in. But I'd like to have you if you'll agree. So I did. I served that one year as principal.

He was marvelous, quiet spoken and in perfect control of the kids. He used to talk so softly. He used to say, "I'm not going to talk loud. They can get quiet and listen to me." You could hear a pin fall when he talked. He taught classes like everybody else. That was true everywhere I taught until I came to Kerrville.

After my one year as principal in Center Point, my husband moved in closer to the city of Kerrville. Again I thought, "Well, I guess my teaching career is over."

Then one day I met Mr. Daniels, the principal of Tivy Elementary. I'd taught for him one year before I was married. He said that he had a teacher that was going to leave at Easter and would I finish out the year for her? Well, I talked it over with my husband, and he said, "That won't be but six, eight weeks. Go ahead and do it."

Once I'd started back in, Mr. Daniels talked to me and said, "Why don't you come over?" So I agreed and started back teaching.

Let's see . . . I taught there until 1951 when my daughter was born. That year I decided, "Well, I'll stop for sure now." But I was back in seven months. I decided to stay with it that time until I got it out of my system, and I didn't get it out until two years ago.

My elementary principal, Tom Daniels, had a school here in town named for him. He would walk around the school yard and put his arm around a little child and say, "John, is your father better now? Is he out of the hospital?" He just knew everything that was going on in every child's life. He was the kindest, most gentle person.

If he ever chose, which was very rarely, to spank a child, he talked and talked and talked to that child. It would be a child he'd had in the office many times. Then he would eventually say, "Now, if you continue to do this, I'm going to have to punish you." So when the child went on and did it, he'd finally say, "All right, now you come on down to the office at three this afternoon." Just as calm, never a word of anger in his voice. It didn't happen very often, though. I'm going to say once every two or three years.

My junior high principal was Jack Murray. I always felt fairly close to Jack, and I liked Jack. He was a different personality all together from Mr. Daniels. He was more a gung-ho, macho type. Mr. Daniels was a gentle, quiet person. I came to be fond of Jack and to understand him, and I feel like he genuinely cared for me, too. I guess we both cried when I went.

I loved Katy, his wife. I taught both of his children. I always felt close to the Murray family.

One year someone told me Mr. Murray was looking for me. It was the first day of orientation. I had just been up there a little while before, but I went back up to the school. Mr. Murray said he wanted me to teach English in eighth grade. I just came unglued. I'd been teaching the sixth. He told me Miss Stevens had decided to resign. She'd had that throat cancer operation. She got up there that day and started crying and said she wasn't up to eighth grade.

I said, "I don't want to teach the eighth, Mr. Murray. I taught the eighth before, and I didn't like it."

He asked, "Will you teach the seventh?"

I said, "Yes."

So he hired Miss Stevens for the eighth and me for the seventh, and that's how I got in junior high. I never did want to teach there. I think that's a difficult age, and I believe only their mothers could really understand and love them at that age.

Mr. Daniels used to be good about allowing me to do things I wanted to do. I would get tired of the fifth grade and say, "I'm tired of being in the United States in geography. I want to go to Europe a while. Can I teach the sixth grade next year?"

He would say, "Yes," and quite often I would get children that I'd had the year before. I knew them so well that really it was a help to them and to me. I knew which ones were performing and which ones were not doing what they could. I'd say, "Oh, you know how to do that. You remember last year."

I would go from the fifth grade to the sixth and from the sixth to the fifth. He let me do that three or four times, and then I was caught in the sixth when they changed it over to the junior high. That was the reason he let me go on over to Peterson Junior High.

I cried because I didn't want to leave Mr. Daniels. I went and I told him, "I'd give anything to stay, you know," and he said, "I'd give anything to hire you back."

This experience taught me one thing in life. Sometimes you resist change, but when you go ahead, you're just as happy there as you were anywhere else once you settle down to it.

When I was teaching English, I gave them a six-weeks study on Funk and Wagnall's book, *Thirty Days to a Better Vocabulary*. We went through that entire book, and, oh, they fought me. After they graduated from high school, three of them went off to Officers' Candidate School. They came back and said, "Thank you. Four of the words from that vocabulary book were on the test. We know that's probably what saved us."

I said, "I figured that sooner or later you'd have some use for them."

I made them memorize poetry, too, and they just pitched a fit about that. One of them later on was interned for a while as a prisoner in World War II. He told me, "I sat there and went over and over those things you made us memorize." Like from Shakespeare. You know, "Good name in man or woman, dear my Lord, is more precious than any jewel" . . . "He who steals my purse steals trash." He said he'd say those things over and over, and I was so glad. He said, "I wish I'd memorized a lot more because it gave me something to occupy the hours with, and I did a lot of thinking about it."

I taught drama and role-playing, and when the kids learned poems, I'd have them act it out. They'd say, "Oh, this is silly!" But one of the boys I had, David—I'm real proud of David—was accepted to theatrical school.

I went to the library the other day and got a list of books that they considered for everyone to have read to be well-educated. I got to looking at that list, and there wasn't one I hadn't read. But a lot of them were things the teacher had made me read back in high school. One was *Pride and Prejudice*. I can't reconcile those two.

All those years in the junior high, part of the time I taught English and part of the time art. It started off with them knowing I had an interest in art. The principal asked me if I'd like to teach one semester of art in the eighth grade, and I told him, "Yes." So the next year he made it a full year, one class. During that time, we switched schools. The high school took the junior high, and the junior high went back to high school. Shortly after we got over there he gave me two art classes, then the next year three classes, then the next year four, and the next year five, and I was just out of English. I always missed that because I enjoyed my English classes.

I told him, "I've never had any formal art training." I'd had a few art lessons in watercolor and a few in oil when I was a kid.

He said, "Well, to keep 'em off our backs you've got to get twelve hours."

So I went back to San Antonio Community College and took "Teaching Art in the Elementary School" and some things like this. Then I took a course in silversmithing and cutting gem stones. Enough to get twelve hours credit. I also at this time began taking classes out here at the Point where they have artists' courses all year. They would allow me to take a two-weeks course and would give me credit for that. During that time I must have taken about eight different sessions out there.

I have wished many times that school books were written by teachers. I don't believe they are. I have bought books that looked like they would be marvelous, and then when you got into them, you have to ask, "Why in the world did we adopt this? It's going to be here for twelve years." It would be just impossible. I'd finally stick them in a drawer and go on teaching. We've found some that had half a dozen mistakes in them. You know, grammatical errors in an English book. They hadn't been edited. This sort of thing.

I have often said that the whole thing should be turned upside down and started over. I can't feel like what's being done is going to improve the situation. And I don't think paying teachers more money is going to make a good teacher. It has to be a caring person. I don't know whether there are too many teachers that don't really care.

I know for one thing I used to give my children essay-type questions to answer because you have to think to answer an essay-type question. When you give an objective test that you can run down the line like on a math or a spelling test, and there's just one answer that's right, children get where they can't write. They can't put an organized thought down on a piece of paper.

And you know another thing—the reading? When we used to read, we read poems by Celia Thaxter. We read about Rosa Bonheur and her paintings in the first grade. But when you say, "See, see, see, run, Dick run," when you get through with twenty pages of that, what have you learned? Absolutely nothing!

I'm ready to go back.

I remember the winter on the ranch. I'd come out with a kettle of hot water to pour on those gate latches so I could slide them back. I'd caution my kids not to burn their fingers with the hot tea kettle. I'd drive to Center Point and leave my daughter, and then make it back to school by eight o'clock.

Today, my daughter gets her children to school late every morning. She says, "I just can't do it."

I say, "You can if you want to. You just never have decided that it was important that your children arrive on time. You're teaching them a very bad habit—a very rude habit of not being places on time."

What's wrong with being a wife and mother? Today if a woman says she doesn't work, people look at her like she's crazy.

Years ago at O'Donnell, I had to make lesson plans for the entire year. I never could stick to those lesson plans. You'd have one section that they'd learn fast, and another section where they'd go slow. You can't plan a year in advance where you're going to be. The principal would come down and ask, "Are you on page so 'n' so?" I was only there once.

Fortunately, I had superintendents who allowed me a good deal of leeway. I hate organization and having to teach the same subject every-day at the same time. You can't just quit something they're really inter-ested in to get out another book and do something completely different. I just never could stand that.

I'd say, "I like broad periods of time. I may want to work three days hard on something, and then I'll catch up with the rest of it."

My superintendents always said, "Go ahead. Do it your way and get it done."

It's wonderful that all the way through I had supportive people like this that allowed me to do my own thing my own way. I always said, "If they get supervisors breathing down your neck, I quit that day because I can't survive."

The best superintendent I ever taught under was Ed Wildman. I liked Mr. Wildman. The teachers felt a closeness there we never felt after that. He let us all go over to the cafeteria, and we had coffee every morning together. We just sat around the tables, and we talked. We knew every-body in the high school. The schools were right together across the street from each other. We all knew each other, and knew what was going on, and felt close to him and to every teacher. But you know, there weren't but about eighty of us then. Later on when the school grew so much and there were over two hundred teachers, I never knew two people in high school. I never knew when people resigned, other than what I read in the paper, and when new ones were added. I never did meet them. I got where about all I knew was my middle school and one or two of the old ones over in the elementary that had remained there when I left.

Teaching was hard work, but it was very rewarding to me. I wouldn't take anything, of course, for the children that I knew, and the contacts and relationships I had with them. That was what was the really important part.

TWO

Knowles Witcher Teel

Knowles Teel, 1987.

My first year teaching was in 1924 in Lake Victor, Texas, where I went to teach for a term of seven months at seventy-five dollars a month. I was eighteen and had completed one year of college to get my certificate. I boarded with an elderly couple who had once been our neighbors on our ranch. She was like a second mother to me and heated a rock to be put in my bed every cold night to help keep me warm.

KNOWLES WITCHER TEEL began her teaching career at the age of eighteen in Lake Victor, Texas, in 1924. She spent most of her adult life teaching, even after her marriage and the birth of her son, until she retired from the Bandera schools in 1972. As such, she typifies the first generation of women teachers to combine a full-time professional career with being a wife and mother. Her pride in this unique status is evident, for example, as she talks about being among the original group to receive a master's degree in elementary education from Trinity College in San Antonio in 1952.

Although Knowles became a dedicated professional, she chose teaching almost by default. "Teaching was about the only decent thing when I was growing up for a girl to be," she says. "If you became a secretary somewhere, well, you got a hard name. They had a hard life. So I never thought of anything else but a teacher. And anyway, I always loved children, and that's what I really wanted to be." It is open to speculation whether she would have chosen teaching had other opportunities been available.

Knowles's views of what it meant to be a lady are reflected in her strong opinions about what was proper behavior for a teacher. Although she resisted the harsh injunctions against teachers and decried the arbitrary firing of her colleagues for dancing (one year she was the only teacher who avoided being dismissed), she hoped to witness the end of lunch duty before she retired (she didn't)—not because it was an unprofessional imposition but because it was inconsistent with her own image of what she held to be appropriate behavior for a teacher: "I didn't think it was right for a teacher to go back into the classroom all sunburned and wind-blown. Children notice small things and appreciate them."

Knowles began her career not in a one-room but in a three-teacher school, at a time when a young teacher was seen by herself and the community as less than fully adult. The transition between parental home and new community often was eased by boarding the new teacher with a family. When the arrangement worked well, as Knowles's first one did, the teacher truly became part of the family. Knowles said of the lady of the house, "She was like a second mother to me and heated a rock to put in my bed every cold night to help keep me warm." When Knowles was unable to mend a pupil's torn pants, she did not hesitate to turn to this woman, exactly as she would have to her own mother, for unquestioning assistance.

Boarding arrangements did not always work out well, however. In her second position, Knowles telephoned her mother to rescue her from living with the school principal and sleeping in the baby's room. The solution was a boarding house, where the behavior of single teachers could be carefully monitored. Although the "teacherage" inhabitants did not always adhere to the rules proscribed in their contracts, the rewards for breaking them usually were not worth the risk of being fired.

Like the families where the young teachers boarded, the church was a vehicle for conveying local community standards. Knowles and her colleagues attended religious services as they were told, but even their "correct" behavior could be misinterpreted as Knowles learned to her chagrin one Sunday when she heard herself being preached about from the pulpit. Her sister-in-law fared worse and was nearly fired when the church elders discovered that she could not play the organ as they had hoped.

The intimate ties between community and teachers was reflected in a closer connection between teachers' and pupils' lives outside school. Teachers who lived within a small community were well acquainted with their students' lives beyond the classroom. Knowles's interest stretched even to pupils who lived in a world "foreign" to her. She traveled to Medina Lake to visit the tent homes of children living in poverty. Indeed, she volunteered during World War II with the Red Cross Home Service and continued afterwards "because I liked it." In that role, she provided clothes to children from Medina Lake so they could attend school. Based on these experiences, the move from country schoolmarm to Head Start teacher seemed less a bold leap than a natural progression by a teacher who sincerely was interested in all her students throughout her career.

The historical significance of events that occurred during her lifetime does not escape her. Knowles's stories about her childhood provide something of the flavor of the "Wild West" she and the other interviewees experienced—including raids by Mexican bandits, the murder of an unfaithful wife and her lover (a crime that went largely unpunished according to the local mores), and a shoot-out after a school play in which a sheriff and his deputy were killed. However, gun fights were infrequent punctuation in the standard routine. Growing up, the usual evening entertainment for Knowles and her brothers was to play "beauty shop" while their mother fixed her hair. Such homely occupations provided comfort and stability in a world where the loss of a barn, a house, or livestock always hovered closeby.

In order to fully appreciate what the interviewees are sharing, readers must infer circumstances that are not always made explicit in the narrative. Behind Knowles's story is the financial struggle to earn a college degree without much assistance from her housewife-mother and her father, who was a sometime livery man, rancher, and foreman on her uncle's ranch. Moreover, the status of women and children was precarious at a time when death was a frequent visitor of the young. Like another interviewee, Gladys Peterson Meyers, Knowles's mother was an orphan who was separated from her brothers and taken in by an uncle with daughters of his own. In Knowles's own generation, polio struck her younger brother, who was disabled for life.

In telling the story of an entire lifetime, details that contribute to a remarkable accomplishment are sometimes lost. Reading about the stories and rhymes Knowles wrote to interest and motivate her youngsters is one reminder of the dedicated hours of service performed by teachers of her generation. It is also testament to the transformation of a once "mean" little girl into an altruistic teacher and thoughtful poetess.

Knowles's retirement has been a continued period of growth. Now in her eighties, Knowles is active in the Retired Teachers Association and her church and directs her creative energies into writing illustrated books of poems for her friends and family.

∽

Knowles Witcher with first- and second-grade class, 1928–30. Florence Elementary School, Florence, Texas.

A long time ago people often said, "Why did you become a teacher?" Well, that was about the only decent thing when I was growing up for a girl to be. If you became a secretary somewhere—well, you got a hard name. I don't know why, but they did. So I never thought of anything else but being a teacher. And anyway, I always loved children, and that's what I really wanted to be.

What was it like when I was a little girl? I was mean!

My daddy worked on a ranch. This was in Rocky Creek, between Lampasas and Burnet, near Leander. It was out in that area. We went to Lampasas to shop and everything, and the first two or three years we lived out there I went to a country school. That's where I learned a lot of things.

The first day we could get the seats we wanted. I always wanted the back seats. They were old lumber seats that had been built sturdy, like a bench with a back on it, and a big high desk that I could just barely see over. But we could hide all kinds of things down in that desk!

The little boys would be excused and go out to "the bushes." There was a knothole behind my desk, and the little boy behind my desk would poke a note back through that knothole. By the time he came back and tapped on the wall, I had the note answered, and I'd poke it back there. Teacher never did catch on.

Every once in a while boys would go hunting and get skunk all over them and come back to school. On a cold day—they always hunted in the winter, you know—their hides were worth something. Those boys would smell up the school 'til you just couldn't stand it. You just couldn't stay in there.

I have written a story. It started when I was about four, I guess. You see, I'm a thousand years old. This was the wagon train days. It started from Sonora, Texas. My daddy was a rancher on a ranch over there, and he married my mother, who was an orphan. An uncle and aunt had taken her to live with them. My daddy was working for her uncle, and they got married after she was grown.

We went by wagon train to a ranch that Uncle had bought close to Marathon, Texas, near the border of Mexico. When we left on this wagon train trip, I was about four years old. We stayed until I was about ten. We sold and left there. Mexico was having Civil War, and every once in a while around the ranches there was fighting. I've got all the battles recorded. This was before 1913 because I had a brother that was born in 1913. It must have been 1908 or '09—somewhere along in there. They were having war in there, and they'd run these peons across the border. That's what they called them. My daddy worked them on his ranch. So we had a lot of experiences with narrow escapes with both people.

My daddy was a goat man. He had thousands of goats. He went out there and took up the school land. He went out there working for my mother's uncle who was quite wealthy and had a large ranch. Daddy was the manager. Then on the side he got to buying up the school land.

There was some land that was set aside by the government for schools. I think it was fifty cents an acre you could buy that school land. Daddy bought eight sections but in different areas. They weren't all together. And then he had thousands of goats and hired these Mexicans. Most of them had come over the border because they had been born in Mexico. They were called peons. Daddy put 'em in camps out taking care of these goats. In the winter time they went down in the valley where it was warmer, and sometimes they built some shelters. But then—about March—when it started getting warmer, they took 'em to summer camp up on top of the mountains. Daddy would go up once a month and take loads of groceries to the camp. That was a big time because we'd get to go with him. Eat goat meat that was dried that they had stretched on lines. Never had any flies or anything like that up there. They always had beans cooked and coffee in big pots, and it was just a fun time. My mother and little brother would go, too.

My little brother was crippled. I didn't have much to play with. And then I had a baby brother, Max. They're both dead now. Scott just died three or four years ago. Both of those boys had emphysema and asthma, and it weakened their hearts. Both of them died of heart disease. I'd be just about out of family now except that in later years my Daddy married Lorena Glimp, who was a schoolteacher.

Every Saturday all these people came to town. Rachael Luna's* daddy, Wird, had a clothing store there, and somebody had a delivery wagon with a horse that bit. My baby brother, Max, was the cutest thing you ever saw. He wore a Buster Brown hat. I'd go to town every Saturday evening holding his hand so proud of him. One day he was walking close to the edge of the sidewalk, and that old horse reached over and bit him. Max was the maddest thing. Somebody saw it and gave him some money so it would make it better where it hurt so much.

Before Lampasas, we lived in Ballinger. But it was Texas all my life. I never did live out of state. When I was a little bitty girl, we lived in Ballinger. My daddy had a livery stable where they kept horses, boarded horses, and kept these wagons we rented out and all of that. That's where I burned the house down!

My mother had just inherited a little money from her parents' estate, and they built a new home with it. It was out at the edge—where the wind was blowing all the time out there in west Texas. A neighbor was moving away, and the wind was blowing so hard that my mother didn't

*Another interviewee.

want to take me and my little crippled brother. The neighbor's house was just a few feet away.

She had said to us, "Mrs. So 'n So is moving away today, and I've got to run and take them over there. You be good and don't play in the fire."

So that planted a seed. I couldn't wait until she got out of the door. During those days we had wood stoves with a wood box. We were packing to go somewhere on a trip, and she had been emptying things and throwing paper in that box, and it was full. So the minute she got out—I can remember this—I was just a little tiny thing, but I got my little chair, and I climbed up high and got in the match box, got me a match down, and I lit that paper. And then it blazed up so big it caught the wallpaper on fire and climbed up the wall so it frightened me. I threw the door open and dragged my little crippled brother out, and then I went back in to get all my dolls and dishes and things. Mother got there just as we got in the yard and I had gotten my things out. It went so fast 'cause I opened that door and that wind just took it everywhere right now before anybody knew it.

So neighbors and people came in, but they couldn't do anything about it. It just went. I guess they didn't have fire departments maybe like we have now.

My daddy was already at work downtown. Somebody came up to him and said, "Mr. Witcher, your house just burned down."

He said, "No, it didn't. I just left there."

And the man said, "You go home and see."

It burned the whole thing down.

Do you believe it? It was wonderful. I didn't get a spanking, and I got to take all my dolls and toys and things that I had rescued. We got to live in a new house, and people were so nice. They brought in clothes. I got new toys. It was just wonderful.

Then from there we went by wagon to Sonora, Texas. We had some adventures on the trip to my mother's uncle's ranch. The goats ran into what they call buckweed. It's poisonous, and some of the goats died. They had to stop several days and try to cure those goats before they could go on. But some of them died.

You know it's hard in west Texas to find water streams? Sometimes you could go up to the ranchers' ranches who'd give you permission, and they would have water tanks and you could get water. But one night we went to a lake in the river. When we got to the streams, it was salt water. All those goats just pawed the earth and howled all night. Daddy had to walk around all night long to keep those goats from wandering away because they were so thirsty. I remember my crippled brother Scott and I climbed out of the wagon and ran so fast down to the stupid river and got a drink, and it was so salty.

And wild animals'd come in to the herd and grab a goat. Even after we finally got to the ranch, they had a terrible time with wild animals. They set all kinds of traps. The herders had dogs, and they had to watch the animals all the time. There was this trail behind the house where we lived on my uncle's ranch, and they finally discovered that that was the trail where some of these wild animals came down to go to the water, and they set traps.

In those wagons, in the backs of them, were what they called *chuck wagons*. It was a sort of a kitchen. It had a big back that stuck out like this and shelves in there and a lid that came down to make a table. They stocked it with all kinds of groceries and cooked on the camp fire. My daddy would cook, and sometimes some of the men.

One of the Mexicans made me a stick horse out of a soto stalk. You know the Mexicans are pretty artistic. They made it big and put on straw for ears and fixed a stick on it so I could ride it. So every night in camp I'd get out and ride my stick horse. They made Scott one, too. He was crippled, and he couldn't use his. Along the way, one of those fell out of the wagon. I don't remember whether it was mine or Scott's, but we lost it.

My mother's uncle was real rich, and he had a big ranch there and also had this big ranch up in the mountains. He prevailed on my daddy to go out there and manage that ranch for him. It was twenty-four miles from Marathon and thirty-two from Alpine.

We went in two wagons with several hundred head of goats and milk cows tied behind so we could have milk on the way. I just had one baby brother then. The old cow wouldn't walk. She just refused to walk. So Daddy had to sell her someplace. I think it took us six weeks to get there.

This ranch is high up in the mountains, just like heaven. And there's a huge tank like a lake out in front of the house where the ducks were swimming all the time. In the winter that froze over solid with ice, and the men had to go around with axes and cut out a big square and give it a shove under the water. The stock would follow and get a drink. If they didn't hurry up and drink, it would freeze again.

We had an experience one Easter Sunday. A big snowstorm hit even though it was April already. There were no weathermen back there, but my father saw the clouds coming. So he got on his horse, and he rode as fast as he could over those mountains to try to get to those goats, to try to move them off those mountains back down into the valley somewhere where they wouldn't freeze, but he got there just as the snowstorm hit. They were freshly sheared. The only goats he had left were the Mexican goats with long hair—mohair. They had just straight hair, and they were in there for meat purposes. The herders were allowed to kill those goats.

So he lost all his goats. That was before the days of insurance. There was a big land company out there that was buying up all the land, and they wanted our ranch, so Daddy sold it. Harmon and Jackson. They own most of that country now.

Two or three years after my daddy had taken up a lot of the school land to hold it, we had to start building. This was government land set aside for the purpose of generating revenues in support of the local schools. He paid fifty cents an acre for it. You had to promise to live on it for so many months out of the year. That was called to *'prove* [*improve*] *up on it,* and people who lived on it were called *squatters.* You had to squat four months.

So Daddy got a bunch of these Mexicans come over the border plus an old white man who had come to that country for his health. He was a carpenter so he could build a little cottage—we called it a shack then—so we could go down there and spend the weekend. Then, as they developed the place more, they built a larger house. Wasn't too large. Wasn't but two big rooms.

Daddy had to go back up to Mother's uncle's place every so often to check on things, and when he went, he usually stayed two days or three. Well, one night he wasn't at home. There had been a lot of trouble in that area with these peons stealing, killing people, and taking their stuff across the border in the night. Mother was kinda sick that night so she went to the bedroom, but my brother and I sat on the floor and played games and played with toys.

I heard something and I said to him, "I'm scared. I'm going to lock the door." Then we went to bed, too.

Later, in the night, Mother heard the racket at the door, and she jumped out of bed. The night was real dark. There were these two Mexicans down on their hands and knees crawling right next to the house.

Daddy and Mother kept ammunition because of all of this. It was in a lard can, and Mother tried to light a kind of light to find the gun and the ammunition. She went over and raised that window and called those Mexicans. They were right next to the screen because there was a stick across the screen, and she raised it and called them to go away. But the rest of that night those Mexicans circled that place.

They would burn down homes Indian style and kill the people when they came out, so she didn't expect we'd even see the light of day. She just thought, "Well, they must have already killed the old Englishman that lived in a tent on the other side of us." He couldn't hear.

That night those Mexicans were circling around our house. Mother could see the pen where the horses were, and they had all the horses penned out there with a horse that could chop the ice. Looked like they were going to take the horses and try to go to Mexico. Guess the good Lord just looked down there.

She tried to get me to open the other window on the other side and put me out, and she told me to run. [But I wouldn't.] It was seven miles to the nearest neighbor. A white couple lived seven miles away.

She said, "You try to go to the Parkers and tell them what happened."

That was funny. That night I had a dream, and I was playing with my brother, and I said, "Scott, somebody shot me! I gotta run tell my mother." And I was screaming, "Mother! Mother!," and she grabbed me and shook me and told me what had happened 'cause she didn't think we'd ever live. So for the rest of the night we sat up in the bed and watched these Mexicans in the dark, circling, circling.

In the morning, the old Englishman came to work. They hadn't shot him after all. The Mexicans went out and got their horses and their plows. They were digging a big tank like a lake near the house. They went out there and went to dig. Mother went out there, and I was standing by them holding onto her dress, and I was scared to death. It was before my baby brother was born. He wasn't here then so I guess I was just five years old.

She put the gun there on the ground, and she said, "You come near my house in the night and I'll shoot you! *Vamoos! Vamoos!*" She said, "You'll stop at this! I'll shoot you if you come near the house anymore!"

They said, "*No sabe, no sabe, no sabe.*" Daddy didn't get home that next night, so I was scared to death. But the next night my daddy came home. He talked Mexican because he had been to Mexico, so he went out to talk to them.

They said, "Oh no, we didn't do that. We were walking in our sleep."

He said, "Well, you can walk in your sleep right now!" And he got on his horse and followed them all the way to Marathon. They put them in jail over there, but you couldn't do much with these peons, you know.

There were bad people in that part of the country, anyway. Kept them isolated out there. Not many people had gone out on those ranches. They'd go out there and check on things. But nothing was ever done. The sheriff told my daddy they tried to escape a couple of times, and one of them fell under the train and was killed. That's all we ever did hear about it.

I had another funny thing that happened there. I guess it was every Saturday or Sunday, all those men who worked for us would come to our yard, and Daddy would cut their hair. I had a whole bunch of little ducks—little baby ducks—and they were out there and nobody noticed them. That night they all started falling over and died. Daddy opened up one of those little ducks, and their little craws were stuck with that hair that fell off those men. Absolutely stuck! Nobody noticed what they were doing.

I don't remember on that ranch whether we ever had any pork. But when we moved out from Lampasas, they had what they called "hog-cleaning" days—hog killings. The neighbors would come in. First Northern, usually. They would butcher all the hogs. They had smokehouses, and they'd hang this meat up in the smokehouses and smoke it, and they'd have it all winter. Big hams and everything.

Then the next week they'd go to some other neighbor's house. And the same thing when the wheat and the oats got ripe. They'd move the big machines from one place to another. Everything that happened, the neighbors all came in, and they all worked together.

We didn't have much to entertain us when we lived on this ranch out from Alpine, and at night, well, my mother would let us play beauty shop and fix her hair. She had long curls, and we'd work and work and fix her hair. I don't know how she did it. I guess we didn't know much about beauty shops. I don't know what we called it, but anyway we fixed her hair nearly every night.

I can't remember that we had any books or things to read. I know we had toys. We'd set on the floor and play. But we had one of these old-fashioned . . . I think they call them phonographs. Yes, Victrolas. We had records that we played all the time.

A funny thing happened when we lived on my mother's uncle's ranch. Well, we were already down in our own home, but he'd come down to see us. He'd come by train to Marathon, and they would hire someone to bring him out there. By the time he got there, he was so drunk he couldn't walk. He drank, and my daddy would have to pour coffee down him half the night and walk him. I still remember those days. Daddy walking him up and down—Uncle Orve. But I was just thrilled. I could take all that 'cause I knew Daddy was going to say, "But he always came with that buggy full of gifts!" He brought all kinds of things from apples to oranges to candy. One time he brought Mother a rocking chair. They just laughed.

See, my mother was an orphan. Her mother and father died when she was five years old. So her uncle's wife—her aunt—raised my mother. She had one brother and another aunt raised him. They didn't see each other much in their younger days. Uncle Orve had four girls. So Mother fitted in just like she was one of them.

During those days, he had lots of cattle on his ranch out from Marathon, and when market time came, they shipped them by train to Chicago. He always went with them to ship the cattle, and pretty soon the packages started to come in. He'd get all drunk and buy gifts for everybody. When he'd buy materials for the girls' dresses, he'd buy a whole bolt of the same material and a whole bolt of something else so they'd have material to last. Dresses alike. It was too funny. I don't guess the money worried him 'cause he was pretty well fixed.

He had come to Sonora by wagon train from somewhere back East. Also his wife had a sister that had a bunch of children. Her husband had died, and they came along too. Uncle Orve always had a house on his ranch for them to live in. This aunt, she had four or five boys and one little girl, and he always kept her in boarding schools and so forth. As the boys got older, he'd hire them on his ranch, or else he got jobs for them. Their mother lived to be, I think, around a hundred years old. We used to go see her when I was an itty-bitty girl. It was always lots of fun to go and see Aunt Bea. She lived to be a real old person.

In Alpine, in third grade, I had to board in order to go to school. Mrs. Starr, the lady that I lived with there, was a friend. They had a great big two-story building that was right near the street. No playground, just the sidewalk. She was a very sweet Christian lady. She took care of me. She took care of my clothes and fed me and got me to school and everything. She had a little girl, and she had a little boy. Her husband had a meat market in the same block. A big pink building. And out just a little ways was the school.

So I boarded with them, and we got many scares. Mr. Spinell—I have this in my book—the Spinells, the couple, had one daughter, and she was in my class at school. One night we went to the movies, and she and I were sitting together in the front seat. There was a big ruckus in the back of the house, and people jumped up and screamed, pushing and trying to get out of there. Some of them were trying to get to the front to find their children. My daddy and mother happened to come in from the ranch that day, and they were there.

This Mr. Spinell's wife was just beautiful. She had worked at the army camp, the USO or something and entertained at that canteen. He got jealous of her, and so he said to her that evening, "Would you like to go for a ride? We'll go by and pick up a friend." That's what they did. He got out on the road and got out his gun and killed his wife and her friend.

That got back to town, and that's what was happening in the theater. Every time they heard an unusual noise, people thought it was a raid from the border. Everybody was screaming, and finally somebody came up and got this little girl—she was sitting by me—and said, "Come with me, honey." It was her mother that had been killed.

About that time my daddy appeared. They got word of it, and I never was so glad to see anybody. He was pushing through the crowd to get me.

Well, for days after that the soldiers—'cause this man was a soldier that was killed—raided. They were out everywhere, every night. They eventually had to take Mr. Spinell out of town, or they would murder him.

They were looking for him. Part of the army had the bottom part of Mr. Starr's building rented. They had a lot of stuff stored there. So they were constantly milling around and coming over there where I was boarding. Except we lived in the back part of the house. And there was the upstairs rooms where people had their apartments up there, too. A couple that lived there had a ranch out towards the border, and one day they found them out there where the Mexicans had killed them.

Mother and Daddy had gone back to the ranch, but those soldiers kept on. One night they were just all over that building—just everywhere looking for the man. It just petrified us.

The soldiers never found him. No, they arrested him and put him in jail.

What happened to my little friend? Her grandparents took this grandchild and changed her name after Mr. Spinell shot their only daughter.

When I boarded with Mrs. Starr in Alpine, it was too far to go home on the weekends, and there were no cars. Mother and Daddy'd come in by hack—something like the old surreys. Had two seats, had a top on it, and had isinglass—things that buttoned on the side to close them all in. They could come in a day. They always stayed a night or two.

Mrs. Starr was really sweet. I had friends, and we went to church and everything. I missed my parents, oh yes, but I wasn't homesick—not as homesick as I got the first year of college.

It kind of varied how long the school year was, depending on how much money they had [to keep the school open]. It might be six months, might be seven months, might be eight. I think it was eight months in Alpine, but when I went to Marathon—when I went to first grade—I think that was just seven months.

Eventually, we sold the ranch near Alpine and moved to this place on Rocky Creek out of Lampasas, Texas. It was too hard to arrange school for me in Alpine. An old man had a ranch. He was so old he had to give it up. He didn't have any relatives, so he sold it to my daddy. It had a beautiful stream and everything, and when we first got there the cotton was all ripe and ready to pick. We got in at night, and they told me about the cotton, and I couldn't wait to wake up for it to be daylight. I ran into the cotton field. It wasn't very far away, and I picked my apron full and came back. I was so thrilled over that cotton. They had a hired man who came in and picked it and put it in sacks and so forth and so on.

When we moved to Rocky Creek, we went to the rural school. Just one room. That's where we passed the notes and played out under the trees and, I guess, went to the toilet a little farther away.

The first year I went to first grade in Marathon. That's when my baby brother Max was born. The next year, my daddy hired a governess to go out and live on that ranch, and he also brought one of the little Mexican boys that had run over the border that didn't have any home. There was one big old two-story store in Marathon at that time. They sold everything from groceries to toys to yard grass. Everything. And also they acted as a bank. That old man, Mr. French, ran that store.

My daddy also picked up a man and his wife, and they had a little child. He knew them in Americus. They had a tent in the backyard, and the lady was supposed to work for my mother, but she didn't know anything. Those people don't really know about houses, washing and cooking and so forth. She did a little, but she was crazy. She thought if that little boy drank water, he'd die.

Daddy'd try to come in at least once a week and talk to the old woman and give her all the instructions for the week. She had her back to the water pan we kept for the chickens, and that little boy ran up there and was taking a drink. So Daddy kept her in the house so she wouldn't look around and that little boy could get a drink out of the chicken pan.

One day Mother nearly scared the little child to death. She heard the oven door slam. She went in, and that little boy had opened the oven door and gotten him out a handful of hot biscuits. She didn't stop him. He got out there with hot biscuits. He had something to eat.

One night we had the nicest thing on the place. We had a brand new two-story barn, and they came in screaming that the barn was on fire. The neighbors from all over the country came. We had a windmill and a great big tanker, and the only thing they could do was stand on the steps around it and dip up that water and try to carry it. Well, the barn burned down, of course.

Well, Daddy didn't stop at that. They finally decided that maybe one of these hired men may have thrown a cigarette. Or else they had hauled in a lot of feed from the fields that had been baled, and they say sometimes green feed will start a fire. They never did know.

The sad thing was my daddy had just come back from Lampasas that day with a big, big load of expensive stock feed. About all they could do that night was to get all the stock out of there. The chickens and the horses and everything that was sheltered in the barn. And those horses were crazy! In a fire you can get one out, and they'll run right back!

Oh, we had lots of tragedies. My daddy had Mexicans living all down on the creek in tents. They were supposed to cut wood, thinning out the land for fields, and my mother would pack a lunch. She wasn't afraid of anything. If I had a child, I'd be scared to let him go down there—afraid he'd get on a snake or fall on the ground. But my crippled brother and I would take our lunch and go down everywhere. My little brother would throw things in the water, and we had a little foot bridge. It was a log. We started back across that log, and I fell in and got wet. I think my brother, he lent me his pants. I can still see him if I shut my eyes—crying and hopping along on that crippled leg with just his shirt and his underwear on. His shirt was long. It came to his knees.

That one little brother had polio, but back then they called it infantile paralysis. My mother went on a trip somewhere with some of her relatives, and on that train was a child just screaming everywhere. Nine days after she got home, my little brother got sick.

Before he died, any time we'd get together we'd have to laugh and recall some of the things that happened. He threatened to tell on me lots of times. That day he promised me he wouldn't tell. I guess they must have known about that 'cause I went home with his pants on. But he was such a sweet fellow. He'd just do anything.

My first year teaching was in 1924 in Lake Victor, Texas, where I went to teach for a term of seven months at seventy-five dollars a month. I was eighteen and had completed one year of college to get my certificate. I boarded with an elderly couple who had once been our neighbors on the ranch. She was like a second mother to me and heated a rock to be put in my bed every cold night to help keep me warm.

The schoolhouse was located at the edge of town, which was no great distance for me to walk as the town had only about two hundred population. Our school was composed of three teachers. I had the first four grades. We had to do our own housecleaning, carry the wood, build the fire, take out the ashes, and get fresh water for our schoolroom. It was in a one-gallon bucket, which often had spit balls floating around when you went for a drink.

And that's where I had the little boy who lived with his grandfather. The grandfather was fat and old. He was the ticket agent at the railroad station. Grandmother and Grandfather were separated, and so were Mother and Father. The two men lived alone doing their own housecleaning, cooking, and laundry work, often which were sadly neglected. It was often hard enough to find enough clean clothes to send Jimmy to school on time.

One day, Grandfather had to go to the store to buy new pants before Jimmy could come to school. At noon that day I found him on the school ground crying. On investigating, I was told that one of the older boys had set him on the barbed wire fence, which tore his pants. He was heartbroken and did not want to come into the room with a hole in his pants. I told Jimmy to bring his pants to me after school, and I would mend them. I could not sew a stitch, but I knew my rock-warming second mother would mend them for me.

Later in the year, a nice-looking man and woman stopped at the school and asked to speak to Jimmy. The lady turned out to be Jimmy's mother, and she had come to take him home with her. He whispered to me that he would like to speak to some of his friends to tell them good-bye. I later learned that he was giving his private store of goods to his friends. His wealth was tied up in stolen eggs, which he had hidden around in various places. He was going to make an investment in chewing tobacco when he put his produce on the market. Life had not been very kind to him, and he was learning early how to beat the odds.

Then the next year I went to Florence, Texas. Did I tell you the story of how they put me in a room to sleep with the baby?

This school the first year I taught was a three-teacher school. A man who was principal of a school in Florence had relatives in this town. He saw me, and he'd heard of some of the experiences I'd had in Lake Victor.

He said, "Would you like to upgrade yourself? I can get you into an eight-teacher school." He got me in over there, and he said, "Now you don't have to worry about a place to stay. You can board with us."

Well, I was young, just going on nineteen. I was eighteen the first year. My mother lived in Lampapas, Texas, and I rode a bus to Florence the day before school started. I got there late that afternoon and got off the bus. He met me and took me to his home, which was close to the schoolhouse—very convenient. But I discovered I was to sleep in a room with the baby. He was in a baby bed, and he cried all night. And I cried because I was so homesick and so disappointed I didn't know what to do.

So I sneaked to a telephone that next morning when I got to school. I called my mother, and she said, "Don't worry."

She came over that day and packed all my things and moved them to the hotel. She did it all. She ran interference for me because she knew it would be embarrassing for me to try to leave and found me a place to stay. I didn't have anywhere to go anyway. She came over in the car and moved my things to the hotel.

The man was the principal of the school. He taught upstairs, but he didn't come down very often. So it was embarrassing, but I got out of it.

The hotel was really a boarding house. As the other teachers came in, it happened that almost all the single teachers lived there. There was really no place else very much to stay. All boarded there. So we almost ended up with a dorm there. It was very nice.

There were four of us single women teachers and a man teacher who lived upstairs. The four of us were downstairs, and we had one long room that was sort of a living room area and then little bedrooms that were off. One little bedroom was just a sort of a den with a curtain across it, but it was private. We each had our beds.

We had eight teachers in that school, and the superintendent. That was the second year I was there. There were three teachers that lived in Florence, and they were staying at home. One was a young man whose parents were elderly so he felt he should go back and stay at home. He was a musician. He taught one year, and then he left there. One was a good friend of mine whose parents lived there, and she lived with them. She taught just one year, and then she left there, too.

All the other teachers—all the single ones—boarded at this hotel. It was an old-fashioned type hotel where they had a long table. It was just filled with food. You could eat all you wanted. The man and his wife that owned the hotel also owned an old-fashioned dry goods and a grocery store. So I think we got better food than we would have, if we could have found it, in any home. And it was nicer because it was a faculty affair. Not many other people stayed there other than teachers.

I don't remember how much it cost to live there. I think maybe that year I drew eighty dollars [a month]. The first year I started over in Lake Victor I got seventy dollars, and that was a seven-months school. But when I went to Florence I think it was eighty dollars, and it was a nine-months school. We probably paid something like twenty-five dollars for board. I'm sure it wasn't very much at that time. It was nice. I was trying to think last night. I guess we only had one bathroom in that hotel. I can't remember. I guess we took turns taking baths. I don't think they could have afforded another bath.

Well, something came up. One of the men who lived upstairs and his wife was the owner of the drugstore. It was a little town, not many stores. He was a Baptist—a staunch Baptist—and it was in our contract that no teacher could dance and teach in that school. So we got to playing records down there. This was the second year I was there, and I stayed there three years. The second year I was there my husband—he was a single man at that time—became the principal of that school. My husband became principal after they fired that principal at the end of the year. I don't know why. He wasn't involved in the dancing. And my husband boarded there. He lived upstairs. So we all bought some records and got us a little Victrola, as they were called then. We'd play records, and some of us tried to dance. None of us knew how to dance. But this trustee upstairs could hear that, and he reported to the board that we were dancing down there. Back in seclusion.

Now my sister-in-law who lives next door to me went to Tarpley, Texas, to teach. That's over close to Bandera. They almost fired her because she couldn't play the piano for the Baptist church. They didn't have anybody to play the piano, and she didn't know how to play. One of the trustees was a Baptist, and when he hired her, she just looked like she could play the piano. He just expected that they were going to make an organist out of her at their church. She went to church, but she wouldn't play. I think she played a little bit, but not enough to play for church. She was that timid. And she almost got fired at the end of that year because they found out she rode double on a horse with a man—rode behind the saddle. So that's what teachers put up with a long time ago.

I guess the other teachers were fired for dancing. I guess so. A conglomeration. But it was in the contract we couldn't dance. They let this old maid go, and she wasn't participating. But maybe they didn't know. They never did ask us any questions. At the end of the year, they just weren't reelected. Those were the days when they could fire you. They can't do that now, but they could then.

If you were a teacher, you just shouldn't go off on night parties. Of course, you couldn't drink. We didn't have so much of that then, but that's what it meant. I know one night we all left. They didn't know what we were doing. So we went on a beautiful creek on a moonlight night and took our picnic supper. And we took our record player. The creek had solid rock all on one side. So that's where we were. And we were trying to dance down there, too. I suppose they never did know that. But anyway, that's how strict they were a long time ago. Teachers couldn't do that.

Anyway, after a year my husband didn't want to teach there anymore. He wanted to be an engineer. So he went back to the university to get his engineering degree. But then he got sidetracked there. He met a man that he became close friends with who was superintendent of the school in Bandera.

So he came back to see me one night and said, "What would you say if I told you I was going to go back and teach school next year?"

I said, "It's your life." We weren't married. I said, "You do what you want to."

So he went to Bandera to teach and got sidetracked. Later, after seventeen years, he went with the Bandera Electric and was an engineer.

My son is a physical education teacher. His father was somewhat against this choice because of the poor salary. We had had to struggle so much with poor salaries. During the depression, they lowered my salary ten dollars a month to eighty dollars because that's all they could afford. My husband got a little more. During the Korean War, my son enlisted in the navy hoping maybe it would help him decide what he should be. When he got out, he said, "Mother, all I want to be is a teacher, but I don't want to hurt Daddy."

I told him it would be all right if that was what he really wanted. His daddy just wanted him to be happy. My son is doing less physical education now because they just made him principal of his junior high. That's a hard age, but my son says he wouldn't change because the children really need him.

From Florence, I went to Mathis, Texas. I stayed there three years. When I got to Mathis, I got a hundred dollars a month. We found an apartment, and there were four of us that stayed together there. I guess that was 1926.

Before we got there a man, a doctor, was called out on a call, and he never was found. He didn't come home. After I moved down there, they found his body buried under some mesquite trees. So all four of us were just scared to death all the time. We lived in a new place that had an upstairs apartment. This man owned a lumber yard, so he had built a very nice home and an upstairs apartment. It wasn't too far from the school. They had just one school. So when we walked to school, we had to go down a trail between some mesquite bushes. We made sure that we all went together. Two of us were Baptists, and two were Methodists, of the girls, so we took turns when we went to church. Everything we did, we did in a body because we were too afraid to walk alone. Because there were no sidewalks. So when we went to church, we still had to go down a trail between bushes. So one Sunday night we would go to the Baptist church, and the next Sunday night we'd go to the Methodist church.

I started going with a boy down there who was the son of a man who had once been the superintendent of the Methodist school. This boy was teaching in Orange Grove, Texas, but he lived in Mathis, not too far away. In fact, he was living in his mother's and father's home there. So I got to going with him. He was not a church member. He would not go with me the night we went to the Baptist church, but the night we went to the Methodist church, he'd go with us. He'd take us along in his car. The Methodist minister was very broadminded, but the Baptist minister was one of these hard, narrow-minded Baptists. He just thought young people were all rotten.

One night I was sitting there in the Baptist church. One of my roommates punched me, and I came to and realized that this preacher was preaching about me!

He was saying, "We have a young lady who's a teacher in the school and supposed to be an upright, fine young lady. She works with the young people here in the"—I've forgotten what we called it, some sort of organization for young people . . . BYPU! That's what it was—"Then she sneaks out, and we don't know where she goes after that. So we don't think she's living the kind of life she ought to live."

That's what he was saying from up in front of the church. What I did was to leave with the girls, and we all went to the Methodist church. It was time to go to the Methodist church that night. So that gives you a little idea of what teachers a long time ago had to go through.

I don't remember whether we had a contract down there where we couldn't dance or not, but at that time they put it in almost all the teachers' contracts.

The other teachers I lived with were nice. One was from Llano, Texas. One was from a town in east Texas. I went through there this summer and asked about her. Somebody gave me her address, and she now lives close to Austin. One lived near Mathis. We had a nice year. Everything we did, we did together.

None of us had a car. Teachers just didn't have cars back then. But the young man I was going with, he had one. I knew I was going to get married when school was out, but my [future] husband was very broadminded and said, "Now, you don't have to stick at home. Go and have fun."

So I got to going with this fellow. I told him I was going to get married when school was out, but he said, "Well, that doesn't matter. The man on the ground is the man that wins."

So I just went on with him.

After school was out that year, I caught a bus and came to San Antonio. My husband met me. We went up to Bandera and got married because we were going to the university that summer and didn't have time to have a big wedding. So we just went up to Bandera where he'd been teaching and got married up there.

I wanted to tell you going from Mathis that night—the bus ran at night after school got out—I got on this bus to San Antonio. They had no paved roads at that time. It had been raining, raining, raining, and the ruts were very deep. We just went from side to side in this bus. It had two seats behind, I believe, or three.

There was a man sitting next to me that kept putting his hand on my knee. After a while we got to a place where the bus driver says, "We're going to stop for a drink, and if you want to get out for a drink, well, do so."

I stayed in the bus, and he got out. I made sure that I slipped way over on the other side. So when he got in, he slid over there right by me again. So I didn't get away from him.

He asked me all about me. "When you get out in San Antonio, where are you going? Could I take you somewhere?"

I said, "No, my mother will be there to meet me."

I never was as glad to see somebody's face as I was to see my mother's face meet that bus that night. That was another thing teachers had to put up with a long time ago.

I want to come to Bandera again. When I was telling you about these children on Medina Lake, that experience was in Bandera, Texas. I came there in 1929. My husband met me in San Antonio. We went up to Bandera and got married. My mother was with us.

In that school—that was during the bootlegging days—one of our best friends, a sheriff of Bandera, was killed because he found a still that was operating and took it into the courthouse. They were going to have a trial, and the sheriff was shot. His sons still live in Bandera.

They had a big rodeo facility out about two miles from Bandera. It had a great big barn and also a big, open-air pavilion where they met to dance. They'd have a rodeo, and then they'd have a dance that night.

Mr. Hicks, the sheriff, went out there after we had a play at school. My husband was principal in Bandera, Texas, and he had put on a play that night with his class. Mr. Hicks's baby son was in the play and was blacked up like a nigra. When the play was over, his father went behind the stage and was talking to him and laughing. He was a very jolly man.

The son said, "I'll get this black off my face and go with you."

The father said, "No, you don't need to. You go on home and go to bed. I'll be all right."

He went to this dance, and somebody tapped him on the shoulder and said, "There's trouble down at the barn."

He started running down there, and a deputy was standing close by. He heard the remark. He watched the sheriff leave and go down to the stock barn, and in just a few minutes, he heard a shot.

He said, "I bet they got Mr. Hicks."

He started running down there. When he got down there, this man who shot Mr. Hicks had gotten in his buggy, hitched the horse, and was circling all around the open space. He was circling by a plow part of the time. Well, Mr. Burns, the deputy, hid behind the plow, and he ordered him to stop. He found Mr. Hicks, and he knew he was dead. So this man kept going, going, going. He wouldn't stop. All the time, he's spotted Mr. Burns behind this plow so he was shooting at him. As the man approached the plow, Mr. Burns stepped out from behind the plow and killed him.

Two were killed that night. That was a terrible experience.

There was another man that lived there who had a still, but it wasn't found at that time. Later, it was found and picked up. He also killed a man, and then he went to the pen for it. Later on, I taught his children. His daughter was afflicted. She talked sort of hare-lipped through her nose. She had two brothers. Both of the brothers were a little older than she, and they were all in the first grade.

One morning, she came to school, and she said, "Miz Til, Miz Til, the boys got liquor hid down here in the ditch."

I asked her some more about it, and she said, "Yep, they brought the liquor in to sell it."

So I slipped out and told the principal of our school. My husband was

also in the school. My husband was the principal, but he had a superintendent. They were young men, about the same age. So they went down
there and found it and called the law and had them come and pick it up.
That was the beginning of that.

Those children didn't go to school very much. They just came occasionally, but they had textbooks checked out. When the end of school was
approaching, my mother came up to visit with me. She lived in San Antonio.

I said, "Mother, I have to go out in the woods and get some books."

I told her where I was going. This man had served a short term, and
he was back living out there. I think one reason his term was shortened
was he was in poor health, and he didn't live much longer after that. He
was living out in the country with his family, and his children didn't come
to school very often. I had to get those books in before school closed. So
mother and I went out there. Mother was scared to death.

She said, "Aren't you afraid to go out there?"

I said, "Well, I have to get those books."

So I got out of the car and walked up to the house, and told the man
that the children had some books, and school was out and I had to turn
them in. So they gave me the books, no trouble.

Later on, those children grew to be fine men. The older boy married,
and they adopted some children, and he made a fine husband. So it
doesn't matter what their background is, sometimes they will come out.
The baby boy joined the navy, and he got an education, too, and came
back a fine-looking young man. The girl married and had some children
that did learn in school.

That was another episode in my life in Bandera, Texas.

One time we had a food poisoning in the cafeteria at school. We'd had
chicken salad for lunch. Another teacher and I were on playground
duty, and all of a sudden children started falling everywhere, fainting
and vomiting. The other teacher had a little medical training so she knew
something of what to do. She put them under the fountain and made
them drink water so they'd vomit.

She said, "Go get the principal. Tell him we need help."

I ran upstairs to his office, but the door was locked. I said, "The
children are all sick, and we need help."

He said, "Go away. I'm sick."

The doctor came and said, "I'll bet those cafeteria ladies were stirring
the food with their hands again."

You see, even if they washed their hands, they might have had something on their nails. Even though my friend and I had eaten lunch, we
didn't get sick for some reason.

In my early years, there was no lunch duty. School just closed down, and everybody went home. In Bandera, there was lunch duty. I always hoped before I retired they'd do away with it. I don't think it was right for a teacher to go back into the classroom all sunburned and wind-blown. Children notice small things and appreciate them. Like smelling good. After I retired, I once got a call from a child's mother who wanted to buy her daughter, now grown, the same perfume her teacher had used. She had liked it so much as a child. I told her I was sorry to say I couldn't remember. I thought it might have been "Evening in Paris."

I went every summer for many years to finish my degree. I think you learn more that way. I only had one long term in college, and that was for my freshman year at Baylor College. I went to summer school every summer and took extension courses and correspondence courses until I graduated with my bachelor's degree in education from Trinity College. It used to be the College of San Antonio. Then I was in the first master's graduation class at Trinity College in elementary education. I wrote my thesis on children's literature. It was worth one course.

One summer I lived in San Antonio during the war so I could go to college. I couldn't commute because of rationing and the scarcity of gas. I lived with a retired man and his wife. The man was supposed to babysit my five year old son. He really didn't have to babysit much because my son just followed him around everywhere he went. I'd run home in between classes to see if my son was all right.

After I did my thesis on children's literature (which included a num-ber of original, illustrated stories), I did a number of stories on my own just for fun because I believe very strongly in teaching phonics. You know there was a time in there when they didn't teach phonics, but I kept on teaching it. I'd give an example of it and make a little story up, all in rhyme, just real silly. "But then my poodle went off his noodle, and took a taste of that gluey paste!" Real silly. But kids like things like this. I would pass these out in the latter part of first grade when they could read. I would make them up and use a ditto machine and primary typewriter I had in my room. On some sheets I didn't put any pictures because they were supposed to do that. Every morning I'd say, "Now, it's a big secret. Don't you tell anybody what's on there. You draw your own picture that you think fits this."

Oh, they had more fun. I passed that out at first for busy work mainly to stimulate the child who excelled in everything else and had time on his hands: "The farmer's pig, did a jig. He fell on the hose, and broke his nose!" They all liked that. Well, that was one of the things I did in first grade.

Then, toward the end of the first grade, I had these little first-graders writing stories of their own and illustrating them. They each had a tablet.

We called it their *permanent tablet*. They weren't allowed to put anything in it except the special story. They wrote these on their own. Yes, first-graders. They illustrated their own stories. Again, this was for the upper-level children. Poorer readers and so forth never got this far. But you have to sort of try when you're teaching a mixed group. You see, this was several years ago, and now they do segregate in a way. Have special teachers to come in and help with those other children. But these would be the upper level of the class.

Then, we had a tablet that was called *teacher's tablet*. Anytime they got finished with their work, they were allowed to slip up. I had several of these. I think one's all I've got ahold of now. They were allowed to put a special story in my tablet that was mine. I could keep it and take it home at the end of school and have it to enjoy. They took great pride in doing those things, too.

This is a story I'm going to give you. This is from Medina Lake. We picked up the children from Medina Lake in buses in the later years. When I first started teaching, we didn't have buses, and they had to get in. But this child came in after we had buses because he wouldn't have had any way to come in. They lived in a tent. That was their home. The land down there was very cheap, and sometimes they didn't buy it. They just went down there and put up a tent.

I worked with the Red Cross besides teaching school. I started as a volunteer during the war, and then just continued afterwards because I liked it. I was with what they call the Home Service. Somebody told me that there's a family down there with some little boys, and one of them would be school age in the fall, but they had no clothing.

So I went down there to see the family, and sure enough, they needed clothes. They had one tent. At that time it was only one tent. Grandma hadn't come yet. There was an open fireplace outside where they cooked right over that campfire. They cooked in one big pot, and they all ate out of that one big pot. There was sort of a table that was piled up. Mostly it was made out of rock. A few old boards across the rocks. That was the table. And their utensils were just piled up there, and that was the way they cooked and the way they ate. They squatted around this campfire. Well, that was what I saw. But I got his size, his age, and so forth, and I went back to town. The Red Cross allowed me some funds to buy clothes so I bought clothing for this little boy.

He came in on a school bus, which was quite an experience for him. He got to school. He didn't know how to participate in anything. He wouldn't have anything to do with the other children. He wouldn't play with them. When he followed me on the school ground as I did the school ground duty, he always squatted right by me and dug in the sand.

One day I said to him, "Richard, what does your daddy do?"

He said, "He hauls garbage, and he's going after Grandma today!"

So that became quite a joke in our school: "Going after Grandma today!"

But what happened . . . Grandma had an old-age pension, so she had her own tent down there. She lived adjoining them, and they shared her pension. When the father didn't make enough hauling garbage, well, they ate off of Grandma.

The first day I went to the lunchroom after Richard entered school, he wouldn't sit at the lunch table with the other children. Our lunchroom had long tables with benches on the sides. He scooted down underneath the table, and he ate with his hands. I put him a tray up there. The children marched by and picked up their trays, but Richard wouldn't. So I got his and put it up there, and told him it was up there and insisted he get up there like the other children. But he never would come out. He was like a little caged animal. He would reach up and snatch the food off the tray and take it under the table to eat. That went on for some time before I could ever get him to get up there and sit with the other children.

Well, what was amazing was that Richard grew up, and the next little boy came. When he came, well, he was tamed and housebroken. Richard wouldn't even go to the bathroom. He'd just go out behind a tree somewhere, if I didn't catch him first. The bathroom was a scary place. He wouldn't go into it. But when his little brother came, we didn't have all those problems because Richard had been the man—the forerunner— and had carried every message home, everything that happened at school.

Then Richard when he got to high school became quite an athlete. After he finished high school, he joined the army and made a right nice man. And so did his brother just younger than he. I kept up with them that long.

There's another poem here I'd written about a little boy that I later was very proud of. I worked in what they called Head Start two summers. My friend and I were sent to Austin to attend a workshop—in the early sixties, I guess—the first year of the Head Start. We had the first Head Start in the summer time to try and get those little children ready for school.

This little boy was living with Grandmother and Grandfather. Somebody said he didn't have a father. I don't know. I met his mother a few times. She didn't live there, but she'd come back to visit. She always seemed interested in him and would come to school and talk to me.

But the little fellow lived with Grandmother and Grandfather and didn't know how to play with other children. So he was something to deal with every day. He just ran and made all kinds of noises. We had some boxes we put down and knocked the ends out so they could make a tunnel and crawl through it. Well, he liked to do that. He didn't have to participate with other children. He could do that as an individual so he liked that. Then, as he got a little better acquainted, he would run in the hall and scream, and bounce the ball, and hit people, and kick people, and pinch them. This is the poem I wrote about him. Do you want to hear it?

Willie

We studied Willie from every angle,
In hopes we might untangle,
the mysteries locked within.
This little chap with the turned-down chin.

We danced, we sang, we played, we read,
we hoarded all the words he said,
In hopes that we might somehow find,
the secret key to this young mind.

We played sand box, we stacked up blocks,
We talked of colors in the rocks,
We tried and tried to no avail
to reach this child. We must not fail!

And then one day we saw a gleam—
He built of clay a perfect stream
With bridge arched high—a work of art.
His chin came up—he had his start.

The years passed by, I glimpsed the sky
And a span of bridge met my eye—
I breathed a prayer, as I bowed my head,
For Willie's name was what I read.

Another one of the Medina Lake youngsters had the measles one time, and I went to visit him. Years later, I ran into him in the grocery store. He recalled that I visited him as a sick child. At first, I couldn't recognize him as a grown man. But then my memory cleared, and I remembered his name. This is what I wrote:

He Spoke to Me

He spoke to me, a handsome lad,
And said, "Do you remember me?
Some years ago you helped me add
And told me stories of the sea.

And once when I was sick in bed
You came to our old wrecky place
And sat by me and stroked my head—
I know you well, I know your face."

I searched his eyes, I traced his frame
For some small hint to free the past—
And then I whispered his full name,
My foggy memory cleared at last.

He told me stories of the seas
And now he added score for score
For men who sleep on foreign leas
Because of fiends who sneaked ashore.

And as I listened to his words
And saw the pain carved on his face,
Because of lameness which occurred
In raids before he reached his base—

My bosom swelled with pride to know
That part of me walked battlefields,
For we share lots with all who go
From our school rooms to fuller yields.

But while I'm on that, I had another little fellow from down the Lake whose little fingers were grown together. He was not well developed and wasn't very bright. But happy—just as happy. I think it is so important for teachers to try to reach the child at every level—make him happy. Every morning he got off the school bus and ran to my classroom. He'd put his hands on his hips and stand there with his legs sort of spraddled out and say, "I's here!" and smile from ear to ear. He was just that happy all day long. But a very few things he could do with those little, knubby hands. They were very poor people, and I doubt when he was born anybody looked at him. I don't know. I don't know if anything could have been done or not, but he was a six-year-old child then. He couldn't even dress himself well.

Of course, he wasn't promoted out of the first grade, but we had three first-grade teachers, and they changed rooms so he'd have a new situation—feel that he had made progress. He went to the bathroom one day. We did have bathrooms that adjoined the classroom. He came back with his pants down around his ankles. The teacher said, "You go in the bathroom and pull up your pants."

He said, "I cain't, I cain't."

She said, "Oh, you can. You go try."

So she had her back to the door because she was sitting in reading circle on a little stool, and she heard the children laughing. She turned around and there he was standing there with his pants around his knees. No underwear. So she said, "You get back to that bathroom and pull up those pants."

He said, "I cain't, I cain't."

So she went with him that time. When she got in there, she found out that he had both legs in the same hole of the ragged underwear that he did have on, and there was no way he could pull up his panties!

He didn't learn very much, but he was happy. I think that's the main thing. I have a poem here somewhere that I'll read you in a little bit that talks about that we never know when we look at a child what in the world he'll be. He deserves a chance, too.

While I'm on Medina Lake, I had a little girl that came from down there, and she looked very nice. Clean and nice. I decided, though, one day that I wanted to go see the situation. She talked about living in a tent. So I took a lady with me, and we had to park in the cedar trees to get through. I broke the aerial off my car trying to get down there.

When we got there, these people were gone. But we saw a tent, and it had a window in it. Sitting in the window was a dog that looked exactly like a picture of a dog sitting there. We couldn't tell the difference until he moved a little bit. We sat for a minute in the car just looking at the situation. When the dog moved, we knew he was alive.

We ventured up there. When we got to the tent, we found out the door didn't even open. You had to get down on your knees to crawl in. So we got down there and peeped in. There was one bed for the man and the lady. The floor was almost solid with beds—just mattresses and quilts thrown down. That's where the children slept. But this little girl came looking real clean every day, and I wondered at that, you know.

One day the father came to school and tapped on the door. He was smiling and real timid. He said, "I'd like to speak to her"—I've even forgotten her name. I said, "Come in."

She was sitting near the back of the room, and I watched out of the corner of my eye. He went back, and together they unwrapped a package. He got down on his knees right beside her. Her little eyes were just popping. And his, too. He was just as excited as she. They undid the package and brought out a beautiful picture book. I found out later that some aunt had mailed it to her from some company. They both had their heads down over that book and were so enthralled with the whole thing.

So I got a different view of the people that lived on the Lake. I found out that he was a veteran and had been injured. He had some severe back trouble, and they lived off a small pension. I sort of lost track of them because later they moved here to Kerrville, but I was living in Bandera at the time. One day I happened to run into them over here in a store, and they were a *nice*-looking family, all well dressed. So I suppose somewhere along the way maybe they'd upped his pension, or he got some help. There's a Veterans' Hospital here. I didn't ask any questions, but it could be he got over here and got some help. Maybe was able to hold a job.

You never know what you're working with with the children.

THREE

Gladys Peterson Meyers

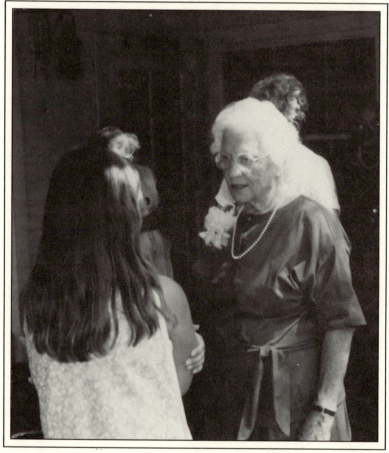

Gladys Peterson Meyers, guest of honor at her eightieth birthday party, Kerrville, Texas.

I don't know whether it's the system, a lack of incentive, or what it is, but my gripe against the teachers nowadays is that when I went to school, in addition to teaching history, reading, writing, and arithmetic, trigonometry, and all that sort of stuff, they taught character. And I don't know, lately, but it seems to me like that old dedication of trying to teach character, too, is gone. Because I can recall some of my school teachers taught me some of the things I try to go by now, more so than any preacher.

—MELVIN MEYERS, HUSBAND OF GLADYS PETERSON MEYERS

GLADYS PETERSON MEYERS started teaching at the age of seventeen in a one-teacher country school in Knoxville in Kimble County, Texas. She never looked back or stopped until she retired from the Kerrville Independent School District in 1963, except for four years when she was forced to resign because she was married.

Gladys was a girl who couldn't be defeated by the obstacles that lay in her path. When told she had to give up teaching during the depression because she was married, she got a job as a social worker; when she was supposed to sit home alone patiently waiting for her soldier-husband to be shipped overseas, she defied convention and went to Bend, Oregon, to be with him; when there was no money for college, she borrowed it. Some people persist because they lack insight about their own limitations or the odds against them. Gladys's self-perception is apparent in her opening statement: "I think the thread of my life has been the desire to learn and a desire to be with people and to enjoy them. Most everything I've done has been along that line."

For someone with those desires, teaching was an ideal profession, and Gladys knew as early as third grade that she wanted to be a teacher. She recalled loving the smell of Crayolas and wanting to teach so that she could always be around them. She also remembered her teacher Dora Nimitz, sister of the World War II admiral and one of Gladys's role models and supporters. Today, in arguing for scholarship money for future teachers, Gladys asks, "Suppose nobody had believed in me?"

Of all the people who believed in Gladys, her mother probably was most influential. An orphan at eight, her mother was separated from her brothers and sent to a family as a "built-in housekeeper and baby-sitter." Understandably, she was eager to escape into marriage at fifteen, but hard times followed. Gladys's father became ill, and her mother supported the family by running a boarding house and cooking meals for businesspeople. Her mother learned from these lessons and vigorously encouraged Gladys to gain skills to support herself. Over her husband's opposition, this "independent person, a ramrod, a motivator" supported Gladys's teaching career emotionally when she could not financially. Her mother's life is a reminder of how harshly life could treat women of that time, just as Gladys's shows how much a woman could accomplish against considerable odds.

Gladys is proud of her ancestry and her parents, and her story is laced with references to them. (In retirement today, she is active both in the Kerrville Historical Society and in the Daughters of the American Revolution.) In her descriptions of her parents, she seeks and finds the best— an approach that mirrors her general attitude toward the world. Although she is not blind to life's troubles, her interpretation of it is positive: "So I've had a good life. I've been fortunate to make good friends. I'm unpredictable. Dependable, but unpredictable. But I've enjoyed life. I have an appreciation of life. Everything I've ever dreamed of, I have it. Some people say it was hard, but I didn't think it was."

Perhaps one of the greatest keys to her satisfaction with her life is her ability to appreciate her own accomplishments. She does not dream of the unattainable. She realizes the value of what she has done and allows herself to enjoy it. "That was satisfaction to me to be able to teach in the same school with my former students. I felt like I'd really succeeded."

Gladys's "unpredictable dependability" describes her willingness to take risks. However, she often minimized these risks by her ability to recognize opportunities when they presented themselves. Her first job was in a jewelry store owned by her Sunday School teacher, which led to his recommending her for a college loan. That first position taught her the skills she needed to win a job far from home in Bend, Oregon. Her risk taking was not precipitous or based on whims. She postponed marriage for five years after her engagement until she could pay off her college loan and spent ten years part-time to earn a four-year college degree. As she says, "I always had to sort of step along to get there. But I was determined." All these traits reflected the self-confidence of someone who from earliest childhood "always wanted to be center stage" and who, even after retirement, "still wanted to be in the act."

Another figure loomed large in Gladys's success in fulfilling her dream of being a teacher: her husband, Melvin Meyers. In fact, none of the married teachers in this book faced their husband's opposition to their working. Although they varied in how strongly they encouraged their wives' careers, the husbands did not actively oppose their wives' working. Melvin certainly was among the most supportive. He was willing to postpone marriage five years until Gladys had paid off her college loan, and he helped in small ways such as playing the piano for a class program. Gladys herself observes, "You had to have a husband that cooperated with you to be a teacher."

Gladys's story reveals the economic discrimination experienced by women teachers. She was forced to give up her job when she married (on the crest of having repaid her college loan), was laid off during the depression, and never received credit for her early years of teaching before the retirement system was established. A teacher's hold on economic independence prior to the initiation of tenure was fragile, as is evidenced by the math teacher who in the middle of the year was fired for flunking a trustee's football-playing son.

Schools as well as teachers suffered from penury, and both city and country schools suffered from neglect. Gladys scraped the mud out of the school in Houston and was discovered by the state supervisor standing in a wastebasket stomping papers and cleaning a classroom in Comfort, Texas. With her usual resourcefulness, Gladys pulled down the decrepit porch of the schoolhouse to provide firewood when her first community refused to provide fuel.

Her story tells of other socioeconomic inequities. She witnessed the differences between schools for whites versus those for Mexicans and blacks and between the degreed and nondegreed teachers who taught in them. Within the white community, she saw the education given to rich ranchers' daughters whose fathers could afford private finishing schools and colleges and the education reserved for the poorer girls like herself. Rich and poor fathers, however, often shared the view that too much education (and especially the wrong kind) was a waste and would turn their daughters into grass widows. After all, "Marriage was the thing everyone depended on."

Finally, Gladys's experiences as an eighteen-year-old first-year teacher, wearing glasses "whether I needed them or not" to look older, is reminiscent of the other stories in this book. Her description of bullies coming to test the new teacher is corroborated by Thad Sitton and Milam C. Rowold's *Ringing the Children In.*[1] Typically, however, Gladys's most vivid descriptions emphasize not the difficulties but the good times of attending "play party dances" (escorted by one of the sixteen-year-old "big boys"), the brush arbor parties, and her cowboy suitor. Her loving description of living within a family in the community is particularly memorable and characteristic of her viewpoint: "It was a great life."

In retirement, Gladys and her husband Melvin enjoy the quiet comforts of their household (including two affectionate collies and a curious cat), the bustle of church and civic activities, and watching the deer graze outside their picture window.

ℳ

"Transportation system" for the three-mile ride to James River School, 1927.

Grades 2–8, James River School, Kimble County, Knoxville, Texas, 1927. Gladys Peterson, teacher.

Gladys Peterson Meyers,
age eighteen, 1926.
Pumping the school well.

Grades 2–8, James River School, 1927. Gladys Peterson Meyers, teacher.

I think the thread of my life has been the desire to learn and a desire to be with people and to enjoy them. Most everything I've done has been along that same line. I did social work during the depression when I couldn't get a job teaching because the married teachers were second choice. There were many singles. Then, even among the married ones, during the depression I was told, "You have a husband. You don't need the position as much as somebody who has little children to be supported." Because I didn't have children.

So I had to give it up. That's when I went into social work.

I was married in Houston on May 29, 1932. I returned my contract to Corpus Christi in August after I was sure the marriage would last! Teachers were not allowed to be married. In Houston they weren't allowed to teach during the depression. That's when I went into social work. I worked as a caseworker for the Texas Transient Bureau for two years. Then during the war they began to accept married teachers. During the war there was a shortage of teachers—World War II. I taught in Houston for ten years. I taught forty years in all. I taught six years before I married, and then I taught in Houston.

I started before the state retirement program. I never got credit for the years before the retirement system. I had to start over from the beginning. I think it started about '28. I married in 1932 in Houston. There were four years I didn't teach. I bought into the retirement system when I went back into teaching after my daughter was two years old.

During the war, there were two sessions. I taught half-time because I had the morning session. That's when I got back into teaching because of the shortage of teachers. You were expected to go home at twelve because if you stayed they'd expect you to do a whole day's work for a half-day's pay.

The school that I was in was on the outskirts of town, and the roads were not paved. They got pretty muddy in the rainy season, and there were times when you couldn't drive your car up to the school. So you'd leave your car on the main road and wait for the milk truck to come along to get a ride to the school. Just on special occasions. Then when you'd see them coming back from their run after two-thirty in the afternoon, you'd ride back to your car again.

You didn't sweep out your room in Houston, but they didn't have janitors in Houston during the war. We didn't sweep them out; we used a hoe to scrape the mud out. The building leaked, and we put buckets on the desk.

My most embarrassing situation in teaching was in Comfort, Texas. I heard the state supervisor was coming. I was tidying up, and I didn't finish in time. Here I was standing in the wastebasket, stomping down the papers, trying to get everybody to clean up!

Then another embarrassing situation was in Houston. The city super-intendent came out to tell them how badly we needed repairs on the wooden building, and it had been raining. The roof was leaking, and I had buckets on the desks to catch the leaks.

The superintendent said, "What's that bucket doing there?"

I said, "Well, the roof's leaking so bad that we had to stop it so it wouldn't ruin the books."

I think he got us assistance from the state because they could see how bad the situation was.

When the supervisors came, they would ask to see your lesson plans. They would sit and observe the teaching and mostly check the facilities. Your contract would be issued for two years—two years probation period—and if you came up to the required standard, you didn't take the teacher test. We were subject to inspection about three times a year. That's why I was tidying up the room. They would observe you, and in addition, they had departmental supervisors. I enjoyed all of them ex-cept the music teacher because I never really was equipped to teach music. But I had to, so I did. It was hard to get a tune out when you were scared to death.

On one occasion in Houston the music supervisor came. I had dreaded it very much because the pitch pipe and I just didn't get along too well together. When you're scared you couldn't get the tune. Just as I was ready to hear the children sing, thinking, "Well, let's demonstrate," just about that time, a child came to the room. She said, "Miz Meyers, you're wanted on the telephone."

I said, "Not now, not now." It was an awful time for the telephone.

The child came back a second time and said, "But it's long distance, and you must come."

Well, I excused myself. When I got to the telephone, it was my father in Kerrville had had a heart attack. So I went back and told her, and she said, "Oh, that's all right. You go. I'll be back another time."

So when I left and got to Kerrville, I saw my father sitting on the porch eating an apple. He'd recovered.

I said, "Oh, Daddy, you saved me!"

He saved me from that supervisor. By the time she came back, I was prepared.

I got a hundred dollars a month when I started teaching. I don't have too much sympathy for teachers who complain about poor pay. They don't know what they're talking about.

A friend's daughter had the same desire to be a teacher. Incidentally, she's now a member of Alpha Delta Kappa. I gave her a recommendation.

She said, "I didn't know you were a charter member." I was a charter member of the Omicron chapter. In 1925–26 at San Marcos, we were a charter chapter of the Bluebonnet Girls later known as Delta Kappa Gamma.

She's teaching now in an inner-city school. One day she had a knock at the door, and she started to open the door, and one of the seniors—this is a senior high in Houston—grabbed at her blouse to pull her out the door. And at about that time, four of her students who were football players came to her rescue, and told her, "Just don't you ever open that door again without letting us go first." She's still very popular.

I think that's the kind of thing that turned my daughter off from teaching. I taught my daughter in school in Houston. One day she said, "Miz Mother," and they said, "Why are you calling the teacher 'Mother'?" She said, "Because she is my mother." She'd been wanting to tell it.

My sister went to teachers' college. Her strong point was journalism, and she went to Washington, D.C., and was a typist. A secretary. She is now retired and lives in Kerrville. So we're enjoying our life together. She spent her time promoting her husband's career.

My brother is a top salesman—a football player and a top salesman in Houston. He didn't get to college, but his daughter is a teacher. So there're two in the family. My mother's relatives were preachers.

I graduated from high school in 1925—Tivy High School in an eleven-year program. I wanted to be a schoolteacher from the third grade on, particularly because I loved my teacher very much. She was sister to Admiral Nimitz. I must have been a nice pupil because she said nice things about me, as I knew her in her nineties, and she was always talking about that gabby little girl with the sweet little smile.

But I enjoyed being around the school. I loved the smell of Crayolas. Does that make sense? I thought, "Well, I'll always be around Crayolas"— The wax Crayolas that fascinated me. So it was admiration for my teacher and the environment that appealed to me.

In order to go to college, I was able to get financial support from the Alzafar Shrine Temple, San Antonio Masonic Lodge—a loan of four hundred fifty dollars and a thousand dollar Aetna Life Insurance Policy as security. I paid the insurance premium myself—eighteen dollars, I think, for one year's premium. Let's see, I must have been sixteen when I took that out. I graduated at sixteen. My Sunday school teacher who was the local Masonic Lodge secretary signed the note, and my uncle who was the local tax assessor was a cosigner. This paid for one long semester and one summer.

After one year in San Marcos or normal school, I taught school at Knoxville, Texas, a very back, boondock-type of a school.

My father didn't think of a female as a good investment education-wise. His real reason was, I think, that he didn't have the money because there were three of us. I was the oldest. He was the only one in his family of eight that had any education past the first few years. He had a business education. He went on to business school in San Antonio.

But he was a great reader, and he instilled a love of reading and quotations as part of our life. One of his main sayings was, "If you have a kindness shown you, pass it on; it was not meant for you alone."

And, "If at first you don't succeed, try, try again."

We used to laugh at Daddy's quotations, but they stuck with us, and they really shaped our lives.

I can remember him talking about Victor Hugo's *Les Misérables.*

He was also a well-traveled man according to the times because he had gone through the Arizona Territory working with the railroad that was pushed into that part of the country. So [he told] great, fascinating stories of life as a railroad employee building the railroad into the Arizona territory.

In later years I was able to go to Phoenix, Arizona. My daddy had inspired that great desire to go West, and my mother said he entertained her many hours giving her his stories of the West.

My mother did not have many years of schooling, but somehow I remember my daddy was shaping her education by encouraging her to read. She would read the newspaper to him, and he would correct her pronunciation all the time. So really, they were sort of a self-educated family. A desire to learn, but maybe they hadn't had the advantages.

Here's a picture of my mother. You can see she was a very determined woman. She had drive. Her brothers, and my picture at three, and my husband's at six [are also in the picture]. My mother's brother married his [her husband's] mother's sister. This [picture] was in Houston. I look a little out of character there. I look a little bit shy, but I don't think I was ever shy. I always wanted to be center stage.

My mother had me reading before I was in school. I think I just memorized it. She also saw to it that I had elocution lessons. Do you remember when they had elocution lessons? And I would recite. My teacher was a neighbor. Kerrville was always a town of retired people, so there was a neighbor who took several of the young children in the neighborhood. I don't remember that we ever paid her anything. She just loved to teach children. But she would have little recitals. I didn't take piano because I never was musically inclined, and that wasn't in the pattern. But in the early years of high school we would recite. We would have Friday programs. Remember how they had those?

One of my favorite stories was when we moved to Kerrville, and I was about three. My daddy took me to show to his friends. He had married this young girl—fifteen years younger—and a very beautiful young girl—an orphan. She was anxious to get to the Hill Country, and he brought her here.

I was an only child until I was five and a little bit of a show-off and mimic. My father liked to take and show me to his friends. He'd say, "Sing something for 'em. Sing something for 'em." And I would. Of course, they all thought that was cute.

My mother had to make a little lady out of me. She never gave up in all her ninety-four years in her effort to rear a proper young lady who knew what *not* to say. He was going to make an entertainer out of me. Oh, we had a great childhood.

The point of all this is that my disposition, my nature, was such that I wanted to show off and be with people, and my relationships with other people was the most important thing. I later became a social worker and was a teacher, so I guess I've always wanted to interact with people. But I was a little bit shy, to a point—not always, but as I grew up.

When time came to teach, I was going to go to a teachers' college. My high school education was adequate for the time. We didn't have a great many courses like the city schools because ours was a small, country town. But they were small classes, and the teachers were able to give a lot of individual attention. That was important, I think, in the shaping of our thinking. We got just almost person-to-person relationships.

The first-grade teacher taught everything. Second grade was a great strong person in phonics, and I'm really indebted to her for her foundation in phonics because years later when I was teaching and phonics was out, I would rely on my phonics background, and I'd just go ahead and teach with phonics as well as the system at the time. I was able to get good results with my students because I knew that basis was so important. We started out with *hat, fat, bat* routine, and I don't know but what that might not have had a lot of merit.

My math teacher was very strong, and we had the same one from the fourth grade. She was a very hard, strict person and unpopular but she demanded perfection. We passed just to get out of her room. Then the fifth grade, who do you think was our math teacher? She had math in the fifth grade, sixth grade, seventh grade, eighth grade. We got to eighth grade—she was teaching algebra! She was a very strong teacher.

I suppose if she would have promoted the football captain without good grades, she would have been there yet. But she bucked the school board, and she was out. She wouldn't pass a boy that didn't make his grades. With her it was, "no pass, no play." That was the first I ever heard of it. They fired her because she wouldn't pass the player who was the son of the school board president. They wanted him on the football team, and he didn't make the grades. She stood her ground 'til she was fired in the middle of the year. She had seniority—Nellie Horn—a very dedicated teacher. Very grim about it.

Tenure? Oh no, you just pleased the school board. You didn't get paid a whole lot. I don't suppose she knew what compromise meant, and she wouldn't give an inch. But she made a wonderful math teacher.

We had different teachers for different subjects in the upper grades. We didn't have a junior high. It was lower and upper, I guess, at that time.

The old building of Tivy High School was restored two years ago. The original building was restored. I was on the Kerr County Historical Commission that helped promote that. It was a real thrill to see it rededicated and the students from way back. Our graduating class had the fiftieth reunion. Last year would have been the sixtieth, but I think there weren't but about five out of twenty-five still living. One of those was dying with cancer, and we just had too much sadness to bring them back in. So we didn't celebrate that one. But that's pretty good—twenty-five in the class of 1925.

A lot of teachers made a great impression. My third-grade teacher was Dora Nimitz, sister to Admiral Nimitz, and she was the one that really inspired me to be a teacher. She encouraged me through all those years. I got to see her again when she was in her nineties in the rest home with my mother right here in Kerrville. She always smiled and remembered me as a pupil. It never left her mind that her student lived with her through all those years. That was unusual, wasn't it? You could see how much teaching meant to her. I think she inspired. She lived next door to an aunt of mine so I saw her inside the school and out of it. She always made a good impression.

And that teacher that taught me phonics stayed with me all those years, too. Some of them I can't remember their names, but the outstanding ones were the ones that had the little personal touch.

As I graduated, my father didn't see how I could finance my education. It wasn't popular to educate the girls at that time. It really wasn't a good investment. Because they'd marry, and then they'd lose all that money. Marriage was the thing that everybody depended on.

I was sort of an independent person, and I wanted to teach. My mother said, "I want her to be able to support herself."

My father said, "You'll make them too independent. They'll make good grass widows."

They called them that at the time. He said, "They wouldn't make a good wife. They'd just be too independent."

But my mother didn't see it that way. She said, "Well, if they have to support themselves, they'll be able to. I want them to be able to have some way to support themselves—and be an independent woman."

I guess she was one of the first women's libbers. Well, we were descended from Lucy Stone, and Dr. Blackwell, the first woman doctor, is an ancestor, a relative. So I guess it came down through there. We just believed in women having equal rights all along. I don't think I've ever gotten over it. I was fortunate enough to marry a man who went along with the idea, who didn't demand servitude.

My father wanted me just to get a local job. About the only thing available was the laundry. I said, "I don't want to be tub number two. I want to be something better than that." But that's not being fair to the people that have to be.

My mother envisioned better things. In order for me to be in college and not stay home and support the younger sister and brother, my mother went to work in the school cafeteria. She spent many long hours and worked hard. Then my father's health broke down, and he was not able to work. So it was a pretty hard struggle for all that time.

I remember when I was little and the *World Book Encyclopedia* man came around. He sold my mother a set for the children. She had a little egg money from some chickens she had, and she told my father it was more important to feed our minds than to feed our bodies. About three years ago my mother died at ninety-four. Her mind was just as clear the whole time, fortunately.

I went to college one year, I'd teach a year, and then I'd go in the summers to get my four years of schooling. It took me ten years to get four years of schooling. At the end of that first year at San Marcos, I knew I had to teach in order to get money to come back for further education. There were several people doing that at the same time.

My first year I had to take a make-up course in the summer. So at the end of the summer school, there were not many jobs available—*positions*, they called them. Somebody told me about a little country school in Knoxville in Kimble County up above Harper. It was a one-teacher, one-room, all-subject school. They were desperately seeking a teacher at that time of year. I didn't know how desperate they were, or why they were so desperate, but I heard about it and got an interview.

I met the school board president downtown, trying to look as dignified as I could. I wasn't but seventeen, and certificates weren't issued until you were eighteen. But here it was. I was still seventeen, and he needed a teacher very badly. He said, "Well, it doesn't pay very much. Seventy-five dollars a month for eight months. And I kinda wanted somebody with experience."

I said, "Experience!" I stomped my foot and said, "How will I get experience if somebody doesn't give me a start?"

"Well," he said, "at least you've got spunk. Let's give you a try."

That's how I got started.

I boarded with him, his family. I rode a swayback mare to school. I wore a divided skirt over my dress because ladies didn't wear pants. And the little eight-year-old son rode on the rumble seat of the saddle while we went to school. We went about three miles to school.

I built my own fires on a three-legged iron stove. The legs were propped up bricks because vandalism had kind of torn up things. Some of the windows were out. They didn't even put the panes in so we had paste board, plywood—whatever we could find.

I had to build those fires in the morning when I'd get to school. I remember we would rake ashes over the coals from the fire at the end of the day so that they would keep, and the next morning it would be easier to start the fire by raking the ashes back from the hot coals. I burned the fur off the sleeve of my coat trying to reach down.

I was just another child. It was 1926, and here I was seventeen. I became eighteen in August, and I was able to get my certificate two months after school started. My students were ages eight to sixteen. There were eight students—two of them taking algebra. Two in the second grade, two in the third grade, one in the fourth grade, one in the fifth grade, no sixth or seventh, but two in eighth-grade algebra.

I think the eighth-graders just came to check me out. They didn't intend to spend the year. The reason the last teacher had left was she went running out the front door because they had decided they could tease her, the older boys, the same ones who came to learn algebra. They didn't care about algebra. They just wanted to chase the teacher out. That was their dedicated purpose—to run the teacher out. They had gourds in the attic, and they would wait until school got started, and then they'd drop those things down the stove. She didn't know what was coming out of that. She went running out saying, "No more of that."

So that's the way it was.

When I first saw them my first day of school I thought the school board was coming. There were these tall boys, taller than I was, and they said, "Well, no, we are your pupils." I couldn't believe it.

Later on, they threw a skunk in my well and stole my Bible, and a brass hand bell that I had planned to use for a keepsake all my life, and a dictionary. I said I hoped they'd look up the word *thief* because that's what they were.

The strange thing, shortly after that, I didn't have any big students. They had accomplished their purpose and decided that I was going to stay regardless of what happened.

About fifty years later I met one of those young men in a beauty shop where his daughter was, and I said, "Did you get my bell?"

He said, "No, and it hurts my feelings that you'd accuse me of it."

He told me who it was, after all those years. But that was just a small group way back.

I would get seventy-five dollars a month—twenty-five dollars for room and board, and thirty dollars on my loan. So that left me enough money to go to school in the summer time. It took me ten years to get my education.

The first year teaching was only an eight-month session. It was a great life out there—living with that family, being part of that family, riding horseback. I loved the country. It's the same area where I'm living now. I guess I've always wanted to get back to that.

It was a very understanding family. The boy was very good. Many a morning, I'd hear a gun shot about daylight, and I'd know to get dressed because we'd have fried young turkey for breakfast—buttermilk biscuits and fried turkey. And for our lunch we'd put turkey, or sausage, and an army canteen. We'd carry our own drinking water because the well was not available because of the skunk. That just took care of our water supply.

Our restrooms were a shanty out in the back. The fuel for the heater came from the wood. At recess time we'd go out to the surrounding area. We'd hobble the horses in the pasture—right over there—and then we'd go out and gather up firewood and pile it up to use it for our fire in the school. We had fun. It was just a bunch of kids out on a picnic. And the teacher was having more fun than the children.

The wood that the trustees—not the school board in those days, the trustees—had left for us was a big pile of felled trees. There wasn't a student there big enough, strong enough to even cut the wood. So we couldn't cut the wood pile, and nobody cared enough to do it for us.

So one day I decided that the little rickety roof over the porch was going to fall, and it was really a hazard. So we started shaking the post, and then we'd have firewood. We shook it down. We used the shingles off of it to start our fire. Broke up the shingles. We furnished our own wood.

See that old swayback horse [in the photo]? And the saddle? That's what we used to ride to school on. One day, just to be ornery, the little boy kicked the horse. He must have thought I couldn't ride very well. I was talking to him about something, and he didn't answer, and I looked back, and he was sitting by the side of the road. So I let him walk the rest of the way. It was kind of funny.

Here's a picture of me trying to look very stern. I even wore glasses whether I needed them or not.

This is a picture of the well. It was an old hand pump. I knew there was a skunk in the well because when I pumped the water, the skunk fur would come out.

I had more fun than they did. It was a new experience for me. Life was good.

We didn't have a superintendent; we had trustees [of the school]. The man I lived with was a trustee. I never saw any superintendent. Nobody supervised me. I was on my own, believe me.

We didn't have any discipline problems except one of the older students. The first week of school he was teasing a little girl in front of him. I think he was sixteen. I was seventeen.

She said, "Make him stop."

So to correct him, I just tapped his hand.

He said, "Oh, do that again, that felt so good."

So I said to myself, "That's not going to work."

Then they had these little country dances. "Play party dances" they called them. I went to one of the dances with him. It was like a date. That was the time moonshine liquor was very popular, and I found out that he had a jug.

They had play party games which was like country-style dances, the old frontier-type. You'd go into a home, move all the furniture out in the yard and dance on the floor. They also would go to another school, which had warped floors. It was a little hard to dance on the warped floors. Waltzing was very difficult over a warped floor.

The date ended because some of the men got into a fight. I didn't know why, but later I found out it was over the jug of liquor they had in the woodpile. One man threw a big rock at his brother. Fortunately, I jumped behind a door at that time. I didn't know how dangerous it was. But they were just having a big fun thing. To them, it was no problem.

I had ridden over with this sixteen-year-old boy. He got me home all right, but then he went back.

I was very naive at the time. I learned a lot about life in the country, and life in general.

They had these play parties quite often. They didn't have invitations. Word would get out there's going to be a party at so-and-so's house. Whether you knew them or not. A huge crowd would appear. They still do that. In fact, they're having a brush-arbor party over there in Shelton right now. Have you ever heard of a brush-arbor? Well, they just build a frame on the top and put branches of trees to keep the weather out.

Then they'd have church meetings. Back then they just had what they called a get-together.

In my first year, there was a cowboy that had gone with every teacher. In fact, he would give them a great rush. He'd come over and sit in the swing on the front porch. All the family stayed in the background.

His first night to come over I thought that I would really entertain him. I made him angel food cake and lemonade. The man in whose home I was staying had told me, "Oh, you just try that."

So I served it to impress him. He didn't say anything.

So I said, "Well, did you like it?"

"Yeah, but I'd a heap rather have corn bread and sweet milk."

He was a great polo player. The Western, country-style of polo player. He was a bachelor and a great catch. He had 10,000 head of goat, but nobody could ever catch him. He married in later years. We didn't go anywhere. He just came and sat on the porch. Maybe he knew I didn't want to go anywhere with him. He didn't have a car. He came on horseback. He came and sat and talked.

He said, "I bet I can hold both of your hands in one of mine."

I said, "No, you can't."

So he did. And while he had my hands, he snapped my garter! But don't tell anybody that story.

The family was such a pleasant experience. We remained friends for years.

The following year, 1927–28, I taught in Comfort, Texas. One day my future husband came to visit me, and we went back to see this family in Knoxville. We went up and spent the night with them—well chaperoned. My sister chaperoned.

Three of our tires were slashed on the way up there. It was a tough country. We had to get to a telephone and have somebody bring us three new tires from town. We waited by a mailbox until the people came home. It became dark, and we were sitting and waiting for them. Finally they got home and turned on the lamps—they didn't have electricity— and we telephoned.

Transportation was rather remote. The roads were not too good. The bus driver from Kerrville brought us the tires.

You didn't teach after you were married. That was an automatic cancellation.

After I went to that school, I went to Comfort, Texas, nearer San Antonio. It was an entirely different situation—modern, well managed, with a German community. I had a second grade, and that was a very pleasant experience. There I lived in a boarding house. It wasn't particularly expensive. Let's see, I must have gotten eighty-five dollars a month. It was a big raise. For nine months. I lived near enough to walk to the school, and I could go home on weekends.

Then in my third year, I wanted to come in my home town, but they didn't have anything available but a small, one-room, Mexican school. All the students were Mexican. It was kind of a pioneering type of experience. After midterm, they had a teacher with the degrees in the main Kerrville system who was having discipline problems. I agreed to trade positions with her. She took the Mexican school at her same salary, and I went into her position with my same salary. She was getting more, but I had the advantage of having a harder class, better facilities. She was not a disciplinarian. No, she couldn't handle the situation.

Those students were a joy. I still meet some of them. One is now a newspaper editor. Another became a sheriff in town. Several of them were World War II casualties. And I was teaching side by side with some of the teachers who had taught me.

Then I went to Corpus Christi for two years from 1930 to 1932.

We were engaged for five years. I wouldn't marry until I paid off my loan. It took me about five years to pay that loan because I didn't have much. They were very lenient with me. I paid it regularly, small amounts, but I had it all paid up before I married.

The country schools were very short on teachers, and they didn't have the facilities or the salaries to attract the teachers with degrees. So there was a program at that time where you could get a temporary certificate after one year of college. You were available if someone would accept you. You would go in the summer and work on the degree. At the end of two years of college, you could apply for an elementary certificate. Now high school was more.

When I married, I had three years of college and still a temporary, elementary certificate. My two years at Corpus Christi were still on the provisional certificate. But when I married and moved to Houston, the University of Houston was just starting its first year. So I was fortunate. I got to teach part-time, or tutor, or whatever was available at that time. I got my degree and later taught in the Houston Independent Schools during World War II. I also got a loan of three hundred dollars then from the Houston College Women's Club. I always had to sort of step along to get there. But I was determined.

The elementary supervisor for the Houston Independent Schools was the one who approved the loan. She said, "Oh, I remember your husband. He was outstanding."

He didn't think she could remember him because she never had him as a pupil, only seeing him as a supervisor, but I believe she could have. When the Columbia University method of teaching reading [sight method] came in, we weren't supposed to teach phonics any more. But she said, "Just teach it anyway."

She was a great influence on me: Laura B. Peck, supervisor of elementary education, Houston Public Schools. I remember her main advice to us as teachers was, "Don't get in a rut. Go out when school is out in the summer, and whatever you do, get new experiences. Find something to keep from going stagnant."

One of my main interests since I've retired has been Home Extension and the Historical Society. I still wanted to be in the act. The Agricultural

Department has Home Extension for the homemakers, particularly in the rural areas—a learning program. Like 4 H Club. So we organized a group out here. It's very active.

Retired Teachers has been an interesting experience. I'm head of Community Service. And Scholarship. In our Retired Teachers' club we had a strange mixture of reactions about the idea of giving a scholarship. Some of the teachers were hesitant. In fact, they were almost belligerent about giving a scholarship to start young people in the educational field.

"Well, we didn't have any help when we were that young!"

That's beside the point. I'm very dedicated to getting somebody started because I know what it meant to me. Suppose nobody believed in me? I never would have thought of the field. But somebody cared about promoting young people. So that's the thing I'm really interested in. Also, I'll be on the Scholarship Committee with the DAR chapter in Fredricksburg because I like to see young people being promoted.

I got my loan to go to normal school from the Masons. The secretary of the Masonic Lodge was also my Sunday School teacher. He also had a jewelry store. My first employment was working in his jewelry store. So he saw a need there to help a young person get started.

I did photo refinishing for him, which came in handy years later because during the war, I went out to Oregon where my husband was with the army. I managed to follow him that far and get out there to spend some time with him. In the little town there was no place to live. I happened to see an ad: "Photo finisher wanted. Jewelry store." I went to them. I told them, "Oh, I had experience. I had done that kind of work before." I didn't tell them how long and how many years ago. So I got the job.

At about the same time I went to the USO. A woman happened to come in with some cookies for the service men. She said, "Incidentally, I have a spare room's going to be available."

I overheard the conversation, and I stepped up and said, "Oh, that's just what I'm looking for." So I got to live in her home.

In the meantime, I sent word by someone who had a Signal Corps insignia. I knew my husband was at the camp, but I was on my own. He told me to stay at the Dalles, Oregon. I'd taken the bus that far. But I knew he was going overseas, and I wanted to stay as long as I could. I told the man to tell Sergeant Meyers that his wife has a job and is living in Bend, Oregon.

My husband had told me to go home because I had a job teaching. He thought I was on my way back to Houston to teach school, but I had received word that the polio epidemic was so bad at that time that they had decided not to open the schools for six weeks. So I didn't lose out on school at all because I got back just at the time it was opening.

You had to have a husband that cooperated with you to be a teacher.

I stayed in this area all my life. I didn't go out of state. I made a lot of good friends, in the war time and in the depression time. So I've had a good life. I've been fortunate to make good friends. I'm unpredictable. Dependable, but unpredictable. But I enjoyed life. I have an appreciation of life. Everything I've ever dreamed of, I have it. Some people say it was hard, but I didn't think it was.

My mother's mother's family moved out West during the Civil War. Of course, they were adventurers. They got as far as Houston. The family was attending church there. She must have been about sixteen or seventeen. And a young man thought she'd make a good wife, and they were married. They had three boys and a girl. The father died when my mother was five and the mother when she was eight. She was a strong character. She shaped my life forever. The boys were sent to work on a farm, and my mother went to live with another family. She was just sort of a built-in housekeeper and baby-sitter.

My father was a policeman in Houston, and he was with a friend and saw my mother. He said, "Oh, that's a good-looking girl." The fellow he was with said, "Come on, I'll introduce you."

So he said, "Sister, this is my friend."

She was just a young girl of eighteen when they married. She was nineteen when I was born.

My mother always wanted to live here. She loved Kerrville. She gave me Kerrville. That shaped her. She died at ninety-four a few years ago in a nursing home right here in Kerrville. I was glad we had that time together. She was an independent person, a ramrod, a motivator.

In Fredricksburg they have a dividing line, and there was a lot of prejudice during World War I because of loyalties. The German families were a little bit cool to anything new. In fact, they're very standoffish. As a girl, as a Peterson, I didn't know many people in Fredericksburg. But after I married and became a Meyers—oh, I was welcomed! I've enjoyed being in the Homemakers' Clubs, and a group of women in the DAR over there just treat me like I'm acceptable because I have a German last name. But they're very strange. Friendly, but hesitant, the German families. So there was a sort of German/non-German group. Kerrville was mostly the non-German group. The Schreiner family—who gave Kerrville the store, the bank, and the college—came from Alsace-Lorraine.

I know a friend of ours that lives in Fredricksburg said when he went to Kerrville they'd say, "Ah, you live on the other side of the Rhine." They call it the Rhine. But most business people traded from Fredericksburg on to San Antonio, and then the Kerrville business drew out of the ranching community—sheep and goat raisers, mostly. So they had common interests right there. Fredericksburg is farming and some cattle, but then there's ranching mostly in the Kerrville area—in the hill country— up towards what we call the Divide.

There wasn't too much prejudice in World War II. We loved Nimitz. He was a German from Fredericksburg, and I think that sort of helped unify it. Come to think about it, there were many Fredericksburg young people who came to Kerrville to work, like in the banking area.

I was here and remember well when the boys marched around the courthouse in 1917 prior to being shipped overseas to war. My aunt's house was near the courthouse, right next door to the Nimitz house, and that was my first experience.

Then I was there when they came back. My cousin did not come back. His mother got to go on a Mother's Trip over to France to see her son's grave. She was very proud of that trip, you know. Well, they couldn't take all of them, now could they?*

Then World War II was a whole 'nother generation. My brother was in the National Guard in Kerrville. Then Pearl Harbor came, and they were activated in the service so that was just history repeating itself. As I said, many of the students that I taught were very much involved in all parts of the world in World War II.

Many people came to Kerrville as a retirement area—mostly because they had brought their children to summer camps out there. That attracted some of those same people who waited until they were able to retire. They're here now, and some of their children who went to summer camps. So it grew as a resort area. A health resort, and then a recreational resort. That's what's caused its spurts of growth.

Many tubercular people were sent to Kerrville for the sunshine and the dry air. Our first Veterans Hospital was called the American Legion Hospital strictly for tuberculars. Then, later on, it became a Veterans Hospital, and it's a pretty excellent facility. I know my husband is eligible to go there. They go strictly by financial ability to pay.

An old friend's brother and I graduated from high school together. Her brother's older than she is, and I heard her just a day or two ago tell me of an experience as a teacher that she had had, and it was so much like one I had had. I had one child who didn't come to school. He went home at noon and didn't come back. I asked somebody to take care of my classroom. It was in Houston, and I said, "He just lives across the street. I'll be right back." So I went over to the house and got him by the hand and brought him back to school.

I thought that was unusual 'til she told me just the other day that there was a little Mexican boy in Tivy Elementary that she sent home with a

*After World War I the U.S. government sent some of the Gold Star mothers to visit their sons' graves in France.

book. At that time they had separate schools for the Mexican families that lived in the town. Our school didn't have but three or four grades. The children didn't have to stay until they were fourteen. Well, they had to go and help their families, support their families. Not any of them were very wealthy.

One Mexican family was outstanding. That was the Baptist minister's son. A very smart little boy. He was named as one of the heroes—a downed pilot in World War II.

So many of my students did not come back. Being in this town again, I can sort of check up what happened to those. I remembered the ones from this town more. I mean it was terrible because I heard of the families and heard of the family backgrounds to start with. I guess that's why I enjoyed teaching in familiar surroundings.

The minister's son was not a dropout. We thought of that later. They could drop out if they wanted to, but certain families had the means and the incentive to go ahead. It was a transportation problem 'cause they were all on one side of town, and the high school was too far away to walk everyday. I'm not sure how that went.

I don't remember any Mexican students in my class when I graduated in '25. San Antonio had facilities. People that had money could send their children to San Antonio schools, to the Catholic schools. Maybe that's where they went—to the Catholic schools, which took them to the eighth grade. So we must have had just to the third or fourth grade at the most. They had a Catholic school in town, and they had facilities through the eighth grade. They had a black Catholic school and a white one. So the Mexicans went to the white because, now, after I came back to Kerrville this time, I taught quite a bit over there.

I substituted recently in the Catholic school and in the Lutheran private school, and this was interesting. In the Catholic school I'd go in the catechism and follow the routine, and in the Lutheran school I could participate in their Bible study and religion courses. But come to the public school, and you're not even allowed to pray or show any signs of religion.

I enjoyed the church private schools so much better because the children seemed to have so much more respect for their teachers. You don't find that on the whole among the public schools. They just do it because they have to. The private schools, they go because they choose that. So I think the most interesting place right now would be the private school.

When I started teaching there was the public school and the Catholic school. And then there was a finishing school for girls: Scofield. A woman was asking me yesterday if I could give her any information on that because some of the women my age now were students in that private school in the twenties and thirties. It was started by wealthy families and the wealthy ranchers to send their girls into a private boarding school to get an education, oh, just a step above the public school. The girls would go to the little ranch schools as youngsters and then come over here to the finishing school. It was just girls. Very strict. I know that some of the Schreiner girls went there, a lot of the prominent families. I don't remember much 'cause I never did go to it, and they didn't really mix in with the local town.

After the depression, in the thirties, many of the ranchers' children that wanted to come to Kerrville to go to school because of the facilities would board with families in Kerrville. My mother helped to meet the family finances by boarding ranch girls. They went to school with my sister. After I was gone, my room was available. They'd come in for the week days and go home on the weekends so it was really convenient. Sometimes my mother'd have as many as four, and they're lifelong friends. They still come back, even after she was in the nursing home. And she had meals for a lot of people—some business people. So that's how she met her needs financially when my father became ill.

Some of the Scofield girls did go to college, but they'd go on to Dallas, to Hockaday School or to Louisiana—a famous one—Newcomb College. They'd go wherever they had to. So we had a lot of highly educated people in the area, but it was just a matter of finances for so many of them. Many of the students that graduated from Tivy eventually came back and taught in the same school. That was satisfaction to me to be able to teach in the same school with my former students. I felt like I'd really succeeded.

When they built a new high school, they couldn't agree on the name of the new high school. Captain Tivy had given this land for the original school. When the high school was built, the Peterson family donated the land to that high school, and they were going to name it Peterson. But the old Tivy graduates wouldn't hear of Tivy High School being changed after all those years. So, they had the junior high named Peterson Middle School, and that was to solve that problem. Then they rebuilt the middle school, and restored the old original building. That's what the Historical Commission just finished. That's used for the administrative building now.

Oh, it was fun to go in the building. I remember that cloakroom where they put me when I was in the first grade 'cause I chatted too much. I was a chatterbox: "If you don't stop talking, I'll put you in the cloakroom." So I spent a lot of time in there.

FOUR

Elizabeth Shelton

Elizabeth Shelton, ca. 1987.

It was all right for a woman to get a college education as long as she was planning to be a teacher. But if it were any other profession, it wasn't. They'd say, "Why was it necessary? A woman needs to stay home and learn to cook, wash and iron, and get married and have children."

ELIZABETH STROUD SHELTON began her teaching career twice. The first time was as a sixteen-year-old teacher in 1922 in a one-room school in a German settlement between Dunley and Quihi in Medina County, Texas. The second time was in 1965 as a retiree from the public schools who started over as a special education teacher in a private school in San Antonio. The story of why and how Elizabeth began a new career at age sixty-five encapsulates the coping styles she used throughout her lifetime. After being widowed young by a man who "didn't believe in insurance" and putting her five children through college, she would have been content to enjoy her family and other activities but found she could not live on the pittance provided by the Texas State Teachers' Retirement System. Financial necessity indicated that she would have to continue to work even though the public schools mandated her retirement.

Failure was not even an alternative to be considered. Typically, she looked close at hands for resources to assist her. She responded to a want ad because she recognized an old home-town name, and a family friend hired her to teach in a private special education school because she was "Jim Stroud's daughter." Never doing anything by halves, she earned her graduate certification in special education because "I just thought it would be nice to have it."

When she walked into a classroom of unruly, mentally retarded children, she restored order by assigning one youngster to call roll and demanding a memorized Bible verse as a response. Again, failure was not a possibility for Elizabeth or for the children, even though many would have considered it impossible for her students to memorize a Bible verse (and do other tasks she assigned). She acted *as if* events would transpire the way she wanted them to, and often they did. Is it too fanciful to think that maybe mentally handicapped children wrote "impossible" letters to their parents because Elizabeth took all the letters—even the orphans'—to the office to be mailed just *as if* there would be loving eyes to read them?

A strong sense of propriety motivated many of Elizabeth's actions. Indeed, it led her to acquiesce to her father's wishes and become a teacher. Elizabeth wanted to be a lawyer, and even today she frequently asks, "Don't you think I would have made a good lawyer?" But it was not to be for a "lady" in her day and age. College was expected—the "right" thing to do in her family. Remarkably, her father put fourteen children through college, though Elizabeth laments, "Poor Pop, he died before he knew whether I was going to be a lady or not"—although she was already established in the profession he wanted for her. Elizabeth, too, was worried about the effect that higher education would have on the men of her day and admonished her friends not to reveal her profession to prospective suitors so they would not be scared away.

Once pushed into a teaching career, Elizabeth entered it wholeheartedly. The story she told about putting flowers on her dreaded stepmother's grave was a parable of how she approached other difficult or odious tasks: "I'll get my revenge by fixing her grave up, and when her kids come up here, they'll know that I've been up here." She solved problems by doing more, not less, than what was expected of her.

Elizabeth's mother died when she was still a child, but there was no lack of female relatives and chaperones to be role models and supervise her upbringing. When a friend accused her of being "the dumbest person I ever knew to be eighteen years old," Elizabeth retorted, "If you knew my father, my brother, my Negro mammy, and my father's brother's wife, and my aunt . . . " Her father also was a strong influence; she defied the dress code for teachers in her first school because it is more than her father required. She also turned to him as a man with enough "influence" to get an outhouse installed so the young teacher and her charges would not have to go out in the "brush."

Elizabeth's description of her first country school underscores the poverty of life and lack of glamour for a sixteen-year-old teacher away from home in a town where "there wasn't any picture show, wasn't anything" and the children ate "old, cold biscuits and syrup day after day."

In addition to the one-room schoolhouse, Elizabeth's story memorializes two other unusual schools. One, at the end of her career, is the private school for special education students before public schools were mandated by law to provide services for them. The other, at the beginning of her career, was the Girls Training School in Gainesville, Texas. There Elizabeth taught "five little girls" ages eleven to thirteen. Three had been sentenced for up to ten years (until they were twenty-one) for the crime of being pregnant, two by their grandfathers and one by her uncle. The punishment for the men involved, if any, was never mentioned.

Today Elizabeth is past president of the Retired Teachers Association, active in her church and Friends of Music (where she both sings and sews costumes for concerts), and an inspiration to her five children, twelve grandchildren, fifteen great-grandchildren, and countless friends.

Elizabeth Stroud, graduation photo, Devine, Texas, ca. 1920.

It was all right for a woman to get a college education as long as she was planning to be a teacher. But if it were any other profession, it wasn't. They'd say, "Why was it necessary?" A woman needs to stay home and learn to cook, wash and iron, and get married and have children."

Teaching was the only profession for a woman. I know I fought rigorously against it. I made my own decisions.

For years I would date young men, and I would caution the other girls, "Don't tell him I'm a teacher." 'Cause I don't know how many of them told me later it was fine, but "Before," they'd say, "I'd have had the feeling that you'd listen to every word I'd say. That I'd make errors in speech."

I'd say, "I wouldn't have done that."

"Oh, I know that now," they'd say.

There wasn't anyone, you know, in all my growing-up years, no one who would ever consider being a doctor. And really, a nurse, a long time ago automatically had a bad reputation. But later on, a nurse was almost the equivalent, for a lady, to a teacher. It took a long time.

Did I tell you all my nurse-daughter was appointed chairman of the board, the State Board of Infectious Disease Control? My number two daughter. She's writing her third book.

As long as you had a teaching career in mind, I can remember this, you didn't even have to go to college. You could go and take a test at the area superintendent's office, and you would be certified to teach. But you had to have college in mind.

I was going to college. I never thought anything else. It was automatically understood. You went to school every day. If you were well, you had to get there. Even if you were on your deathbed. And then you automatically went to college. There were no ifs, ands or buts. My father had fourteen kids, and all of them went through school, to college. I didn't really want to be a teacher. I wanted to be a lawyer. Pop wouldn't hear of it.

Well, my dad sent me to college, and I got my temporary certificate I taught on. I was in school twelve years, and it took me eight summers to get my degree.

I think the reason Pop was so insistent we go to school, he was taken out of school in the fourth or fifth grade. He was taken out of school to help make a living. He said they were so poor, and they didn't have very much. 'Course there was several of them, and they had to raise everything that they ate, practically. Very few clothes—no shoes—and he said in cold weather he'd have to walk to work barefooted. When it was real cold, his mother would have to wrap his feet with rags and newspapers. I think he was about, oh, in his late teens, and he was sent to Wealder. At that time they were living at Lockhart, and they sent him to Wealder to be an apprentice under a blacksmith who happened to be my mother's father.

Now that's where he probably met my mother, but they didn't want him to marry her. They didn't want my mother to marry my dad because they didn't think he was, you know, upper crust—as good a stock as they were. But in the long run, in doing the genealogies, we come from dukes and duchesses and lords and such-like on my daddy's side, and on my mother's side we go way back to Suzanna Wesley, mother of John Wesley who founded the Methodist Church. My friend Nova Marks says she understands now why I'm like I am. She says, "You're like Suzanna."

Pop took us to San Antonio once a month to the dentist 'cause our town didn't have a good dentist. If we were real good at the dentist's office and didn't fuss or complain, he would treat us afterwards. He'd take us shopping. We bought our shoes, our clothes, our groceries. We bought everything in San Antonio. He wouldn't buy just a dozen bananas, he'd buy bananas by the stalk. Apples by the box. Oranges and apples in those barrels. It'd stay on the back porch, the sleeping porch. You could eat as much outside or laying around the house. He'd chase you down to find out who, say, ate half an apple and threw the rest away. You wouldn't get any again for a week.

When I taught in the little one-room school in this German settlement between Dunley and Quihi in Medina county in 1922–23 we had to walk through this black mud. And we had to cross a creek. They cut trees, saplings I guess you call them, and lay them across that creek.

When it rained and the creek got up, well, they would come after us on horseback. Four of us would ride a horse back to town. The man that I lived with—he and his wife—would come for us. He was the most prominent family in town, his family was. He was an old German man.

I paid sixteen dollars a month for my room. They put a one-burner oil stove in the bedroom, and if you've ever smelled coal oil, it's horrible. Smells terrible. Particularly when you turned it out. It's worse than a candle when you snuff a candle out. And that's what I had to cook on. I had to cook my own meals.

They didn't cook for me, but they insisted I play Forty-two [dominoes] every night. We would have a table all set up, and you had to play. I was just part of it, I guess.

I was supposed to wear my skirts two inches from the floor and two petticoats. I insisted, "I'm not wearing two petticoats, and I'm not wearing my skirts that long." I said, "My father didn't make me do that," and I said, "I'm not going to do it here!"

That was the rules they had set up for the teachers.

We didn't have any trustees. We had the county superintendent and this old man kinda ramrodded everything. I can't even remember his name. I was trying to think of it the other day. He was back in '23–'24. That county superintendent would pop in on me ever once in a while. You didn't know when he was coming. He'd park down the road, and he'd walk up.

In winter time, when they butchered, they made this blood sausage. I would go back there and play Forty-two. And on this heater, they would have a big pan—about so big, so deep—and that blood sitting up there gurgling and a-boiling! Oh, it was sickening. I had a finicky stomach anyway, and to have to sit there and to have to smell that stuff!

"Don't you like blood sausage?"

I said, "No, I never did eat any and just looking at that turns me." So I got to where I'd give an excuse. I couldn't go play Forty-two while I knew that stuff was boiling up there. And it seemed like every time I'd turn around, they had a pan of blood boiling on the stove.

I brought my food from home. There was a little store—a little, tiny store and a post office together. I guess both of them were about as large as this room, and if I ran out of anything I'd just go there and buy it. Pork and beans, sardines, or something like that I didn't have to cook. If I went home, well, I always stocked up on stuff. I wasn't supposed to leave town unless I got this man's permission. There wasn't any picture show, wasn't anything.

I brought soup for my kids 'cause I couldn't stand to see them eat old cold biscuits with syrup. Some of those kids would have nothing to eat but cold biscuits with syrup day after day.

I had to be janitor. I had to build all the wood fires of a morning, sweep the building in the afternoon, and mop it ever so often, and wash the windows. I wasn't supposed to ask the students to help me do any kind of the work like scrubbing the floor. It had to be scrubbed every night before I walked out and locked the door.

The water had to be brought in from the well, and at that time I didn't know anything about paper cups. If I had, I'd have bought them because, oh, I hated to drink after all those kids. We had a bucket and a dipper. And runny nose and all and I'd grab something and wipe their nose. We didn't even have paper towels. I'm not sure if we had Kleenex.

What was so bad about going to the restroom, they had to go to the bushes. Even in rainy weather. Boys on the right, girls on the left. The kids didn't want to go. Out in the cold, and no place to go. I didn't either. No wonder I had a kidney infection!

I'm telling you, having a father that had a little influence did a lot of good. The first time I went home, "How's school?"

"I hate it." I said, "You got to do something." I told my father, "I'm not going in the bushes." I said, "I want you to see Mr. Saahtoff." That was the name of the county superintendent. I said, "You got me in this. Now you see that we get an outdoor toilet."

Well, we did. I had to scrub that everyday, and I finally got smart. I got the boys, and I said, "If y'all get here before I do"—I told them where I was going to put the key—"you open up and build a fire in the winter time." At recess in the afternoon or if they'd get through some work before school was out—we went until four o'clock—I said, "Why don't y'all go out and get your exercise? Go out and chop some wood and bring it so it'll be dry." That way I wouldn't have to cut the wood. But it took me two or three months to get smart—'cause that was my first school.

I was sixteen. I was seventeen in March, and I was teaching in September. I didn't know anything about teaching. Sibyl Sutherland said she didn't know anything when she began teaching, and I thought, "Well, where did she think I learned it?" Because, of course, we had practice teaching in college, but it didn't prepare you for all this stuff.

See, I got out of high school in three years and finished in May. Aunt Mattie said, "What are we going to do about Baby?"

She had stayed with us until I was about thirteen. She and my step-mother couldn't get along, and when Aunt Mattie left, my nigger mammy Delia left, too. She wouldn't stay with us. See, Aunt Delia came with my mother when she married. So Pop set Aunt Delia up in a barbeque stand about a block from our house, and Aunt Mattie went clear across town. Then she got a better job in San Antonio.

Uncle Earl, my mother's youngest brother, was a doctor of English at Sam Houston College, and he wrote Pop and said, "Send her to me." So I went up there and stayed with them and went to school that summer, and went right on in September. I went all the way through.

I had to stay with my aunt and uncle 'cause I was too young to be out in the world. I guess Aunt Emma had a maid. I guess they did the laundry because I didn't. Then when they let me stay in the dormitory, I don't know who did the laundry.

Then I transferred from Sam Houston. I was ready to quit, and I transferred from Sam Houston to Southwestern University, 'cause that was our family college. Everybody in the family had gone there. Southwestern was Ruttersville College at first. It was known as Ruttersville College, and it was at Chapel Hill. Then it was . . . let's see . . . what did they change it to? I don't know the name. I forget. They moved it from Chapel Hill to Georgetown, and then it was Southwestern University. Southwestern is at Georgetown, and the one at San Marcos is Southwest Texas.

Even after I had taught a year at that one-room school, they thought I was too young to be out in the world on my own. All of them—my father, my aunt, my mother's brother, and my mother's sister, and my dad.

My Aunt Mattie, a dietician at the Girls Training School in Gainesville, Texas, said, "Send Baby up here. I'll look after her."

So I went. I was eighteen in March, I finished my school in April, and I went there in June. When I left there, I was nineteen. So I went through that year. I finished college in '22, taught in '22–'23, and went there in '23–'24.

I had five little girls who were eleven to thirteen years old in my class. Three of them were there for being pregnant—two by the grandfather, and one by the uncle. They'd stay there until they were twenty-one, unless it was proven they were eligible for parole and could take their place in society again. Most of them were there through their uncles or their father or a friend of the family. There were some girls there that had committed theft—cigarettes or whatever. The county, the courts, sent them there. They thought the kids were delinquents. That's what the school was for—delinquent girls. They could be there up to ten years or more.

I was inexperienced in that type of work. That's what got me interested in young people—working with them.

There must have been about a hundred fifty girls there because they had five dorms. Each dorm had a house mother and a dietician. The girls took turns cooking, cleaning, working in the office, and so forth.

I taught the kids in the morning and worked in the office in the afternoon when the children had to rest. They were taught a trade, working in the laundry, in the office, in the kitchen, or gardening the greenhouse with flowers and all. My students were mostly in the third, fourth, and fifth grade. I think maybe some of them had been kept out of school for some reason. Back then they did that.

Every Saturday I worked in the office in the morning, and in the afternoon I had to chauffeur the superintendent of the school around town while she bought groceries and such as that. She was a crochety old lady. I had been driving for two or three years, and she thought I drove too fast. It was an open touring car. She'd sit with a hat on, this old-timey hat, and hold that hat on as we'd go whipping around the curves in that old Ford. It was an open touring car, with a top you could fold back that you put on when it rained and put on those window curtains.

On Sunday, I had to take my aunt, the dietician, to school to prepare the meal. See, the girls were taught to do the cooking and all.

They locked the girls up every night at nine o'clock. I noticed these two girls that I was really fond of kept edging up to the door. They tried slipping out and got caught at the gate.

I don't know what happened to the babies after they were born, unless they were put up for adoption. They had a nursery there, but they just suddenly disappeared. When I asked my aunt about it, she said, "You're too young to know." And here I was, you know, eighteen. Girls back then were pretty well sheltered and taken care of.

So that was my experience there.

Aunt Mattie retired shortly after that and moved to Fort Worth. See, Aunt Mattie had left college to come home and take care of us kids when my mother died. She left home when I was about thirteen and got a job as a dietician at the girls training school. After she was there twenty-five years, she retired and went home to Fort Worth, and she died there.

My experience at the girls' training school was an eye opener you might say, having been protected like we were. We couldn't play with just anyone, and if any girl had a shady character, they were not allowed in our place. My father and my oldest brother saw to that. And my Negro mammy, Aunt Delia, she wouldn't let anybody on the place. She was 104 when she died.

Every summer when school was out in May, Pop would put us on the train and send us to my mother's people at Wealder, Texas. So we had too many bosses. We should have all turned out better than what we did.

At first I didn't know why those girls were in the trade school, but after I was there two or three months, 'course I had heard tales from kids in school talking. That's where you get your education. They were not open. You didn't hear anything about sex like you do now. So I'd ask my aunt questions.

I had a companion teacher, Ruth Lawler. She taught sixth to eighth grade, I believe. She would insist that I was old enough to date. But Aunt Mattie would say, "No, she's too young."

But anyway, Ruth would get me a date to go uptown so I learned quite a bit from Ruth that way. She went with a real nice fellow, and he had a younger brother my age. I was still being protected, and Ruth told me one day, "You're the dumbest person I ever knew to be eighteen years old."

I thought, "If you knew my father, my brother, my Negro mammy, and my father's brother's wife, and my aunt!" Because Aunt Mattie, Aunt Delia, and my dad and my brother kept an eye on me. Poor Pop, he died before he knew whether I was going to be a lady or not.

I think Ruth was about twenty-two or something like that. When you think about it, she was my English teacher at Southwestern, a private Methodist college. She got tired with Southwestern. She got disgusted. The pay wasn't good. She got more pay at the training school. You worked for the government, you see.

My father had fourteen children. I hasten to add he had two wives. There were five by his first wife, and I was the youngest. And he had nine by his second wife. They are all living but one. Two of my half sisters and I are real close. They come by quite often. They come by when none of the rest of them do. I just don't take anything off of them. Like when I was wanting to put the curb down at the cemetery, I couldn't get anybody to help me.

Pop died the second of July. We buried him on the Fourth. He had gotten out of his sick bed the Sunday before to go and put flowers on the grave, and we buried him the next Sunday. His flowers were still pretty. I thought if he could do that as sick as he was, the least I could do was take care of the graves.

So I got hold of this Mexican man that worked with my dad a long time, and he made me a cut rate of seventy-five dollars. So he put the curb all around these graves. I couldn't get anybody to help me pay for it. It was going to be more than seventy-five dollars until I told him, I said, "Well, Jim, I can't get anybody to help me pay for it, but I'll get you the rest of it when I can."

"That's all right, Mrs. Elizabeth. You're a good woman. Anybody that'd come up here . . ."

Every time I'd go down on change of season and take flowers and clean off the graves. I had narcissus and irises and mums and roses. Every kind of flower. Something was blooming all the time.

One time I was angry with my half sisters, and I felt, by George, their parents are buried here. Now, why don't they do something? So I put flowers . . . I have two little brothers buried there, and my mother's parents, and a niece, and my father, and my stepmother. So I put flowers on everybody's grave except my stepmother and I got back in the car. I looked over there, and I said to my cousin Agatha, "That's tacky. I can't do that." So I got out of the car and got more flowers and put them on her grave.

Agatha said, "I don't know why you did that. That woman hated you."

I said, "I know she did. But," I said, "I'll get my revenge by fixing her grave up, and when her kids come up here, they'll know that I've been up here."

I was named for my grandmother, both my grandmothers, in fact, on both sides of the family. I got my grandmother Stroud's Stradivarius violin and, well, Agatha has it now. But I'd go down there, and she'd play the piano, and I'd play the violin. We grew up in our house playing the organ. We had one of these old pump organs. Everybody had to learn to play it. Anyway, I said our childhood was hectic, kinda like.

Every time I go out there to Big Foot I put flowers on the grave, my cousin and I. I had one cousin send me ten dollars, and he's in California. His grandparents are buried there as well as mine.

So my cousin and I would go down to Big Foot where Grandpa and Grandma Stroud were buried. He was married twice. We cleaned off the graves, and we managed to get a Georgia marble headstone for Grandpa.

We got back in the car and my cousin said, "I'm not going to clean that old lady's grave."

I said, "You mean his second wife?"

He says, "She was mean as all get out."

Oh, she'd fuss at us kids! They lived up the hill from us, and we would have to take their meals to them. If we were five minutes late, she'd chew us out about it.

They were both so old. He was in a wheelchair. His legs were shot up in the Civil War. He drove the stage coach after he got out of the Civil War. He was captured by Santa Ana and kept in Mexico in prison for a long time and managed to escape. He and some man thought they were swimming to San Antonio, but they ended up in El Paso. Somewhere along the road they got guns, rifles, and somebody gave them flour. They made a paste and wrapped it around those guns so that when they were in the water the guns wouldn't get wet. The Indians were still roaming the country.

So when they got to El Paso, they hiked back to my grandmother at Lockhart. She was living in Lockart at that time. Lockhart, Texas. Which is above Wealder, not too far from San Antonio. My aunt had dressed up to go to a party. She had married.

So Grandma was out working in the garden, and Aunt Ellen came out, and she said, "Mom, there's a strange-looking man coming down the lane."

Grandma didn't look up. She just kept on a-hoeing and a-weeding. When Grandpa got within hearing distance, she kept on a-hoeing—never did look up—just said, "What took you so long, Pa?"

He'd been gone two or three years, but the war had been over for some time. He'd been in prison, see?

Anyway, tales like that . . .

Grandpa's the one that perfected this recipe for liniment. Us kids had to peddle it around town at a dollar a bottle. He wouldn't even give us a nickel. He wouldn't give us the recipe—the receipt. He called it a receipt; we call it a recipe.

My aunt's daughter came to see him and while her husband engaged him in conversation, she prowled through his chest of drawers, dresser drawers, and found it. And that today is a well-known liniment. I said right there we'd missed a chance to have a little bit of money.

And then we had the fruitcake factory, you know. That's out from where my youngest daughter lives. Grandpa had gone into town to get flour, coffee, and sugar. They raised everything else on the place. He was gone a long time, and he finally came back. He went with the wagon and the mules, and when he came back, he was walking.

Grandma wanted to know what had happened to the mules and the wagon. Well, he had traded them for this stuff. So it angered her, and she put him to picking pecans—shelling them out, you know—and she began making fruitcakes and selling them to the neighbors. It just developed, and now they are shipped all over the world. They make fruitcakes, bars, cupcakes. They sell pecans and everything.

Grandpa Stroud was given a land grant when he was mustered out of the service in the Civil War. It took in what I call the holy city, Devine, and Big Foot and Pleasanton, and on down to Three Rivers.

So when I was teaching down in San Antonio, I would go down to Devine and pick up my cousin Agatha, and we would go down to Three Rivers. I would go down on Friday night, and Saturday morning we'd head out to Three Rivers where one of my half sisters lived.

Every place that was Grandpa Stroud's that we passed by, they had oil wells on them. Agatha would be so angry. She'd just cuss that man out something terrible.

When he came in, he'd say, "Pack up, Ma, we're moving!" He was always trading—you know, moving.

"Where're we going?"

"To Big Foot."

She says, "I'll never paint another picture, I'll never paint another dish, I'll never plant another garden," and she didn't. She just sat in her rocking chair, and she died.

She was buried at Big Foot. That's the worst . . . It's just one little dinky store. It's kind of a farming country, you know. People scattered all around. It's named for Big Foot Wallace, and they have the Big Foot Museum down there in his honor. Well, we went to the museum, and I didn't see much.

When we first started, we had truant officers. The county superintendent, of course, we had, but we had a truant officer, too. What happened to him? They just did away with him. We don't have a truant officer any more, but you can't enforce anything anymore. Truant officers used to get them by the ear and take them back to school.

In the sixties Tommy McDaniels used to do that. I said, "Tommy, how do you know so well where they are?" I had taught his brother and sister, too.

He said, "I guess it's 'cause I was just like one of 'em, and I knew all the places they'd be. All I had to do was drive down under the bridge or wherever, round 'em up and take 'em back to school."

Tommy got down there lots of time and got those kids out. He'd go down in the basement where it's so pitch dark you couldn't see. I worked with the, uh . . . oh, what was my title? Anyway, I worked with the young people. Tommy was a police officer, and he'd come by and say, "Come on, Grandma. Time to go."

I'd say, "Where are we going?"

I said it was a good thing my kids were all grown 'cause I'd have been afraid I'd a met one of mine down there.

I got my special ed training in San Antonio. I went at night at San Antonio College. I went three nights a week for a year in 1971. I'd drive home, and then I'd go back the next morning.

I didn't necessarily have to have a special ed certificate. I just thought it would be nice to have it. I'd teach all day, and then I'd go to school at night. I was sixty-five, and I taught special ed there six more years 'til I was seventy-one.

I wish now that I had taught a little bit longer and bought me a new car, but it wouldn't have made any difference because now I can't drive anyway. There are days—I was telling my daughter Jimmy last Saturday— there are days when I feel real good. I'd do anything if I had my car, and I could just get in it and go where I wanted to, when I wanted to.

And she said, "Well, you don't have any business driving."

I am so sick and tired of hearing, "You don't have any business driving. We want you over here where we can take care of you, watch over you."

I said, "Well, how do you think I got to where I am? I didn't have anybody watching over me all these years."

See, when the kids' dad died, my youngest daughter was a junior in college, and the youngest, my son, was a junior in high school.

Jerry was a music major, and she said, "Mother, I'm going to quit." I said, "No, you're not!"

Their dad didn't believe in insurance, and he left quite a few bills. We had two bulldozers. One was paid for, but it was mortgaged to pay for the other. We knocked timber and built dams and spillways and roads, whatever.

He would call me from Leakey where he did a lot of work, and he'd say, "I'm so tired. My back hurts. Can you pick me up?"

I said, "What's wrong with the pick-up?"

"It's out there."

Well, I'd drive to Leakey and get it, and the next morning I'd have to hit the floor running at four o'clock, get his breakfast and lunch, and take him to Leakey so he could go to work. I had to come back and get the kids up. Get their breakfast and get them ready for school. And I'd go to school. I'd go to teach.

Well, I tell you, I had retired, and my legs broke out up to my knees. My arms—see these pits? I'm allergic to so many things, and the doctor made a mistake and gave me penicillin. I almost died from it. My finances got to rock bottom. I owned a big three-bedroom, two-bath house, swimming pool, and everything right here in town. I thought, "If I don't do something, I'm going to lose my place."

So I was reading the paper one day, and there was an ad in there. I thought, "Well, I know those people. They used to be in Devine."

So I went down to San Antonio in pouring down rain. I had a half sister that lived there. So I went down and visited with her and drove on out to the school.

Mr. Bledsoe said, "Sure. Jim Stroud's daughter is welcome."

They wanted me to go right then. So I went to the classroom, and a young Mexican man was teaching. The kids were walking around. They were knocking things around. They'd walk by anybody's desk, and they'd just take their hands—everything was on the floor. They threw erasers, they threw chairs, they threw books. That poor Mexican man could not control them.

So Barbara, the principal, said, "I'd like you to start in the morning."

I said, "That's not cricket." I was just getting up from what they call the Asian flu and I was as weak! I didn't think I'd make it to San Antonio. I said, "I feel like you should give him two week's notice. That's the proper thing to do."

She left to go next door, in one of the other classrooms, and he said, "I'm afraid I'm going to lose my job."

I said, "Not for two weeks you're not because I'm not coming in here tomorrow." And I said, "Look around for something else."

So the first day I went down there, two weeks later, the kids were still misbehaving. That night I drove all the way back to Kerrville. I had really planned to stay with my half sister. Coming home I thought, "Well, I cannot take that. Those kids walking around, screaming at each other, throwing things." So I thought, "Well, we're going to fix things!"

I went back the next morning, walked in, and they were still throwing things around. I gave my Indian war whoop, and everybody got quiet.

I said, "Everybody sit down. I mean at your own desk." And I said, "Don't open your mouth. I'm not going to speak any louder than I'm speaking now." I said, "I'll have no more walking around, getting up out of your seats, unless you first raise your hand, and I give you permission. You are not to walk by and touch a thing on anybody's desk. And if I see you throw a book, I'm going to throw a book and hit you right in the head." And I said "You are not to throw erasers, and we are going to begin this morning."

I called to one boy. I said, "Come up here." He was scared to death. I said, "You stand right here, and you call roll. I'm going to write the name down as you call it, and if they cannot respond with a Bible verse, they are going to have to learn one before the day is over." After that I had no more trouble.

They knew a Bible verse because every Tuesday afternoon Mr. Bledsoe would have the nuns come over. I don't know what they taught them, but they did teach them the Bible. It was nondenominational.

The school was all just special ed—handicapped. When I first went in there I had about thirty in my classroom. I told Barbara, the principal, I said, "Barbara, I cannot teach this many." I said, "Twelve is the limit." So we kind of weeded them out to twelve, and I ended up with twelve. Anything I wanted, I got.

The only reason I got in at my age was it was a private school. And the fact that Mr. Bledsoe knew my father. He was asking me about different people in Devine. He said, "Call off some familiar names, some of the old timers."

I was rattling off, "Keaton, Haliburton, Thompson, Whitworth."

"Yes, I know, I knew all those people."

He had a saloon at Devine. He had a mentally retarded son. That's how come he opened up that school. First he moved to Center Point and tried to start it there. But he couldn't get any financial help from the people in Center Point, or Kerrville or Comfort, so he sold it and moved to San Antonio. He bought . . . oh, I forget how many acres he had . . . quite a few . . . because he needed a place for his son. He didn't want to place him in any private school. It was supported by the United Fund and private donations and some board. The children were boarding students. They stayed there all the time.

I would take mine shopping. I'd tell Barbara I was going to take them shopping. I said, "I want them to look nice."

I saw to it that the boys had little white shirts, bow ties and slacks, and the girls were neat and clean. They loved hamburgers. So we'd eat, and we went to Joskey's. They loved the escalators. People'd look at me, and they'd say, "All these children yours?"

And I'd say, "Yes, every one of them."

And, well, in truth they were. I had them for so long, you know, that I . . .

I had seven students to be rehabilitated and go back in the public schools, and we promoted quite a few.

A lady came from New York. She was inspecting the special ed schools, the set-up and format and all. She looked around, and she said, "I feel so sorry for you."

At that time I had three mongoloids in there. She said, "They will never learn to write or read."

I said, "Well, sure they will."

It happened to be on Friday, and every Friday we wrote letters. They'd write them home. Some of them didn't even have parents, but they didn't know it, so I let them write letters anyway. I'd take them over to the office, and I don't know what they did with them.

But anyway, I asked Annie—she always sat on the back seat—I said, "Annie, come on up here and bring your letter."

First I think she brought her reader. I said, "Read for this lady."

"Ok, Mama 'Telton." They all had speech impediments except two.

She came up and read beautifully, and that woman was amazed.

"Well, she could read, but she can't write."

I said, "Annie, have you finished your letter?"

She said, "Yes, ma'am."

"Will you bring it up and let me see it?"

So she goes and gets it. She's a little pigeon-toed thing, and she came about to my shoulder. Just as happy as she can be all the time. She brought that letter up. She had a beautiful penmanship—backhand.

That lady said, "I just don't believe this." She said, "I would give anything if I could take this back and show them in New York. They won't believe me."

And Annie said, "Mama 'Telton, give it to her." I said, "OK. You want to write another one?"

She said, "Sure." So she went back and wrote another letter.

I would like to have heard the outcome of that, but I never did.

We would have busloads of people coming around from, say, the telephone company. When it was time for the United Fund drive, they would maybe send two busloads of people out.

One little ol' boy sat at the back seat. He still calls me. I get calls from Michael at two or three o'clock in the morning. He would look out the window and he says, "Mama 'Telton, here they come. Coming to look us over just like we were a bunch of cattle."

I said, "Well, Michael, don't get upset about it because that's where we get a lot of our money to operate this school."

"Well, I don't like them coming in here and looking through my things."

I said, "Well, you don't have to show them your things. Just put them in your desk and get your book out, and if you want to read and if you want to color while they're here, I'll take care of it."

So that's how I managed with many of the students. They resented the public coming in. I know one day a bunch of San Antonio teachers came in from the public schools, and they were looking. Barbara, the principal, had gone around that day, and I heard one woman say to her, "That has to be Mama Shelton." It was Emily Powell, one of the girls I had in the Methodist youth program here in Kerrville. Her father was county agent. Cynthia was teaching in the San Antonio schools at that time, and she was with the group that came in. She wanted to know about the different students.

I said, "Well, go back to the boy in the very back row seat and talk to him." I said, "His name is Paul, but he likes to be called Michael." And I said, "Just go back and talk to him, just like you were talking to me."

Michael was born a very sane person. His mother was ill in the hospital, and his daddy took him to the playground. Before he could get up in the swing, someone that was swinging let go of the swing, and it hit him in the head. He had a concussion, so he had a plate in his head. But he was smart. He was just as smart as he could be.

His mother died, and his dad remarried. She didn't like the boy. I had a lot of kids that were from broken homes. Maybe they weren't really retarded then. Maybe they were . . .

Some of them were not. No. That's why I could rehabilitate them and put them back in the public school. They didn't belong out there.

This school started before they had the laws that required the public schools to take care of these kids. Now, of course, they have to take care of them in the public schools.

Mr. Bledsoe died, and he left everything in trust for Barbara, his daughter, who was also principal, to stay on with the school as long as her mother lived. When Mr. Bledsoe died, the school reverted to the military, which was a branch of each service organization. They called it *Champus*. You know, the marines, air force, army, and all that. They are the ones that have charge of that school.

I had two of my children to marry down there in the chapel in the same little school.

What's this disease that makes the head so big? Anyway, Bobby had the hugest head I ever saw, and he was in a wheelchair. But he and Holly were madly in love. She would come in and say "Mama 'Telton, what am I going to do? He wouldn't speak to me this morning."

Maybe the kids would be having roll call, and if they didn't say the right scripture, Holly'd correct them.

They knew the times tables. They could say all of them up to the twelves, and they wouldn't make a mistake. Barbara brought someone around after school—from the board of directors, I think it was. I had to put my work on the board for the next morning before I left. We taught until four, and while they were having play period or drawing or coloring, I was putting things on the board. I would just draw maybe "one tree plus one tree," and then I'd draw "equals two trees," you know. I'd draw houses, or dogs, or rabbits, or whatever came to mind. I had that on the board.

Barbara called me to the office the next day. I had an intercom in my room, and she said, "Can you come over for a minute?"

I said, "Well, yes, but keep the intercom open 'cause I want to hear the children."

So I put them all on their guard. I said, "Y'all be real quiet 'cause I can hear every word you say over there, and if you're quiet, I'll buy you all a cold drink." I was going to anyway, but I thought, "Well, I'll just call it a surprise, and I'll just get it for them," 'cause they had very little money. Some of them had nothing.

Well, Barbara says, "When did you start teaching new math?"

I said, "New math? I don't even know new math."

She said, "Yes you do. You've got it all over the board."

I said, "That is 'new math'?" I said, "That's my invention. That's the way I'm getting the kids to do math. If it's called new math, I'm teaching new math."

She said one of the board of director's members was upset 'cause I was teaching new math.

I said, "If they are learning it, what's the difference?"

Then I started with those that had never had any math at all and began with the zero. Long time ago that's the way we started—one zero, two zeros. Then we went on up to ten zeros. Then they wondered what to do 'cause you didn't have but ten fingers. So they decided that instead of two zeros they'd put two ones up there. That's where you get your eleven. And so you have your one and your two and that was twelve. Well, that's the way I taught the little ones that were just starting out. That book's around here somewhere. I should give it to someone that's teaching. But anyway, I got called on the carpet for a lot of the things I did.

When I first went there, they didn't even observe the Fourth of July. Christmas Day was the only day they had off. We taught twelve months year round.

I started in March. I said, "What are we doing on the Fourth of July?" Barbara said, "Oh, we're teaching."

I said, "Oh no, we're not."

I drew a flag on the board, a Texas flag, and I put, "March 2 is Texas Independence Day, a state holiday." And over here I drew an American flag and I put, "Fourth of July is the national holiday because it is United States Independence Day."

Barbara came in and she saw that, and she said, "Shelton, what are you trying to do?"

I said, "I'm teaching history."

So the closer it came to the Fourth of July, I said, "What are we going to do for the kids on the Fourth of July?" I said, "I don't like the Fourth of July because we buried my dad on the Fourth. It just does something to me."

She said, "Well, we teach on the Fourth of July."

I said, "No, we're not." I said, "These kids deserve a break. They go to school five days a week, and they have to be in church on Sunday." They had no time at all on Saturday. They had a field, oh, as big as all this up in here, where the boys worked, and the girls worked round the dorms. I said, "Why don't we have a barbeque?"

So that's what we did.

She said, "What would you suggest?"

I said, "Hamburgers and hot dogs and chips. And let's put record players out there, and let's have a street dance."

So from that day on we had a fun time on the Fourth of July.

And they didn't observe Thanksgiving. So we get closer to Thanksgiving, and I'm drawing turkeys all around here, you know, and pilgrims and all. So I say, "Barbara, I am not teaching Thanksgiving Day. That is a family holiday."

So all the teachers got off at noon the day before Thanksgiving—first time in the history of the school.

But first, we went through Halloween. I said, "What do you do for them on Halloween?"

"Well, nothing."

So they had a big gym, and I made a scarecrow out of a broomstick and a mop and a pumpkin, and I took old clothes. I put turkeys and pumpkins all around and made me jack-o'-lanterns.

We had a big party, and we had a dance. Bruce Hathaway, one of the DJs there on the San Antonio stations, came out and gave all the kids a record apiece. Old records, you know, that he didn't have any more use for. But they loved them.

Then we go through Thanksgiving and then Christmas. We had a big Christmas tree. I took each one of the kids a gift, and a barber came out a certain day of the week to cut the kids' hair.

I had this little ol' mongoloid girl in my classroom had this long, red hair. It never was combed. I'd send her back to her housemother. Oh, those housemothers hated me, because if they were dirty and their hair wasn't combed, I'd send them back. Barbara went along with me, she and Mr. Bledsoe, because they believed in kids being clean. They had plenty of clothes. The housemothers just didn't care about keeping them clean. They didn't want to fool with them. So I said, "Barbara, I'm going to cut Dotty's hair."

"Oh, you better not. We need permission from the mother."

I said, "The heck with her mother. She hasn't been out here in months."

Dotty had long, red hair, and she was the cutest little bow-legged thing, pigeon-toed. In she'd come, "Morning, 'Telton," just a-grinning, you know. So I took her over there, and I had her hair cut just like mine. It was real thick and red as it could be. So I bought her a little pink brush and combing mirror. She'd sit there and comb. She looked so cute.

I took her over, and I said, "Barbara, doesn't she look cute?"

"Shelton, her mother will kill me."

I said, "No, I don't think she will."

This was on Thursday. Friday her mother came after her—the first time in months, naturally. Anyway, her mother liked it. She said, "I wished I had done that a long time ago."

If it was their birthday, and I was there—it was a school day—I'd take them shopping and buy them a gift and take them to lunch. It was their special day. 'Cause that's the way I did my kids. On their special day they didn't have to do a thing. I brought their breakfast to them in bed. I cooked what they wanted. If it was a school day, of course, they had to go to school, but they were allowed to do whatever they wanted to on their birthday. We took a lot of stock in birthdays, anniversaries, and holidays. Still do.

FIVE

Rachael Luna

Rachael Luna, Tivy High School, ca. 1960.

I'm sure some single ladies gave up getting married or delayed getting married so they wouldn't lose their jobs, but I can't tell you about anybody personally 'cause I was too busy falling in love.

EVER SINCE SHE was six years old Rachael knew what she wanted to do. She wanted to have a career on the stage. Instead she fell in love, got married, and then, in an unusual reversal of the typical order of events, became a teacher. It was 1930, the heart of the Great Depression, and the only job either twenty-year-old Rachael or her husband could get was for her alone as a teacher/governess on an isolated ranch outside of Telegraph, Texas. Perhaps the rancher's wife felt that having a married teacher under her roof was less threatening than a young, single woman.

After this unusual start to her career, a second job in a traditional country school soon led Rachael to realize that teaching was a fulfilling career for her. Her substitute teaching well after her official retirement in 1969 and her remarks about hardly being able to wait during the last two weeks of summer vacation for school to begin attest to that. An old, misguided saying goes, "Those who can, do; those who can't, teach." Rachael never gives the impression that she became a teacher because she *couldn't* be on stage. Teaching was a good choice for Rachael because it allowed her to pursue her various interests: to be "center stage," to be in love and married, and to work full-time outside the home.

The emotional need of some married women to work outside the home even when there was no financial necessity was as compelling in the past as today. A critical factor in whether a married woman was able to fulfill this emotional need appears often to have been whether she could win her husband's support and approval. When Rachael remarried in 1934 she needed to convince her husband how emotionally important it was to her to have a job. Her husband eventually did accept her need to work, but his support perhaps did not come without cost to him; through the 1950s, at least, men were expected to be the breadwinners and support their wives.

111

Once a woman teacher had found a husband who would actively support (or at least tolerate) her career decision, she had a bigger obstacle of community standards to overcome. Even when it was not official school policy that married women could not teach, in poor economic times the trend was clearly against them. Rachael says, "I was scared to death when I got married—and didn't make a big splash about it—that maybe I would lose my job."

Rachael's vibrant personality and tolerant humor enlivened teaching for many of her colleagues. She attributed her ability to stand up to the unreasonable restrictions imposed on teachers to her parents: "I got half my sass from my mother, and the other half from my daddy." Dancing, drinking, and playing cards were prohibited for women teachers even in the company of their husbands. Rachael was one of the teachers in her community who began to defy and break down such restrictions. Perhaps other teachers who delayed marrying until later in life were finding their own ways to defy convention.

In spite of her usual tolerant humor, Rachael expressed anger about community interference with teachers' personal lives: "They used to think teachers were never supposed to get hungry or thirsty or fall in love. We were just teachers. . . . I don't know where the idea came from that teachers were not supposed to be human. It used to be that way." The feelings that Rachael describes must have been shared by at least some other women, including those women who considered but then eschewed teaching. This perception, however, was only one piece of the puzzle; it existed side by side (even within the same person) with the viewpoint that teaching was a highly regarded profession and the only one suitable for a "lady."

The changes for married women were not the only differences noted by Rachael between the beginning and the end of her career. Her description of substitute teaching in a special education class after she retired underlines Elizabeth Shelton's accomplishments at about the same age when she earned a master's degree and began a second career in special education. Rachael notes, "When I first started teaching, they wouldn't let children like that go to school."

The biggest change for teachers of Rachael's generation, however, was desegregation and not special education. Her words bring alive the tensions and fears felt on each side of the color line and also the goodwill of many in both communities who sincerely wanted a smooth transition. Because the decision had been postponed so long, desegregation had to begin in Kerrville in the high school. Although many people realized this was not ideal, cool heads planned a smooth, trouble-free transition. Rachael recalls, "As I look back on it, it was one of the most exciting things that happened to me 'cause I believed in it."

Rachael's retirement is filled with volunteer work at her church, the Retired Teachers Assocation (which held its first meeting in her living room in 1969), and her two "adopted" grandchildren, Roxanne and Suzanne, to whom she is related by love.

∽

Grade 4, Tivy Elementary School, Kerrville, Texas, ca. 1935.

Like I said, it was a terrible no-no for a lady, a teacher, to smoke cigarettes. Well, my friend had never smoked a cigarette in her whole life. One day she had a sore throat. We had a nice little store right across the street which sold hamburgers. It was just a general grocery store. At noon she asked one of the little girls in the second grade, "Do you think maybe they'd have Sucrets over at the Red and White store?"

She said, "Oh yes, ma'am, I'm sure they do."

She said, "Would you go get me some?"—'cause children were allowed to go over there at noon.

The girl got clear out the door, and she said, "Do you want a box of matches, too?"

This was in Kerrville in about 1935.

I got my teaching certificate accidentally. I didn't mean to teach forever. I was just taking education courses, and it came along with it. I had no more idea than a spook that I was going to be a teacher. I fell in love with teaching.

At first I really wanted to be on the stage. But like I said, I fell in love.

My parents said I could do anything I wanted to do. I come from a family of teachers. My mother was a teacher, and my aunt was a teacher for many years.

I quit teaching a few times, but I couldn't stand it. I get calls for substituting now. I do it when I can, but I've gotten all these little freebie jobs, working in church in our little thrift shop.

My mother told me stories about when she was a teacher in Lampasas [Texas], the little town where I grew up. My father was in the clothing business there. The boys were very big then. A seventh- or eighth-grade kid was a grown man way back then when she was teaching. This one fella, she had to do something to discipline him in some way. He was furious about it, and his father was furious. The boy went about bragging around that he was going to take his pocket knife—they all had pocket knives at that time—and he was going to carve her up in small pieces and throw her out the window. She was shorter than I am—less than five feet.

The next day he got his knife out and started honing it up and telling her about what he was going to do. She had the chair between them. She said he got a little too close so she just picked up the chair and hit him over the head with it. It surprised him so that for the rest of the year he was her personal bodyguard.

The father came up to bawl her out about something one day. They took things in their own hands in those days.

She was married then, but I don't think I was there. She would stop teaching and start up again. She kind of did like I did. When they needed a teacher, she'd go. They let my mother teach even though she was married.

In Lampasas, I remember my daddy stayed late at work on Saturday night. We, the poor families, grew up around the square, and Daddy would get so puffed up at my mother if she didn't get us down there all dressed up early in the afternoon. Then we just sat there. We'd go into the store and visit awhile. Then we'd go sit in the car. We saw everybody we'd ever heard of. He was upset if we weren't down there.

My first teaching job was out on a ranch. It was a district school, but there was only one student there the year I taught. That was in 1930 and '31. Everybody was so poor then. That was the depression, which had knocked the props out from under everybody. It was out of Telegraph, Texas—way out in the boondocks. I lived in a home with this one student.

They had a little district school about five miles down the road, but at that time there weren't any other students. There had been some Mexican families that ranched out there, but there weren't any children of school age then. So he built a schoolroom off of his garage, this rancher where I was living. I only had one girl—in high school.

I played a little piano, and I sang. I was a speech major, trying to get started in that. But I ended up on this ranch as a teacher.

They thought that I would teach the whole family everything I knew, all the time. For twenty-four hours a day, I was on call. The food was wonderful. The lady was wonderful. The man was pretty much of a dictator.

My social life was Saturday afternoon high tea. There were a lot of English people around that ranch. We thought nothing of driving fifteen or twenty miles through the pastures for tea. Guess who opened gates? I did! The lady of the house had a little baby under a year old, and the student managed to take care of her all the time. So Rachael got out and moved the gates.

The girl was fourteen. I was twenty. We rode horses a lot. I think back now, I was miserable at the time. But at least I was living.

I think my salary was fifty dollars a month, and I paid fifteen dollars a month room and board. It was supposed to have been the district that was paying me, but I think it ended up that rancher was paying me most of it.

The rancher found out that we were doing outside reading in English, all sorts of things. I would read to her sometimes, and then I would give her a page to read. He thought that was horrible. He said, "This is not to go on during the school day!" I thought the extra reading was what I should be doing.

I taught algebra, English, Latin, science. Every day—8:30 A.M. to 4:00 P.M.—with nothing extra. Once or twice we'd take some light calisthenics in the room—just anything to pass the time. History and English and math and Latin.

I got a pony [translation] for the Latin. I had four years of Latin in high school, but that doesn't give you the right to teach it.

I also taught her piano. I taught the little sister piano, too. There was a little sister besides the baby. She was too young to go to school. Any time, day or night, they came to my room for any kind of help that they might need.

I found out later that the man was quite a womanizer. I was so young I still believed in the Easter Bunny and Santa Claus.

It was very boring—very boring. Every Saturday my job was to help clean all the lamps. And they were rich ranchers.

I don't know why they got rid of the teacher that was there before me. She was there quite a while. I don't think the lady liked me much 'cause I was too young, and I think she was afraid that he was going to try to get involved. I was so dumb I didn't know it, 'til later I found out.

I was there less than a year. They just closed the school down after about five months.

I heard about the job from a good friend of mine who's still living in this area. She's quite an elderly lady, but going strong still. She told me about it and gave me the names, and I called and was thrilled to death to take the job.

I'd been to college a year and a half. At that time, there weren't many teachers with degrees. We would go to school in the summer and take more courses to renew our certificates and then go back and teach. It was a long time before I finally got my degree; it was after the war. During the war years, they called so many people out to be in the service that they didn't care whether we'd gone to school or not. They just wanted us to teach.

I just went out and applied for my second job in Ingram. I didn't know anybody there. I had a whole lot of nerve, but I didn't have a whole lot of confidence.

Ingram was little. I was about three years older than my oldest student. I went through the tenth grade so they gave me the English part 'cause I liked it, and I was kind of turned that way all the way through. I think I had fifth through the tenth. There were five teachers, I believe.

You know about Schreiner College? It was Schreiner Institute at the time. They took high school kids and had a junior college. It's always been a fine school. In 1932, when I was in my second job in Ingram, I didn't need to go to college as far as my certificate was concerned. Ingram was a little school then, but the trustees required that I did go that summer. I didn't have any money. I was broke as I could be. I went out to

Schreiner, and I talked to the registrar. I said, "I have a job, and I have to go to school. But I don't have any money. I want you to help me do something about it. Can I make a note?"

Tuition wasn't very much then, but this was still poor times.

He said, "No, you can't make a note. But you can go to school and take whatever you need and pay me when you can."

They just trusted me to pay. Of course, I've always felt very loyal to them 'cause they kept me from going hungry.

The registrar was Mr. Junkin, who was the father of Sam Junkin, the president of the College now. I was his third-grade teacher. I remember he told me he probably wouldn't have gotten this far if it hadn't been for me. When he was in the third grade, we were studying Texas, and one day I found out he couldn't spell Schreiner. He lived on the campus, you know. He said I gave him a wonderful opportunity for using his recess period for learning how to spell it! Now he's the president and a real wonderful fellow. I just love him to death.

We had a minstrel [show], to make money. Of course, I was willing to star! I tell you, it was something else! I remember some of the practicing we did. Of course, it was all pretty country, but fun. They made money. They were doing it for some cause.

I had a crazy little act that I did. Nobody knew about it, not even the master of ceremonies. I dressed up like a hillbilly in black-out and old shoes. I guess I should have warned him. When I came out, he looked like he was going to drop dead!

You know, I still see some of them up there, and we have a real good time. I check with a lot of them. Some went away for years and then came back.

I went on a trip with one couple last summer that I had had in school, and she told me something that I was not even aware of. I used to read to them in the English classes to try to interest them in reading. She said, "You know, Rachael, you introduced me to literature, to the world of make-believe and literature." I didn't know I was doing that.

My husband used to say no matter what I was teaching, whether it was Latin or algebra or what else, I was always teaching speech. He was a great help to me. He was always saying, "Rachael, what year did that happen? Let's look it up in the *Antler* [Tivy High School yearbook]."

In Ingram I lived at the home of the principal, the principal and his wife. They had two young babies. They didn't have a big house. It had two bedrooms, and I think they had their bed in the living room. The man teacher that was there that year had the other bedroom. It was very crowded, only one little bathroom.

The lady said, "Here's the key to your room, and I want you to lock the door and keep the key in your possession." I think it was a skeleton key.

He could have gotten in my room with a hairpin. But we made sure we locked that door.

She was a good cook, and she'd fix our lunch for us. She didn't make it in the morning and let us take it and let it get soggy. She came and brought us a lunch every day at noon. Sandwiches a lot of time, but freshly made.

That was in '32 and '33. During the depression. We were all struggling along, but these people where I lived were really poor. They needed to keep us; they needed the little money that we brought in. We were getting paper [scrip money] then, too. The principal would discount the paper. I guess he had to get money.

It was more fun then than teaching out on the ranch. I would go to Kerrville on the weekends. I had me a boyfriend then. Well, several!

I was twenty-four when I married in 1934. My husband was thirty-three, nine years older than I was. I wasn't going to tell you this, but it is part of my history. I had a brief first marriage. That's how I happened to be in Kerrville in the first place. I think maybe, well, the times and the family . . . I had met this boy at college, this first one. It didn't last. I tried. I did my best. In fact, I was even married when I was on the ranch, but he wasn't working 'cause he couldn't have a position. I was making a living. All that was me. He was in Kerrville, living it up. I felt like I was old at twenty-four.

One teacher I know married when she was fifty. We belonged to a dance club at that time together. I met him briefly. Now a lady at fifty marrying for the first time, that is unusual. He had been married before. She's cute about it, too. She says, "You know, he is the speaker of the house!" I think they were married twelve years, and she says it was the happiest time of her life. That always thrills me! I think she is a delightful person.

When I taught in Ingram we were expected to be active in the community and take part in prayer meetings and such. We lived just seven miles away, but we were not allowed to live in town. We had to board in Ingram. Of course, that's all gone by the board, but that's the way it was then. I came to town on weekends a lot 'cause I had some friends here. Everybody knew when you had a date, and who you had it with. The news went out pretty fast. They knew what you were going to do when you'd get home.

They didn't like it too much when teachers went out on dates—just narrowminded. Teachers were then very much on display in the size of town that Ingram was then. They were very much different from other people. They were not supposed to get hungry or get thirsty or want to dance. Dancing was taboo, you know. Times have changed, of course. I know when I started here—this was after I married—we had a superintendent who was very narrow about things like that. We were not to play bridge, and we were not to dance.

He told me, "In your contract it says you won't dance."

I said, "I'm going to sign the contract, but I'm going to dance whenever I can 'cause I don't intend not to dance."

Then he said, "Do you take a drink?"

I said, "Whenever I feel like it with my husband, and that's none of your business."

He tried to make it his business. He wouldn't let us have school dances for the kids. I think that before he left that changed a little bit. He mellowed somewhat. They used to think teachers were never supposed to get hungry or thirsty or fall in love. We were just teachers.

Yes, some of the teachers were very strict and straightlaced, but I don't know where the idea came from that teachers were not supposed to be human. It used to be that way.

It was even worse for my mother. In her day, goodness! She came to Lampasas to visit her aunt and met my daddy. It kind of got to be habit-forming for both of them. She told me one time, she said, "Oh, honey, Daddy was so fast when I first met him!" She said, "He tried to kiss me on the night we first met."

I said, "Did you let him?"

She said, "Don't you have something you have to do?"

I think my mother had taught a little before she was married. She had a permanent teaching certificate from Hunstville when it was a Normal School—a Teacher's Normal. She'd always say, "When I was in Huntsville . . ." 'Course we never let her forget that. Huntsville is where the state penitentiary is. We'd always ask her what she was in there for.

When she was a little girl she lived in Huntsville. Her daddy was a preacher. She used to tell us about the bloodhounds. When somebody would escape, they'd turn the bloodhounds loose. She was so frightened in the night if she heard them.

My parents were very supportive. I read today in "Dear Abby" where a lady said that there never was time to do anything when she was little. Her daddy was going to do so and so, but something else came up, and he didn't have the time. It made me think about my mother and daddy. They always put us first. I never quit being grateful for that. When I was doing speech contests when I was a little kid, they'd take off and go right with me. 'Course my daddy thought I was the best anywhere.

My mother, I'll tell you how much of a teacher she was. Daddy's really one pleasure was going fishing, and when we would go to the creeks of the river, she'd sit on the bank and teach all the nieces and nephews—the folks in the family—she'd teach 'em all how to swim. And she never swam a stroke in her life!

She taught in Lampasas and another time she took over teaching in a rural school near where Knowles went to school. She went out there on the bus. That's where they always traded lunches, you know. She did that with the kids. I went out there at Christmas time. I was dressed up to give readings. I was all in costume. We got hysterical going out there thinking what would happen if we'd ever have a wreck. There'd be me in this crazy costume and Santa Claus.

Then during the war, we had to move to Port Arthur. My father worked in a clothing store with my uncle, but they both couldn't make a living there during the war [World War I]. My uncle was single. He could have gone away easily, but he was a selfish old man that everybody catered to.

But it was an experience when the war was over! Of course, you know, we were always so patriotic. By the time the war was over, we had moved from a tenement apartment to an apartment in an old house. The people that owned it had lived in Lampasas and were friends of ours so they let us have that upstairs part for us to live in. They called us that night and said, "The war is over! The war is over!" So Daddy got his double-barrel shotgun and ran out in his nightshirt on the little tiny balcony off of the bedroom. All the guns were going off and everybody was going wild. He shot the gun one time and absolutely raised the dead! Then it jammed on him, and he never could shoot it again!

Oh, it was wild! They shot off the cannons and broke all the plate glass windows in Port Arthur.

My daddy was thirty-seven at the time. I was seven. The next time they were calling men at thirty-eight, even with families, if the war hadn't ended. Of course, he just couldn't wait to get in. He just wanted to go start shooting Germans, you know.

Coming home we had a Model T, and we ran into all sorts of bad weather. All kinds of things happened. We ran into people, and Daddy would ask permission to park in their backyards and just camp out and sleep, and they wouldn't let us. They thought we were all foreigners. I guess they were just not friendly down that way. I don't know.

We got stuck in the mud one time. Cars were backed up a block or two, and they couldn't get across a big mud puddle. They had a wagon and team finally to come down, and, of course, charging more than people had to pay just to get 'em out.

Daddy was sitting there in that old high Model T, and he said, "I believe I can make it." So we battened down. It wasn't raining, but the water was high and *muddy*. No pavement or anything. You know, we were the first car that got across there. You never heard so much whoopin' and yelling. 'Course the other cars followed us when they found out we didn't go down.

They had twelve grades at Port Arthur and almost all of Texas had eleven. So they double-promoted me the year we came back to Lampasas. They had high and low grades in Lampasas, which we didn't have in our Port Arthur school, so Port Arthur promoted me up a half a grade. When I came back to Lampasas, then they upgraded me another half to keep me even with the grades. And that kinda went to my head! I *liked* that promotion—movin' on up, you know. So before I got through, I think I had skipped two grades. I studied with someone and took a little exam. It didn't hurt me doing that. You heard Scottie* say she didn't believe in double promotion? Well, it was good for me. It made me want to work a little harder. I didn't have much of a challenge in school.

Now I have no idea when I learned to read because my mother had a little kindergarten at home. Now that's when I was about three years old. So of course, I stayed with her all those days of kindergarten. I just learned how to read. I can't remember not knowing how to read. Of course, I was falling in love with all the boys that went to kindergarten. They were about five or six years old.

My mother had a lifetime permanent [teaching] certificate. She had gone to Sam Houston Normal. That was strictly a teachers' college then. I think she went two years and then took an examination and got a permanent life certificate. I was born in 1910 and my sister in 1906, and she married in 1904. So it must have been before then.

My grandfather was one of the signers of the Declaration of Texas Independence. He was kind of a big shot in the freedom thing. I had an aunt who was a teacher like my mother, and the other aunt a music teacher. One little brother died of diptheria when he was about four. I used to hear about him from my mother's mother. She'd say, "Now, Rachael . . ." and I'd say, "Now, Grandma, hush."

My grandfather was a preacher, and I think, as much as I can tell about him, he must have been very broadminded for a preacher in those days. His great-great—I don't know how far back—grandfather was born in Oatmeal, Texas. I remember hearing about the scary Indian stories from there.

I guess my grandmother—she never had any college—but she was quite a scholar in her day. I know she used to help us with our homework. 'Course it didn't cost much for college then, but nobody had any money.

My mother was the only one of the three sisters who married. Not too long ago a cousin of mine asked me, "How did it happen that they never got married?"

I said, "My mother was the only one who would stand up to 'em."

*Ethyl Scott, another teacher in this book.

My youngest aunt liked a boy real well, and—let's see, what was the matter with him? He played baseball on Sunday afternoons, and my grandmother and grandfather thought that was a horrible thing—to play baseball on a Sunday afternoon. So she just quit trying. And then my other aunt, she was in love with somebody, and they criticized him. My grandmother would have murdered somebody if he just so much as misspelled a word. I'm always teasing people, you know, and making up stories. I'd always say, "Now, when so-and-so comes in, don't say a word. I'm gonna tell 'em so-and-so." Grandma would say, "Now Rachael, that is not right. Just keep quiet. Keep your lips buttoned up tight."

I'd store up all those wild tales. I got half my sass from my mother and the other half from my daddy.

So my aunts never married and taught all their lives. After my daddy died, my aunt who taught in the high school in San Angelo wanted my mother to come live with her and keep house for her—to keep her going. So she did. When my aunt retired, she didn't have social security or a pension. The schools could choose then whether they wanted to give it to you or not.

Have you ever heard of the Gilmer-Akin Act in Texas? One was a schoolman, and I believe they were both in the state legislature. They had the bill—first time they ever had an organized salary scale for schools. Before then every little school was on its own, in charge of everything. I remember telling my husband when that passed, "That means that we will lose our independence as a local school." And it went on from there 'til we don't have a say much in anything, anymore.

When was it? Well, I was married, and I married in 1934. So it was between 1934 and, well, three or four years in there. It was a wonderful thing; I don't mean that it wasn't. But it began to centralize all of the government.

After she retired from teaching, my aunt got a job at the *San Angelo Standard Times* proofreading. She had taught English. Eventually, she got some social security from her job at the *San Angelo Times*. She got a little teacher's retirement, but it wasn't much—like under a hundred dollars a month. Of course, then you could choose whether you wanted to go into the retirement program. She was talking about wanting to buy a house. She had rented all her life. So my mother told her that she wouldn't stay with her any longer unless she decided to buy a house with her, and so she did. They both came back here in 1955. My mother died in 1962, and my aunt in 1966, I believe. I think she felt like she'd done the right thing 'cause life was sure good to them.

I had one sister. She was older than me, and she's dead. In fact, everybody in my family's gone. My sister taught for a while, but she hated it. She went into secretarial work and was an executive secretary in

Washington, D.C. I tried to learn to type. I went to this little school there in Lampasas where they taught you by music. I was just climbing a tree. I couldn't do it. They say they don't teach it that way anymore, but Cissy just took to it. She went to college, too.

After Ingram, I applied at Kerrville. They didn't give me very much encouragement about getting that job, but I got it. Later on, when I told my high school students what I worked for here the first year they said, "Who would take a job with that little money?"

I said there were thirteen people who wanted that job. I was lucky to get it.

I started in Kerrville at Tivy Elementary in 1933. That was the only elementary then. Now we're going to get our fourth one here next year.

We got paid in paper. It was scrip. We didn't get money, and to pay our board we had to discount it ten percent. They finally gave us four separate checks. I made the sum of six hundred and seventy-five dollars a year in Kerrville, and that was in paper, in 1933 and '34.

When I first started teaching during the depression, they did not hire a man and his wife for school at all. During the depression if your husband had a job, it was harder for a woman to get one. I think that was up to the local school board. I don't think that was a state law or anything like that.

I know when I first started teaching in the depression, we had a rule in this Kerrville school that a man and his wife couldn't both hold a job here, but that's strictly economical. We felt like—by *we* I mean the school felt like, and I think I must have to agree—that if a man was working, his wife couldn't work in the same system because somebody else could have that job and keep another family from starving.

Kerrville didn't feel the depression like some of the places in Texas, and I don't think Texas felt it quite as bad as some of the other states.

The school board felt that way, yes. I think that if you were a wife, and you had a good job, maybe like ninety to a hundred dollars a month, and if your husband was working, and you could support your family on his salary, then give your job to somebody else.

I got married in August 1934. I knew I needed to work, and Lloyd didn't want me to work, but he didn't realize how much I needed it. He just didn't want his wife to work. That was back there a while. I was scared to death when I got married—and didn't make a big splash about it—that maybe I would lose my job.

In Kerrville I think the objection was purely economics. Now at Ingram, out there, I think they were morally opposed to anything. Well, they were! They put teachers in an entire different category.

I'm sure some single ladies gave up getting married or delayed getting

married so they wouldn't lose their jobs, but I can't tell you about anybody personally 'cause I was so busy falling in love. In Ingram they didn't
want me to have dates really, but I kept on doing what I had always done.
I kept on dancing and kept on having dates.

We had a school superintendent here when I first came to work in
Kerrville. Everybody was eyeing all the young teachers and everything.
One day the superintendent and I were talking, and he said, "Are you
going with anybody now?"

I said, "Well, yes, I'm going with Lloyd." He and Lloyd were very good
friends.

He said, "You don't drive through town so everybody can see you
every night during the week, do you?"

I said, "No, we don't let everybody see us at night driving through the
streets." So he was on our side.

The superintendent was a little older than Lloyd. Lloyd was nine years
older than I am. They had fallen in a sort of an older circle before.

I think Kerrville was very broadminded in its attitude. Now, San Antonio had a lot of funny rules, too. I think Kerrville was not like most little
towns. People came here to retire and on vacation. It was that sort of
place. It wasn't as tight as a lot of little towns, I can promise you, 'cause
I've lived in some of the others.

I always wanted to go to [the University of] Texas. My mother and
daddy had gone to TCU back when it was Adran College in Waco. They
didn't meet there or anything 'cause they went at different times. They
wanted me to go to TCU, but I couldn't see anything but Texas. We lived
about seventy-five miles away, which was quite a long distance when I was
growing up. We'd go to Austin when I was in speech things. Austin was
town to us like San Antonio is to us here.

When I went to Texas, it was as big then as it is now proportionally. I
think there were about five thousand students, which was a lot back in
1926.

I graduated high school when I was fifteen. We just had eleven grades.
I was anxious to get out, I'd study a little in the summer and take a test
and skip a grade. I went right into college so I was a young college
freshman. I don't know how I survived.

I started out at the University of Texas in Austin. I hadn't ever looked
at any other schools since I was about six years old. I had always wanted
to go there. I wanted to go on the stage. I had a major in voice and
speech and drama. I wanted to do that, but I also wanted to eat. So I got
this job on the ranch, and I figured I'd finish school later.

Then I changed colleges after the war. The University of Texas at that
time didn't have anything in the way of speech or drama that would

interest me at all. I had already taken any little thing they had had. They took it out, one of the governors, I think, the fine arts department. So after the war was over, I went up to Denton to the Texas Women's University, which was a very fine fine arts school. Went in and got my degree in a couple of summers.

I was married then, but it was too far to commute. I stayed six weeks only. I never did stay a full three months. I would come home around the Fourth of July holiday. They were very strict about doing double cuts around the holiday, but I'd do it anyway.

My daddy, he paid all college expenses that first year, and for my sister, too. They sacrificed an awful lot to send us. Then the next year I felt like they didn't need to send us any more. So I decided to stay out a year and have a private "speech" class. I had had a private teacher. They didn't have speech in school then, and they called it *expression*. 'Way back yonder, it was *elocution*. I was very fortunate. I had a wonderful teacher that had all the fundamentals. It was solid; it wasn't artificial.

I had my little private speech class in Lampasas. Got a little money together and borrowed it from somebody else. But I did it. The man let me have it 'cause I was who I was. He knew my daddy would make me pay it back.

After that, I really started the next year. I didn't goof off, I knew I had to make it then. That was at Texas the second year.

Later on, after I'd been married several years, I went to Texas Women's University to go on with my degree. I'd had two private teachers since Texas. I went right to the head of the Speech Department to register. I said I would like to know if I can count any of the work that I did 'cause I was just starting off even. I asked if I could take an examination or anything. I'd had all these private lessons. They took a very dim view of private teachers 'cause so many of them were artificial. He said they'd let me try. He said, "We'll see."

So I took a course in Advanced Interpretation and Advanced "This" and something else that summer. I didn't know how good my teacher was 'til that happened. I was lucky. At the end of that six-week term I had really worked myself to the bone, but they gave me enough back credit that in six-weeks' time I had earned almost a year's credit. I didn't take an exam or anything. My grades were good enough.

My superintendent here said, "That's the most ridiculous thing I've ever heard to think you can get advanced credits."

I said, "I'm going to try anyhow."

He never did like me 'cause I like to dance. Of course, my husband and I both just dreaded that time. It seemed like six years every time. But I made it.

I never did go for a master's even though I've taken a lot of courses. I just never was much interested in it. I took courses from then on, just what I wanted to take. I still like to go to school.

I never tried to make it professionally in the theater because I kept on falling in love. You know you have to be willing to sacrifice everything. I think I could have made it in like musical comedy, but I didn't have that dedication.

When I was teaching elementary in Kerrville they needed somebody to direct the senior play one year. That was 1938. There wasn't anybody else to do it, so I did that. We put on *Adam and Eve*. We did a lot of things that I was proud of. I know that they were very amateur. But if you saw when we started out, and then saw when it was put on, it was pretty wonderful. We did *Pride and Prejudice* and *Death Takes a Holiday* and *Dulcy*.

I'm trying to think when it happened, in the early sixties. It finally worked out all right, but, you know, we had several faculty meetings to just talk about what to do 'cause we all knew it was going to be a very tense situation. The principal of the black school helped a lot on that. We talked about whether to seat kids alphabetically, which we had done before, or to let everybody find his place.

See, we knew we should have started in the lower grades, but that was law. So we just decided to let people come in and sit where they wanted to sit. It was really tense for everybody. As I look back on it, it was one of the most exciting things that had happened to me because I believed in it. A lot of the people, the Negroes, took speech 'cause they knew they could probably pass if they did their best. I worked on the basis of having to improve yourself. They knew that if they did what I asked of them, they would pass. That may sound chicken, but it wasn't 'cause I didn't grade any kid for luck. You can't do that in speech class. You can come in being brilliant and some other little student could just sit there, and she'd learn to get up and talk a little bit, and she'd make a good grade. Do you understand that?

One day this boy stood up and gave this very good speech all about the Negroes, and when class was through he asked me, "Miz Luna, I want to ask you something. How would you feel if you were a Negro?"

I said, "Sam, I can't tell you; I don't know. But," I said, "I want to tell you this. If I were a Negro I would pray every day that I would be the proudest Negro that ever walked on the earth."

He said, "You sure stepped up to that." See, he was a little bit defiant of all of this. He was sixteen or seventeen, I think.

In speech class we learned how to make announcements, how to think on our feet, how to get up extemporaneous remarks, how to plan speeches. Then we read different things and memorized them.

We talked about how we'd treat each other and how to treat them and what to expect. We decided not to give any favors, to treat them as if they had always been in our shcool if we could possibly cut that. And we managed pretty good. It turned out, I think, it was a very successful transition period.

Another thing you may not even realize, the girls, the white girls, started a flirtation with the Negroes, and it frightened me to death. I used to go home and tell my husband that this could be the problem. But it worked out just fine. I think some of these little girls really were touting these little boys. I said, "The boys will get blamed, and it won't be their fault." But I guess that's the end of that.

The Mexican schools had been integrated earlier. But the first year I taught here, in '33 or so, they had the first and second grade down there in a Mexican school because of the language barrier. Their parents just would not teach their children English.

We had a good community of black people here, or else we would have had more trouble with things. One night when my husband was still on the city council, they brought some people from San Antonio in to kind of organize things. Some of our black people here finally told them, "We're getting along just fine here. We'd appreciate it if they'd just move on back to San Antonio." So you see we had it pretty good. It could have been a problem.

When they first integrated, we had a young teacher named Martin come from Doyle, the nigra school. Has anybody told you about him? Martin and his wife were in the Doyle school, and they brought him into the high school. He was a good-looking fellow, so young and interested in everything that was going on. His wife chose to go to work in Austin 'cause in her field she could get a lot better job there. So they commuted. He was killed one night. She was just getting ready to have a new baby. He had gone to see her after school that night and was killed in a traffic accident. He was coming home. They have quite a few things named for him, memorials.

He was such a thoughtful man. One time I was sitting in the cafeteria eating at the teacher's table, and I noticed this little girl, this little white girl, was kind of upset. But none of us were getting excited about it; we didn't know enough. Martin finally came over to my table, and he said (you see, this told me how sensitive he was—he wasn't going to do it by himself), "Miz Luna, I think that little girl needs you to talk to her." I thought that was very understanding. So we went over there. Of course, it was a boyfriend problem. Most of them that age are.

The bad kids I had in school, I loved them. I guess 'cause they were bad. I had one boy scared me to death one day. He had a knife in his pocket. They see us and want to go to carving. I don't remember what he had done, but he had been very rude to the class. I insisted that he apologize to the class, and he wasn't going to do it. The kids were scared to death of him. They kept on saying, "Apologize, Danny, please apologize."

He started toward me with fire in is eyes and his fists doubled up. I kept on moving toward him with a chair between us. I wasn't going to hit him 'cause this chair was too heavy, but I was scared to death.

He yelled, "I'm not going to apologize."

I just kept right on walking toward him. I said, "We just don't need you here if you're going to insist on being rude."

When we got pretty close he looked at me, and the kids they knew that he could hit me if he wanted to. He said, "I'm sorry."

I said, "I accept your apology, and I'm sure the class does, too. You can sit down now." I was so relieved.

At the end of that year, he joined the navy. Quit school and joined the navy. I was going to lunch one day. I went out to my parking space, and this car zoomed up to me. Someone jumped out of the car with the car still running and came over to shake hands with me. It was that boy in the navy.

A lot of them got to me. All of them.

I was the first one to start the Retired Teachers Association in Kerrville in 1969, but it wasn't my idea. This lady in San Antonio got my name and started calling me and wanting to know if I'd round up all the teachers so they could organize. I told her I'd round them all up if I didn't have to take an office. I got all the lists and called up everybody, and we put up one or two little things in the paper about it. Lloyd helped me get everything. He said, "How many people do you think we'll have?" and I said, "Not very many."

So we got the chairs all ready, and I had a little refreshments. It was in the morning.

Mr. Daniels had been the principal at the elementary for so many years. I said, "He'll be the only man there." I said to Pete, "Why don't you stay and keep the man company?"

He said, "Do you think he's scared of women after all these years?"

They came in droves. I didn't know there were that many people. They were sitting on the floor. Some had seen it in the paper. This one "little old man" came over and wanted to know if he had the right house. That was Bliss Mapes, and before the thing was over with, we had elected him president.

We certainly have had a wonderful response here. There are about a hundred and fifty members. And we do things. We sponsored the historical marker for Captain Tivy, the man the school was named for. Captain Tivy came here about the same time Captain Shreiner did. He had been in the army, in the Civil War, I guess, and he was a member of the legislature. He was first mayor of Kerrville. He had acquired all this land and money, and he gave both so that we could have a school.

He had two sisters. They had all made a pact that they would never get married, the three of them. When he did meet a lady that he wanted to marry, the sisters were so upset, both. Then one of them came back to live with them.

You've heard of Tivy mountain? That's where they are buried—Captain Tivy and his wife and his sister and their pet cat. They didn't have any road or anything up that steep hill. At the time, people said it was terrible getting the caskets up there.

The Retired Teachers raised the money for the historical marker. We couldn't decide where to put the thing, whether at the top of the mountain or at the foot. B.T. Wilson* said we should put it at the foot, and if you think about it, it makes sense. Who would ever see it at the top of that mountain? We were the first group of teachers that had ever put up a historical marker for a benefactor. I'm a member of the Historical Commission and am interested in such things.

I quit a couple of times during my teaching career. I thought I was through, and I'd just stay home. I just got bored out of my skull. I wanted to go back. I was missing it. I'd stay out two or three years, and then I'd go back. I always substituted all over.

One time I had this one English class. They were lacking in some of the fundamentals of English—good kids, but kind of on the wild side, some of them. I tried so hard to teach them just manners, etiquette. We were writing invitations one day, and I had said, "Your presence is requested," and so on. I gave them a little example. One of the boys said, "Miz Luna, I didn't think it was polite to ask for presents." And that was high school! It took a whole 'nother half day to clear that up.

I started out in the third grade, and then I went on up. Of course, I wanted to get into speech right away.

I was not trained to teach primary grades like kindergarten and first grade. My youngest was the fifth grade. But I substituted all over. I substituted one day in primary school, and they never got through kidding me about that. I had the babies. I had this first-grade group. They divide the children up into groups just barely six and the older ones. I was trying so hard to do just what the teacher had written to do. I said, "Get your math books out and turn to page fourteen. They stared at me, and I said, "Let's get started now. Get your math books out. Turn to page fourteen."

*Another interviewee.

They just kept staring. I said, "Aren't you all going to follow my instructions?"

One little one got brave enough. She came up to me and said, "Teacher, we don't know where fourteen is!"

I realized what a boo-boo I'd made. I said, "Well, of course you don't. Wasn't that dumb of me?" They were so relieved that I took the blame. Then I wrote *one* and *four* on the board and went around helping all of them. The other teachers thought that was so funny of me. I opened the door and hollered at my friend next door, "What am I supposed to do with these little children?"

I had two there, when I was substituting, that were in wheelchairs. Muscular dystrophy. Those children—that kind of tore me up. You had to take them to the bathroom, and somebody had to feed them. Of course, they began to cash in on that, little tiny children. One time when I asked somebody about them, they had died. They don't live very long. There was one little guy who was real sharp. He always got his work done very well. It breaks your heart. When I first started, they wouldn't let children like that go to school.

Let me tell you 'bout my latest substituting job. The principal called me and said, "I don't know if you are going to want to take this job or not." They don't call me all the time to substitute cause they know I can't do a whole lot, and I can't stand up to it physically. He said, "To be honest, I can't get anybody else to do it."

I think it's a federal law that they have to have these children in public schools, and I wasn't prepared for it. They had to be diapered. There are the ones that are fourteen years old that don't know any more than . . . they don't respond to you. There was one little autistic child. I did that for two days, I believe.

He called me twice again. They have to have a certified teacher in the room, but I just couldn't do it. He said, "I don't blame you."

"It isn't that reason," I told him right away. "I can't lift them."

I did try to help feed them.

We had these buses that took them all around. It was close to Christmas, the first time I did it. We took them out to the Inn of the Hills to see the decorations and somewhere else. They went through the kitchens, and they all got cookies. I never had anything get to me like that. The young teachers they won't touch it. But the aides did it.

They used to die laughing at me every time when about two weeks before school started I always—you know, we wore washed and ironed dresses then—I had all my washing already done and my school shoes all broken in. I could hardly wait 'til school started. There's still that same thing going on those last two weeks of August.

SIX

Ethyl Scott

Ethyl Scott, ca. 1980.

I had just finished high school when I started teaching. I was seventeen, I think, because I was a little late starting because my birthday was in November, and I had to take the exams to teach. I knew the county superintendent, and he was in charge of hiring. We went to the same church, and he knew that school needed a teacher.

ETHYL "SCOTTIE" SCOTT never married and pursued a teaching career all her working life, but her story makes it plain that her decision to remain single was not due to lack of opportunities. Although she does not speak in detail about her romances, we learn a little about them. In her first teaching job in 1921 in Evergreen, Texas, a seventeen-year-old Scottie used her boyfriend's red sweater to beat out a fire that had erupted in the one-room schoolhouse's chimney. In that same community, a seventh-grade boy used to walk her home from school every night. His schoolboy crush was so powerful that years later he sought her out and took her to dinner. She also recalls writing to a boy in San Marcos while she attended college and hopes she didn't act as foolish as some of the girls did while they were dating. In an untaped meeting, Scottie told the author that, like other teachers of her generation, she became engaged later in life and planned to marry. Her fiancé died unexpectedly before they were wed, but today she remains lifelong friends with his sisters.

Choosing to remain single is not the only way Scottie differs from other teachers in this book. She alone practiced her profession in settings outside the traditional classroom. By past and current standards, only she would be said to have moved up a career ladder. First, she was recruited in 1941 as teaching supervisor at Stephen F. Austin College (SFA), where she taught education and psychology courses and supervised student teachers. She also taught children in a demonstration laboratory school at the college where student teachers and visitors could study the methods of master teachers like Scottie. Then in 1948 she became one of the first supervisors in St. Augustine, Texas. Characteristically self-effacing, Scottie said, "Some of my teachers had asked me to do it. I wouldn't have gone into it if they hadn't asked." In 1950 she became supervisor in Johnson County, Texas, from which she retired in 1964.

Scottie clearly enjoyed her life as a professional woman. She paid her own way through Baylor College "for female women" in Belton, Texas, by mopping and dusting, waiting tables, and working in the library. Once employed as a teacher, she "didn't have much time off, day or night." In her entire working life, she took only one summer off. The others were spent taking courses and working at the campus lab school. She liked to attend different colleges "just for the experience," and she recalls with pride attending Vanderbilt University, "one of the most advanced schools in the South." After summer school finished, there were always trips to take (including one to the Chicago's World Fair) and teachers' conferences, where she met some of her best friends.

Although Scottie worked hard to achieve her successes, the history of how she obtained her positions often shows the way the "Who do you know?" network operated. Without applying for it, she was offered her first teaching position by the local superintendent who knew her from church. He needed a teacher and thought she might need a job. She later was appointed to the faculty at SFA in a similar way. When the job at SFA became vacant, it never was advertised, and she never applied for it. SFA's president knew her when he was a superintendent of schools and offered her the job at home by phone. Similarly, she was asked to take a position as one of the state's first county supervisors and did not apply for it in advance. She simply followed a friend from SFA into her new role.

Even though Scottie was qualified for each of these positions, the way she obtained them is in striking contrast to the affirmative action procedures implemented in the 1960s and 1970s to safeguard competent women and minorities from being overlooked in favor of less qualified individuals. Other women in this book were equally qualified, but none were selected for supervisory positions. Perhaps this reflected a societal perception that married women did not "need" to advance in their careers (just as there was greater "need" to hire married men during the depression) or that married women were less serious about their careers.

It should be noted that the practice of providing jobs for those who most needed them benefitted some women who otherwise might have faced grave financial hardships. For example, an interviewee whose story is not included in this book was offered a teaching job in her hometown of Kerrville after her husband died an untimely death and left her a widow with small children to support. The schoolboard president knocked on her door and, unasked, offered her a position when none had existed the day before. That sort of community responsiveness to its members' needs has virtually vanished.

Scottie's story raises other issues of equity. Her accounts of administering some of Texas's first standardized tests in segregated schools vividly illustrate that separate was not equal. Her reservations about the limitations of these tests for measuring individual student's true capabilities have been echoed by most educators today.

Scottie's early teaching experiences must have helped her greatly in understanding and assisting teachers in her role as a county supervisor. Gladys Meyers mentioned being visited by supervisors in Houston who rated her performance and whom she had to please to maintain her certificate. Rural areas were assigned supervisors later than the cities. Their purpose was to bring support and in-service training to teachers. Scottie notes, "There were supervisors who thought it was their job to be critical and things like that, but I didn't feel that way. We were just trying to help them. We just wanted to give them ideas to help." It is a tribute to these early supervisors that the teachers in this book spoke positively about them.

In Scottie's first teaching experience, she encountered the multifaceted roles of rural teachers, including public health, when she brought her students from school to the local doctor to be vaccinated against an epidemic. Other interviewees taught their students not to drink water from a common dipper. Teachers also had a major responsibility for providing entertainment for the community. The importance for Scottie's career of "doing what she could" to entertain rural citizens scarcely can be imagined in this day of television, VCRs, movies, and radio. Making paraffin Christmas trees and putting on the annual Christmas program was literally front-page news in Scottie's little town.

Today, Scottie continues to be active and full of fun. She keeps regular hours at the Deitert Claim Senior Citizens' Center in Kerrville working in the Gold Mine craft shop and keeping the accounts. She enjoys visiting with friends, swapping jokes, and attending monthly meetings of the Retired Teachers Association.

Ethyl Scott, high school graduation photograph, 1921.

My mother had had a stroke. This woman in the neighborhood who was a little bit off, kept on coming over to the house, and even though we locked the screen door, somehow she'd shake it and get in the house. We'd come along and find the woman on her knees praying and praying over Mother.

So I called up my younger brother and said, "You gotta do something about this woman. It just won't do. What if Momma wakes up and finds this crazy lady?" I said, "I'm gonna see if I act crazy. That might scare her away."

So I went to the door and got down on my knees and kept barking and barking. The lady came over and said, "Oh you poor thing, poor darlin'!"

She didn't come back again for a real long time.

I started teaching in 1922 in a little rural school called Evergreen. In my first year of teaching I was the only teacher, and I had most of the grades. I had all the elementary grades, one boy in junior high school, and two girls in high school. Back then we only went through the eleventh grade.

I had two girls in the high school, and they took Latin. I loved Latin. I had a neighbor that taught me Latin during the summer, and it gave me a wonderful start. She was one of the new teachers, and she wanted to practice on me. She also taught me algebra, and I made A's in both.

Anyway, one winter day we were all working. They had an old-fashioned stove, and it was about the first time we'd made a fire that year. All of a sudden, down came some sparks of fire. That fire was coming from the pipe. It had separated.

I said, "Boys and girls, we're going outside. Let's go. Don't stop for your books." I just wanted to get them out because I didn't know what might fall or how bad it was. I could see the fire was smoking out on the shingles of the roof.

The school had these old-fashioned desks, and the children stacked up about three of them. The junior high boy climbed up on top.

We didn't have running water. We had a tank, a cistern. I had on my boyfriend's football sweater. I took it off. We had a long stick, and we wet that red sweater, and put it on a stick and used it to put out the fire. This old boy did a good job—a boy that walked home with me every afternoon. He put the fire out.

I was worried about the inside of the school, and we didn't go in at once. A board member's son happened to come by to see if everything was all right. I told him about the fire, and he went up on the roof and checked on it. It was out.

He said, "Just don't make a fire anymore!"

I said, "Good gracious, no!"

He stayed with us awhile after we went back in. We didn't do much work. We tried to calm the children down. The children all loved him. They didn't question him.

My boyfriend never knew I used his sweater to put out the fire. I cleaned it. I didn't see any point in telling him. He was living where I used to go to school so we would write to each other, but I didn't write and tell him about it. I think I finally told him about the fire, but not about his sweater. In fact, we didn't go together much longer after that.

I did give his sweater back when we broke up, but it was a while before I got it back to him.

The seventh-grader? Well, he went home my way so it was just natural to walk together. It wasn't too far—about half a mile. There were two or three others, but he was older and could talk more than the others, you know. He always liked to find out things. It's funny, years later, when I was supervisor in east Texas, he called me. He came to town, looked me up, called me, and took me out to dinner. I couldn't believe this. I don't know how he ever found me. I guess someone from my home town.

That year there was this five-year-old. Back then, they couldn't go to school at five years, but he wanted to go to school, and I decided to let him come. When the real schooling started, he decided he wanted to take off. They weren't supposed to leave the school grounds without permission until time to go. I saw him and called, "Johnny! Johnny, come back!" He could hear me 'cause he wasn't any further than that. He just kept going faster. Well, my hair felt like it stood up. Oh, that got me! I thought, "You can't miss a thing."

The next morning he came back, and I was ready. I wasn't going to spank him at first. I talked to him and said, "You don't have to stay here." But he said he wanted to so I had to spank him for what he'd done.

His uncle, this young fellow in the seventh grade, told me his mother said if he got a whipping he'd have to quit school because he was too young, and he had to behave. Well now, that was a mistake on the mother's part.

But I couldn't let it go. In other words, I had to spank him. But I didn't hurt him. Except his pride.

His mother came the next morning. I said, "I'm sorry, if he comes to school, he'll have to obey." If I had let him get by with it, it would have kept happening the rest of the year. I said, "I'm really sorry," I told the little boy I was sorry, but he must obey.

So he got that little paddle, and his mother let him come back to school, and I was glad she did. I don't know whether she spanked him at home, too.

The five-year-old and his uncle, the seventh-grader, were real close.

The uncle was the one that talked to the mother. He didn't know for sure I was going to spank him, but he knew I might.

Back then they had to have spankings. You had that in those days to show you had control, but that's about the only one I ever spanked. I believe in kindness and firmness. That's what I thought, and what I tried to teach.

One time when I was at this one-teacher school, a group of children was up at my desk. There were two brothers, one about a year older than the other. All of a sudden, I looked up. One boy was turning pale, and he started slamming all around. I rushed to the side of the desk, and I just caught him as he fell. I couldn't keep holding him up, but I let him go down gradually. He had fainted. Oh my, he was just as pale as could be! I could tell the way he looked that something was wrong—that he was sick. Thank goodness his brother knew what to do. He took care of him, but I was right there. It must have been a slight touch of epilepsy.

That was the first time that I was with a pupil that had that. The parents were lovely about it. They said they didn't want to frighten me, and that's the reason they hadn't told me before. They knew he had spells. Anyhow, it worked out okay, and after that he didn't have any more spells like that. But I was worried about him.

Another time, there was an illness, I forget what the disease was, a children's disease that was contagious. Oh, it was bad all over the country. The doctor got in touch with me, our family doctor, and said that he was coming out to my little town.

The family doctor came out, and he told me to meet him at a certain distance from school, not far, and to bring the children and have them vaccinated. I got word in time to collect permits from parents. We met him, and he vaccinated my pupils. I had to hold them while they got vaccinated. None of them took whatever it was. Thank goodness we took that time.

One time we were going to do a play, but measles were going through town. They weren't vaccinated, and so many took the disease that we didn't finish out because we only had two or three days to go, mostly exams and things like that. Of course they couldn't do them, and so they passed their year of class.

I was very young when I started teaching. Too young. I had a special permit. I know I graduated from high school in '21. Then they had only eleven grades, but I was in public school only nine years. That's because the principal put me ahead in sixth grade. I didn't want to go ahead because I missed things I felt I never made up. I am real skeptical about double promotion unless it's very, very, very extreme that they are special. And then I made high school in three years. I did a couple subjects

139

in the summer. I didn't want to rush, but they wanted me to rush. I didn't want to, but I did.

I had a smart pupil once that was very special. He had trouble seeing, and I asked the school nurse to check him. She found he needed glasses so badly.

I had just finished high school when I started teaching. I was seventeen, I think, because I was a little late starting because my birthday was in November, and I had to take the exams to teach. I knew the county superintendent, and he was in charge of hiring. We went to the same church, and he knew that school needed a teacher. He asked me if I would like to teach school because they needed a teacher, and he thought I might need a job. He knew I was interested in teaching.

I was quite happy and said, "Well, what about this test?"

He said, "We can give you a temporary [certificate] and let you take the test." In those days, you could take an exam and get a certificate. Then I went to summer school to get the courses I needed.

It was probably '22, somewhere around there, I don't remember dates. I do remember my favorite year.

It wasn't my first time away from home. In the summer I had visited my grandparents and my aunt in a nearby town many times. I would spend the summers sometimes with them. Mother and Granddaddy owned the store. They'd always get me something. My aunt would go with them. They lived in Cherokee, a little town near Llano, where I went to high school. I grew up in Llano, a town only about sixty-five miles from Kerrville. That's where I went to high school, and then I taught at this little school.

I was fortunate in my first job. My roommate was related to a neighbor. She had come down to Llano to visit, and she went with my uncle, who was just a little older than I. I stayed in her home. Her father was also a board member, and she was familiar with the school. That was my first time in, but she was familiar with everything there. She was wonderful and wanted to help.

I was concerned about making a schedule and thought, "Now, how will I get in all those classes?" Of course, I couldn't give them as much time as I wanted to each period, but I gave them a great deal of personal help. In high school there's more individual help than elementary. My roommate helped me get a schedule. I believe I would have worked it out, but she helped. She wasn't a teacher, but she had gone to school there. I had one of her friends in a middle grade.

It was a rural community, but it was a nice community school. There was no town there, just an established community. My first job was only half a school year. They just had so many months—six months. Smaller schools are like that.

There were four or five school board members. Four at least. I met with them to begin with, and I would see them occasionally but not formally. They'd take care of business and left teaching up to me.

I just taught one year in that one-room school in Evergreen, Texas, and then one year in a one-room school in Glick, Texas. Then I went to Baylor College in 1924–25. I had been to San Marcos and done some of my work over there. I lost a little credit at Baylor, but I didn't care. I had learned things that I needed to know. I went only one year. I would say I worked a great deal, too, that year. But I would get more than I needed at a teachers' college. So I started back to San Marcos and got my bachelor's degree there during the summer, and at home, and by correspondence. I went every summer until I got my degree.

My mother was glad for me to be a teacher, and she was glad when I went away to school. She was also glad when I quit going with that boy that lived out there. She thought he was kind of a smarty. He came to see me at San Marcos. It was a school where we had regulations. We were supposed to stay on the school grounds. She told him I couldn't go with him into town. I got upset and called her, and she said, "Just don't leave the house." So we sat on the porch.

At Baylor I took English and things of that nature. Basic things. In one course the professor wanted us to be there ten minutes before class started. They had a five-minute bell, and she wanted us to come in before the first bell. I worked at my job up until the first bell, and then I'd dash across the campus.

So when I had to write a paper, she said, "Well, a D-minus is the least I can give you on this."

I thought, "Why the least you could give me? Why not just what I deserve?" I didn't say it, but I really thought it strongly. I said, "Why?"

She said, "Well, you've been coming late to class. Did you make this paper up? Where did you get this idea?"

I said it was based on San Marcos, where I went to summer school. I told her I was describing San Marcos, and she said, "Why are you always so late coming in?"

I said, "Well, I've been working. I hope I wasn't late. I work until time for the first bell."

"Why didn't you tell me you work?" she asked.

She was nice after that, but it was the end of the term. Anyway, it was kind of hard going with her.

For jobs I'd take anything they'd give me—in the library, in the journalism department, just about anything. Shelving, checking out books, even dusting and so forth. I'd wait on tables. Anything.

When I enrolled, I told them I'd like to work as much as I could. They had someone in charge of helping students find jobs because quite a few students in the dormitory worked. In the dormitory where I lived, a lot of them worked. In the most expensive dorm, none of them worked. On Sundays I had to mop and dust, and I did that before breakfast. Up and at 'em! They didn't pay me any money. They gave me credit on my tuition.

At Baylor they used to joke about Baylor College for "female women." It wasn't Baylor University. It was Baylor College. Baylor University was in Waco, which was not far away—about fifty miles. Baylor College is in Hilton. "Female women!" They really did say that!

When I went to Baylor, I was writing to a boy in San Marcos. Some of the girls would have dates, and some would act so foolish. I hoped I would never act that way. I was a little old for my class. Well, I was. I had responsibilities. I was the only girl. There was a brother much older than I, and there were two others close to me. I was the only one in my family that became a teacher, but I had relatives that were teachers. I had a cousin that went to Texas University. She was a principal and taught school. We were real close, always sending something for Christmas.

After Baylor I went to Temple, Texas. I was in summer school there, and the superintendent gave me a job. I was planning to teach again in the rural school.

In Temple I had children that spoke German only. They were adorable. I loved them. They had been speaking German at home in that community, and I didn't allow them to speak German at school because they had to learn English, and that was the only way they'd ever learn it. So they weren't allowed to speak German. I wished I could have learned German then, but I preferred that they learned English. Their parents would have helped me, but that would have spoiled my helping them, so I didn't bother with that. I did get a German book and couldn't read it.

One Christmas those little kiddies made these beautiful Christmas trees. Each one of them had made a Christmas tree of paraffin, a foot high. They had to plan their own colors, red or green. One little girl wanted a white one, and I let her be last because I was trying to get inspiration, too. I had a little fourteen-inch mirror for cosmetics, and I thought, "Why not set the tree on that?" She did and had the prettiest tree of all. She put some silverish colors around on it and sprinkled it. It looked as though it had really snowed on it. She had dripped it real like it had snowed.

We had so many evergreens out on the campus. Holly, sprays, and—oh, just everything! I knew we were not supposed to go get it, but it was so pretty. We just trimmed them a little. They had to learn to make an arrangement, in other words.

We had to get up a program the day before Christmas vacation. We wrote a little note of invitation to mothers to come to the party so mama could carry the tree home. The children couldn't carry those home.

All the mothers came, every one of them. They saw everybody's tree, and they seemed quite happy. They wrote it up in the paper. It was on the front page.

At the end of school, we were going to have a program by the children to do something for the community. We were planning a big play, but right before we were to have it, one of the various diseases that children have started and the board had to close the school. I forget what disease it was. There were only a few days left, and they had to try to control it. So we had practiced for that play, but we couldn't have it.

I worked on my master's from Texas University in Austin part-time, summer times, and corresponding. A thesis took more personal effort. My thesis director was out of town my first term, and the one he assigned me to was a visiting professor from California. He didn't have any idea of what he was supposed to do. My thesis was about the relationship between personality and reading. The department let me go sit through different grades, and I was comparing personalities in different schools. Then I used personal studies and took correlations of different things.

When I got my master's in 1953, I didn't actually have to have it to teach. I wanted it. I liked going to school and finding out new things. One summer I went to Vanderbilt University in Nashville. That was one of the most advanced schools in the South. I had some good courses, and I loved it. I liked to go to another college somewhere just for the experience, and I was learning to teach, of course. After summer school, some friends came by, and we went to Chicago to the World's Fair. I always went to summer school until I went to Nacogdoches to teach in the demonstration school. Then I taught in the summer.

From 1941 to '48 I was teaching at Stephen F. Austin (SFA). That's a college in Nacogdoches in east Texas. I taught education and one ecology class, and I had student teaching. But the education was more in the lab school. We didn't call it that then, but that's what it was.

I was at SFA for seven years. I went to my first public college there. I don't mean to be bragging, but I was considered one of the best in my class. You learn by experience. I learned more there than anywhere. I learned by teaching.

The president of the college needed a teacher [for the lab school]. I had been to Texas University, and he recommended me. He was the superintendent at one time. He recommended me and got word to me. He called me on the telephone at my home. That's the only summer time I didn't work.

I didn't have much time off, day or night. If I didn't go to summer school, I was busy at teachers' conferences. Some of my best friends have come from the meetings we had there.

College isn't what it used to be. Teachers used to be the instructors. They had teachers that wanted to teach in the summer, and they specialized in education in different programs. Teachers were teaching others. That's one of the reasons I had gone into supervising. Some of my teachers had asked me to do it. I wouldn't have gone into it if they hadn't asked. At the end it was so different from when I first started. Then we were so afraid we wouldn't do what we should. I got over that, of course.

I taught second and third grade at SFA. That was my preference. The little kiddies are so sweet and anxious to get into learning and so interested. Well, I learned along with them. I didn't know a lot of things at first. I'd let them know I was learning, too, and we'd find out about things together. We had a good time with it. The quieter, nicer, and more helpful they were, the quicker they'd get to work on something they liked. I used that instead of spanking. It was more pleasant.

The children loved animals. They weren't always the kind of animals we'd want for pets. One was an opossum, and that I didn't care for. But he was fascinating. They brought it in, but we couldn't feed him. So I said we'd keep it until tomorrow.

We called the opossum Nosy. He was nosier than nosy—into everything! We had a little children's library over in the corner of the room with books and all with a little table. I tried to make it attractive for them, with interesting books out where they'd find them and shelves all around.

In the morning, I came in the classroom, and all the books out of the library shelves were scattered out on the library floor. The opossum had gotten in behind them and rooted around, and it was the biggest mess. Bedlam!

We found Nosy in back of the books, and the janitor helped me to get him. We let him go. That's one pet I didn't want. He wasn't too anxious to stay very long anyway.

We had two alligators that we kept for over a year. They were eight inches long. One of the little boys' father was teaching science. Someone had brought the alligator eggs and they hatched.

So this little boy said, "Daddy said we could have them if we'd like to. They're not going to keep them."

I said, "Yes, we'd be glad to have them."

We had an aquarium, about two or three feet long. So we fixed that and had those two alligators in them. We called them Nip and Tuck because it was Nip and Tuck that we wouldn't give them any peace for them to rest.

We had trouble feeding them. They wouldn't accept our food. They got by, though. Somehow they must have eaten when we weren't looking 'cause we kept them for over a year.

I took them home with me for summer vacation. I wasn't gonna leave them there, and I wasn't sure what anybody else would have done. Anyway, I took them home. I was to be at home two or three weeks. I didn't know my mother was so interested in alligators. But she had lived in Louisiana, and she was familiar with them and thought they were cute.

When I went back to school, I put those alligators into a box and took them with me.

Mother wrote me and said, "Did you get back with both your alligators? I keep hearing a noise under the house and it sounds like the alligators." She had someone look, but they never could tell.

I wrote her and told her, yes, I had them. It must have been armadillos.

Mother was as interested in things like that as I was. She saved *National Geographic*s for me, and I had the most beautiful pictures to put up in the classroom about things we were studying because pictures were important to get them interested.

We used to take the *Weekly Reader*s,—they're for children, a newspaper. There was this little dog in the *Reader,* who would write letters to the boys and girls. They wondered, "If this dog could talk, then why couldn't Nip and Tuck, the alligators?"

So the children had the best time writing a letter to the *Weekly Reader* to that little dog. The *Weekly Reader* published it and sent a letter back to us. I don't remember what it said, but, anyway, they answered it. The children were so thrilled!

One little boy's daddy worked at the post office, and he saw that letter addressed to the class. He told his little boy it was on the way, and we should get it tomorrow. The little boy just danced into the room, his eyes sparkling. I didn't scold him for jumping up; I was glad to see him so happy. The children were all anxious to get the letter the next day. We had fun. I learned with them.

We had caterpillars once. Somebody brought in a caterpillar, and they wanted to keep it. So we raised it through all stages. The supervisor said she had never known anyone to get it through all the stages. We fed it everyday. Somebody, one of the children, would bring a handful of leaves, so we didn't have trouble feeding him. But we had trouble getting too many caterpillars because others would see a caterpillar and say, "Your caterpillars got out," and they'd bring the ones they'd found on the school ground. We had more caterpillars than we could take care of.

One time, in the spring, I went out to the lake out there. We took the whole group of us—about thirty people! We went out on a picnic, and we just had the best time. There was a swimming pool with just a little water in it because they weren't using it right then, and there were frog eggs in it. So I said I'd like to take some of those back to school. They laughed at me, but I did.

My principal bought us a little tub I guess about three feet. We filled it with water, and we watched them as they turned to tadpoles and as frogs.

I was giving a demonstration lesson, and about thirty teachers were in there beside my big group of kiddies. It started raining, and these visiting teachers were all jammed in. It just poured, and we closed the windows. We didn't have air conditioning then. And these tadpoles started changing to frogs!

The principal had brought us some Easter lilies and water lilies, too, and they were hopping out on the lily pads. The children got excited, and so did the visitors. It was pouring down rain, and we had to pull the windows down. But we were still interested in the frogs hopping out on the lily pads. You had to see it.

When they first started having supervision generally in this state, they asked me to be a supervisor. A friend of mine had been doing the same work in the demonstration school that I did at another level. She went into supervision, and she kind of got me acquainted with supervision and that helped me. She and I would go to state meetings together.

I was supervisor of St. Augustine in 1948 to '50 and then in Johnson County from 1950 until 1964 when I retired. I had a lot of teachers, and I tried to show them that I appreciated them. I loved them and wasn't trying to be critical. There were some supervisors who thought it was their job to be critical and things like that, but I didn't feel that way. We were just trying to help them. We just wanted to give them ideas to help.

I never had to evaluate them. That wouldn't have been fair to do because you couldn't be with them enough. But you can see their needs, and they do come to ask you for help. I got a lot of requests.

I enjoyed being a supervisor. One thing, I had a wonderful superintendent. He was great. I'd take him home from school. He would always call on me. If they had a big meeting, something special, I had to take him. He was county superintendent of Johnson County. He was the superintendent of all the rural schools in the county, but not the independent schools. My first year, I had about fourteen schools, but that counted independent schools. So he would have been superintendent of maybe eight rural schools. He occasionally went out to the schools, but not very often.

My first year there, the high school supervisor took me around to all the schools and introduced me. They said they'd show me the ropes, and they introduced me to everyone. It did make it so much nicer to find the way. I could have found that way, but it was nicer.

Those rural schools under the superintendent, they had sometimes eight teachers, other times less. They didn't have high school, only up through junior high. When they would get through junior high, they had to go away to high school.

I liked both the rural and the city schools. I didn't like one better than the other. I did have one independent school that just seemed a lot nicer.

In St. Augustine I was the only supervisor at the time. One of the [school board] president's little girls came to my house around Christmas time. The courthouse where my office was had never had a Christmas tree, and I couldn't stand that. I said to these two little girls that had come to visit me, "Would you girls like to help me make some decorations for a Christmas tree?" Oh, they'd love it!

I showed them how to cut and fold and make snowflakes, and we trimmed the tree—a pine tree, a good one. They came to my office and cut out snowflakes and hung them on the tree. Everybody came to look at it. It was the first time we'd had one. Everyone said, "See what they did." It wasn't so beautiful, but it was something the children did and enjoyed. We loved having a tree.

One thing I tried to do most of all was to help the teachers get the children to love to read. One teacher said, "They just hate to read," and that made me sick. I said, "Reading can be so much fun and a pleasure. What will they do later? How can they be independent? They have to read some things to get by."

This one high school asked me to show a teacher how to get started giving standardized tests. I had to be very simple with the children. There was a sample, and there were several answers, and one was right. They did their test, and I said, "Don't hurry because you have to do all you can." I had to be very simple.

The children did well on it, and this teacher was amazed when she found out they could do it. She had been an English teacher, and at one time she was assistant county superintendent. She had strayed too far away from the classroom. When they don't know how to do it, you have to show them. But I didn't mean to teach how to teach.

I wasn't doing anything special. I learned myself.

I knew this lady that was assistant superintendent. The first day the teachers came in, we had a meeting, and she said, "Oh, you're making a big mistake, dear. You're putting yourself on their level. You can't do that, 'cause that doesn't do any good."

I thought, "If you don't work on their level, how can you be understood?" Even with a child, I work on their level. I still do.

I want to tell you another story about a colored girl. When I first went in that room that morning, the teacher had the child come up to the front and lead the prayer. She said the Lord's Prayer, and she said it in a chant, and it was the most beautiful thing I'd ever heard in my life.

When I went back, I had to show them how to take the test, and those poor little colored children couldn't do it. They worked on those math tests. I told the teacher I had gotten them started, but it took longer than I thought it would. When I went in there, I had asked this principal if he would watch the time and stop them, but I had to do it for myself. I had to make them stop. I went in twenty minutes late, and they were still struggling over this test. They couldn't do the first part. I was just perplexed. They just didn't have the foundation, and they missed so much school. Most of them would be absent the first time I went out there.

But the junior high girls were so cute. When I started to leave I had all sorts of stuff to take back. Those little girls would walk me down to my car and help me. So I enjoyed that day.

The teacher had on a white suit that day. I guess the superintendent found out about the test. The blacks and the Mexicans had the same superintendent. The superintendent told the teachers, "The state is going to come down and administer tests so you be sure to keep up your papers and evaluations. And be sure to raise that flag!"

There was another school that didn't raise the flag, and the superintendent didn't notice it. I said, "Oh my goodness, he didn't raise the flag. Suppose someone from the state department comes in and finds that?" I went ahead and raised it.

They were beginning to do testing all over the state. It was reading, arithmetic, spelling, and IQ tests. All of them did it. I was a little leary of it because IQ tests can be so misleading as to exactly what they know. And if they hadn't been going to school, or started late, and so on that didn't seem very right.

I wasn't going to tell them I was retiring. Someone told that I had retired, and they found it out, and we had a party.

I always tried to teach that learning can be fun.

SEVEN

B.T. and Itasco Wilson

B.T. and Itasco Wilson, Barnet Chapel, United Methodist Church, Kerrville, Texas, 1987.

My husband was the first high school black principal in Kerrville. So I was very excited and wanted him to succeed. So I had a very interesting time. I loved the little children. They all wanted to be just like him.

—Itasco Wilson

When I came to Kerrville in 1940, they had a garbage man up here. He took out the garbage—a colored fellow. They paid that garbage man a hundred twenty-five dollars a month, and they were paying his assistant a hundred dollars a month. And they paid me to run that school down there, paid me seventy dollars a month. It's still short of taking a tooth out.

—B.T. Wilson

Nowhere else in this book is the unspoken heard more loudly than in the story told by husband and wife B.T. and Itasco Wilson. The Wilsons began teaching together in the segregated Center Point Community School near Pittsburg, Texas, in 1932 when they were in their early twenties. Their personal and teaching lives continued to be intertwined until their retirement from the integrated Kerrville schools where they worked from 1940 until the mid-1970s.

They are black, and in addition to the gender discrimination and poverty experienced by other interviewees, race created obstacles to achieving the Wilsons' career goals. Unlike most of the parents of the interviewees, B.T. and Itasco's mothers and fathers had above-average educations for their day. All four parents attended at least one year of college—enough education to be teachers. Yet even with their educational advantages, their parents were not better compensated than the parents of white teachers in "the other community."

In spite of their parents' financial difficulties, B.T. and Itasco were among the few teachers (Elizabeth Shelton was another) whose parents expected them to attend college as part of the usual course of events. When B.T. and his brothers "started piling up on each other" waiting to go to college, B.T.'s father accepted for the first time a better-paying job in a public school instead of the "missionary" teaching he had been doing in poor, private black schools. If viewing a college education as a right and not a privilege is a hallmark of a middle-class individual, then B.T. and Itasco met that standard and passed down the tradition to their own children and grandchildren.

Altruistic service to others was another legacy of B.T. and Itasco's families. B.T.'s father accepted a free college education with the understanding he would do "missionary" work as a teacher in Southern black schools. Not all of his children continued this legacy. Two of B.T.'s brothers went into business, and B.T. often remarked that the ones who chose teaching were the ones still living. If he or Itasco had dreams other than teaching, they do not say so, but their life histories are testimony that they channeled their energies into altruistic service for the children in their community. They took their lessons from Mrs. Christine Case, principal at their first school—a lady who "believed that anything could be done."

B.T. and Itasco brought this philosophy with them when they went to Kerrville, Texas, in 1940. B.T. became the town's first black high school principal at the all-black Doyle School, and Itasco was a teacher working closely with him. They built a close-knit academic community of black students, teachers, and parents until court-ordered desegregation forced the closing of the Doyle School in 1966.

Without exception, the teachers interviewed in this book give most of the credit for the successful integregation of the Kerrville schools to B.T. and Itasco Wilson. Their thoughtful, evenhanded actions in both the black and the white communities were remarkable and clearly appreciated by their peers and contemporaries. Much of their personal perspective on integration is unspoken in the following testimony, but what is told is poignant. Despite the benefits of desegregation, there were seldom-mentioned costs—the loss of opportunity provided by a caring faculty in a family-like setting. In their important book *Ringing the Children In,* Thad Sitton and Milam C. Rowold address a similar issue.[1] They are speaking of rural schools for white children, but the principles have much in common. They point to the little-known Great Texas Educational Survey of 1924, a study undertaken by school reformers wanting to prove that small rural schools should be eradicated in favor of "modern," efficient schools. Much to the reformers' dismay, the survey actually showed a slight superiority in the academic performance of students in smaller, rural schools, and the report was buried. As Sitton and Rowold state,

> The losses incurred by the concealment of the report are incalculable. None of the survey findings have ever been used to expand the dialogue

related to the recurring and unresolved questions of schooling. A striking example that lay buried for sixty years may be found in the final summation of the survey commission: "The finding that rural schools are not inefficient leaves open the possibility that the small school has compensating advantages which enable it, with the very obvious handicap of poorly trained teachers and less adequate facilities, to compete with the larger schools in the final product." What were these mysterious, "compensating advantages" at work in the country schools of sixty years ago? . . . Today, long after the school reformers' fondest dreams were realized, there is great dissatisfaction with public education. That simple, yet basic question still remains unanswered: What makes a school good? (18–19)

Whatever makes a school good, part of it was lost with the closing of Doyle School under B.T. and Itasco Wilson.

In retirement, B.T. and Itasco remain active in the Retired Teachers organization, attend Doyle School reunions where the choir sings again under B.T., and participate in numerous church and civic activities. At eighty, B.T. still works every Saturday night playing the bass fiddle with the Just Jazz Combo at a Fredericksburg restaurant. The Wilsons also enjoy visiting their children, grandchildren, and other relatives near and far, and taking special trips with friends, like the author, to the nearby birthplace of President Lyndon Baines Johnson.

Grades 1–2, Doyle High School, Kerrville, Texas, 1947. B.T. is in back row on far left. Itasco is kneeling behind seated children.

B.T.   People who head the educational programs in this country are inexperienced as far as any reaction with students on an extended basis. They just don't know. They've got the answers—"sit up, stand up, do this, that, and the other." But as I said, Who are the administrators?

Administrators are usually former coaches who have never been in the classroom, and all the knowledge they've got about education, they got in grad school. They weren't in service when they got it. They might have been in service as a coach, but they weren't in service in the classroom.

That's the reason why teachers are feeling alienated. Here in Texas there's quite a bit of alienation. Of course, salaries were raised and pushed by the governor—first by the governor and carried through by the legislature. But there's a lot of alienation in school teachers from Texas [Texas State Teachers Association] and these other teacher groups. I'll tell you what. That temerity of theirs and insensitivity on the part of the policy makers—that can come home to roost, you know.

Three of us—there were five brothers—went into education. My two older brothers—one stayed in education, one got in and got out in business. One never did get in. They both completed college. There weren't any graduate schools in the South. So my oldest living brother, the one in Oklahoma, he got his master's degree from the University of Michigan. The next received his master's degree from University of Kansas. My wife and I received our master's from Our Lady of the Lake down in San Antonio.

I met a young fellow who just had finished St. Mary's. I asked him, "Where do you work?" He said, "Well, I got out of service and I went back to St. Mary's."

So I decided what I'd do. I'd go and get my master's degree. Then I'd get a job teaching. This was a pretty good while ago, way back then in the early fifties.

So this class we'd signed up for there was taught by Sister Theresa. She had her doctorate from somewhere. Sister Theresa liked for you to come out of the classroom to her class. The first day we were in there, everybody, each person, had to introduce himself or herself and where they worked.

This one old boy said, "Well, I just finished St. Mary's University, and I haven't taught."

She said, "You don't have any business in here." She told him that. She said, "Well, you're here, but I don't know where I'm going to put you."

That old boy flunked the course.

Everything referred to some situation that these people had experienced, and this old boy hadn't experienced it. He wouldn't know how to give an answer because he hadn't known any of those snotty-nosed kids and all of that, and those that were very cooperative, and those who are

155

very uncooperative—all those things that you start learning when you shut that door behind you, and you're in that room by yourself. That's when teaching begins. That's the type of situation it was. Sister Theresa wanted us to have some experience in the classroom as a teacher to be in her class. She gave that old boy a hard time, and I couldn't do fiddle about it. She based a whole lot of her instruction—her requirements—on applications that you had had experience with, experiences if you made a mistake, you'd try to make something out of it—that type of thing.

A lot of these administrators never had the experience. They went to graduate school, made good grades, but when it comes down to the nitty-gritty, I call it, because they wanted the administrative field, rather than the classroom.

ITASCO   Do you want me to talk a little while for you? I'll start from my beginning. Both my parents and a lot of my relatives were teachers. That's all the professions there were back then. You could take piano, be a teacher, or be a nurse. That's all we knew about then.

I began to realize I'd like to be a teacher—especially those who were handicapped. Seemed like I would take to them. So I took the literature and the teaching.

Well, I finally finished school. I thought I didn't know a thing. I was just prepared to go to work. I was ready to go after four years.

I went straight through. My town was a small town, and we didn't have a complete high school. So I went to a college that had from prep school on. I finished high school at the college. I went four years straight through, and then I went out and started teaching. They gave you a license when you graduated. That was in '31. Yes, we had to do practice teaching in whatever you wanted to major in, and I majored in elementary education. My husband can explain that to you. Now, explain how they did that. My mother and your mother went—wasn't it one year? And then they'd give them a certificate.

B.T.   It was a temporary certificate. It was the normal way. The requirement in Texas used to be just one year above high school, and you could become an instructor. They had a temporary certificate. You had to keep going to school to keep it, of course, but finally in most school districts they only accepted degreed teachers.

ITASCO   What year did that happen? Do you remember?

B.T.   No, that's too far back.

ITASCO   It had to be in the fifties 'cause Mama had to go back to school. She went to a little college. I think that was in the fifties. Anyway, they finally did reach a standard.

B.T.   Both our mothers were teachers, but my father more so than my mother. Father spent forty years as a teacher. Thirty-two of those years were in church-related schools, though.

ITASCO   My mother was the teacher. She was forty-eight years in the system, teaching. She started in 1906 in a little rural school.

B.T.   Father never knew he had a payday coming until the last nine years. He supported us by going into business—rug cleaning business—with my brothers. My two oldest brothers—one was twelve years old and the next one was ten—and they vacuumed carpets. This was way back yonder.
    He had a wagon with a gasoline motor and a big vacuum and real long hose. He'd drive the wagon into peoples' yards and run the hose through the windows and vacuum the furniture and carpets. This was way back before the time of Hoovers and machines like that. So he did that while teaching in order to put food on the table.
    Finally, after I don't know how long, he got out of that. We were piling up on each other as far as going off to school was concerned. My oldest brother finished at Fisk University in Nashville in 1922. My two older brothers started piling up. Here came somebody out of high school, somebody out of college. There was a whole lot of messing around and hanging around, staying out of school, that sort of stuff. One would get hit by another one, and all that sort of stuff.
    So finally we all got through school. I went straight through because at that age we didn't know who the biggest was. And then my father was the principal at the black high school in Waco. He was getting a payday then. I don't know why he didn't want to go into public education earlier. I don't know what it was.

ITASCO   I think he had the missionary spirit. He'd seen people being enslaved. He said in some sections where the cotton was, they were really badly treated. He went into this religious school because he wanted to help.

B.T.   Well, conditions made him what he was. My father was the first black to finish high school in Galesburg, Illinois. When he finished high school, there was a man who had the missionary spirit. He wanted to do something for the education of the blacks in the South. There were no public schools except in large cities. So they had a lot of little academies set up all over the South. Some of them survived and still are black private colleges. But most of them—when public schools began, when black public schools began to get funding—they would disappear. So public schools began to take over.

So this man told my father, "If you promise me you'll go South and teach school for two years, I'll send you to Lombard College."

Well, at that time there were two colleges in Galesburg—Knox and Lombard. Finally Lombard and Knox were combined. Knox retained the name for both schools.

Anyhow, he came down to teach at Sequin. There was a little black school set up down there.

So he came South and went to work there. He and my mother were courting. She was from a little town outside of Knoxville. It is in Knox County. Carl Sandburg was the most famous graduate of Knox College.

My father went right on, and when he came to Texas, he had a master's degree in mathematics. He remained at Guadalupe College in Seguin nineteen years, and then he left and went to another church school in Waco when I was a year old. I'm the youngest. He stayed there thirteen years. We were growing on up so he had to have some money. So he got out of it. About that time, an opening came in the public school there. They had to beg him, but my father took it. Then he stayed at that job until he became ill in his sixties. But he enjoyed it and he left a lot of memories in the public schools there in Waco.

And then my mother taught, too.

My oldest brother taught a couple of years, and then he went into the insurance business. He died when he was in his fifties. My middle brother went to school at Bradley University in Peoria, Illinois, but he never did go into teaching. He went into business. He took the business over that my father started and operated that until he died. He died in his fifties. The rest of us got in the public schools and stayed. I'm the youngest one, and I've been retired since 1973. The school teachers are the oldest ones of us still living.

ITASCO   My husband was the first high school black principal in Kerrville. So I was very excited and wanted him to succeed. So I had a very interesting time. I loved the little children. They all wanted to be just like him.

I moved out of home in '31. I went out in this small school near Pittsburg, Texas called Center Point Community School. Mr. Wilson was my boyfriend then, and he's the one that got the job. Pittsburg, Texas— that's in northeast Texas. And he's the one that got the job for me. He started me to work right away.

B.T.   The principal told my father, "I'm looking for a teacher." And my father asked me about my girlfriend. That's how I got her the job.

ITASCO   When he met me, I was at Bishop College in Marshall, Texas. It has moved to Dallas since. It was a long first year for me. He didn't teach that year. He stayed and worked in the rug laundry. The next year he came out there, and he decided, "Well, why don't we just go ahead and get married? Let's get married." So in December, the 30th, 1932, we got married. That was during the depression. We weren't paid anything then. We had vouchers.

B.T.   That year we got married, we got paid the first four vouchers. The last five we didn't get money for about three or four years after . . .

ITASCO   . . . after my baby was born.

B.T.   We were working in a common school called Center Point Training School. See, there are hardly any common schools now. Most schools in Texas are in independent school districts. The state superintendent is over the county superintendent, and the common schools are administered by the county superintendent. But they have just about disappeared.

ITASCO   You know, the reason for that was in a large area you didn't have any high schools. Well, these schools were established, and these children would come in. A lot of them would board there, and the few that were in the community would attend. Well, you wouldn't have very much in your first grade, but up in the upper grades, you'd have quite a few 'cause they'd come from all surrounding little communities. That's how they got started: there was no high school close around.

Schools like that at that time were called training schools. They were common schools, which meant they were state controlled, but locally controlled. Instead of busing children into the city like they do now, they would just go into these rural training schools. There was a shortage of high schools, and this was one way for them to get a high school education. A little black school in the country would only go up to eighth grade.

They had regular women—housemothers, matrons—just like you do in college to look after the children who boarded. The teachers didn't have to look after them. They'd cook, too.

The head lady of the school, she was a smart lady. Real smart. Her name was Mrs. Christine Cash.

B.T.   She made some mistakes, though. She went to this community, Center Point, a rural town in Camp County, Texas, and she set up a school. I mean, she went there as a teacher, and I don't know if she knew what the conditions were in these sections—that there were only four four-year high schools in northeast Texas, one in Marshall, one in Long-view, and one in Tyler, and in Texarkana. Those were all. The rest of the schools were just not four-year schools. In the school she set up, three teachers taught the first seven grades and ten taught the last four. That sounds funny, but the largest class was the senior class because there were more schools that didn't have the fourth year of high school in east Texas and parts of Louisiana and Oklahoma.

The youngsters came there to finish high school. So this school didn't serve the community. It didn't. The community didn't appreciate it.

That woman fixed things. What she set up was a little Tuskegee out there. That's what she did. We had a home economics department and one of the few high schools in the state of Texas for trade carpentry. It taught the boys how to build houses. But it didn't affect the community. It didn't. Because most the pupils there were from other places.

Everybody who taught there had a degree. All they needed was that. The principal got her doctorate from the University of Wisconsin, and they offered her a chair there in rural education. She was an expert in rural education. But she wouldn't take it. She went on back to that school, and she stayed too long. Some of those old dropouts in that community, the ones who never did finish, got on the board and fired her. That's the reason why I say she stayed too long. She ended up teaching at Bishop College.

ITASCO   When you got through with her, you were ready to go to work.

B.T.   Each teacher passed by the office on Monday morning to put his or her lesson plan on her desk. During the week, she'd walk in and stand at the doorway and listen to you awhile. She'd tell you where you were supposed to be, and I didn't even know where the hell my lesson plan was. But she had it in her head. She believed that anything could be done. There wasn't anything that couldn't be done. So a lot of the science department and other innovations went on. Equipment we couldn't buy, we'd make.

ITASCO   My most embarrassing moment was soon after school opened that year, 1931. At noontime, one of my students lost his lunch. I looked. Some of the pupils helped. Finally I said, "Where is your coat?" He said, "Hanging in the closet." I went to pull something out of his coat pocket and a mouse jumped out. I ran all the way to the schoolyard, children behind me. The principal and other students joined me. Can you imagine? I just knew I would be fired!

Now, in Kerrville, when my husband came here as principal in 1940, this was a . . . well, would you say it was in a rut? How would you describe Kerrville? Isolated?

Now, today, only about five people with degrees, blacks, live here in town. There were others who had nice jobs and things, but they weren't living here.

Of course, when he came in he had to devise ways to motivate the children and keep them in school. We had taught before, but this was the biggest job where we taught together.

B.T.   They didn't have any public school where we taught that was named after a black. The first for us was when my husband was principal in the Kerrville Public Schools. They named it Doyle. It was kindergarten up.

Mrs. Doyle was a lady who was dedicated to education. She came from Louisiana—Shreveport, Louisiana. She worked real hard here and stayed longer than any other teacher, so we thought she deserved some mention. I think she only taught children to the seventh grade, and then another teacher came in and taught them to the ninth grade. They couldn't finish high school here. They had to go somewhere else.

They had to leave here if they wanted to finish high school. So when he came, he decided to put on all the extra grades that we needed. It was 1940. There was just three of us. Three teachers then. I had three grades.

B.T.   We started school at eight o'clock and set them out at four. Combined the top grades into three levels. Of course, some would flip-flop. Kids that would transfer in would get into trouble, but the kids who went all the way through got it all.

ITASCO   We turned out the primary children, I think, at two-thirty, and then he would send the freshman English to me. Just one class. No, I taught the senior English at first. Then later on we added more teachers, and I didn't have to do that.

In my experience with the youngsters, some nice little sweet thing that I remember is valentines. One of my little students—he was from a broken home and the mother began to be ill after having five children. Everybody brought me a little valentine card, and I was giving them all a stick of candy or whatever. And so he sat back there, and I kept watching him. So finally he got a hold of somebody's valentine, and he wrote on that, "I love you, valentine" and wrapped up a nickel in it. You know, that's too sentimental for me, but I kept a straight face in class. I knew I was all the people he had, so I decided I'd keep that nickel, and I wouldn't give it back to him. But during the noon hour when they'd go and buy a little candy for me, I'd offer him some.

"Don't you want this piece of candy?"

I kept that nickel for as long as . . . I don't know. I might have it yet 'cause I rolled it up and put it away. I do have some old nickels. I might have it; I don't know. But I kept it for a long time. That's the way you get.

Sometimes you get a little experience with children. Always will be one that will think you mistreat the teacher. There were sisters and brothers. The girl had been in my purse and got five dollars out of it.

So I'd say to them, "Well, now, I'm not going to bother." I'd say, "Whoever's got it—I'm going to do my work—just quietly go on and leave it in the cloakroom."

So finally one little girl slipped through and said, "Mrs. Wilson, it's in there! It's in there!"

So I went to get it, and I said, "Mary, did you do that?" She had a brother who was a tattler. He said, "Mary, what did you go into Mrs. Wilson's purse for?"

Well, I didn't bother him either. I didn't punish them. I gave them a talk. Now that girl is a . . . Well, she sent us fifty dollars for our fiftieth anniversary and a dollar to grow on. I kept the dollar. I put it up there with our anniversary picture. I spent the fifty dollars, though.

That's my son in the picture. No, that's my grandson. He finished Texas Southern. He wants to be a lawyer.

B.T.   There was a hundred eighty students in Doyle School. Twelve grades. Only had seven teachers, though.

ITASCO   In building it up, first he had a homemaking teacher. He felt that was necessary—to have a homemaking teacher. I could play the piano and he knew music, so we decided we needed what was in line with the community. I think he organized the choir first, or was the band first? The choir—which was very outstanding. The choir was asked to perform for the Lions' state convention down in Laredo and for the state black teachers' organization in Fort Worth, Dallas, and Waco. And in San Antonio at the State Home, and after that at Brook Army Hospital. It was a very close harmony choir. It really was good. He was the director.

B.T.   Tape recorders were just beginning to come on the scene. That was some years ago—'49. You're talking about a small school. Some-

times you have programs going on, and sometimes you can't get anything going on because you don't have enough youngsters. So we were in
and out of things. In and out of football, in and out of baseball. Well, we
got into basketball. And the choir, I don't know where! A bunch of
youngsters came along, and they had fun. When they went through
school like that, there wasn't much in front of them as far as talent, and
there wasn't much left behind. But in this group just about anything I
tried to get that group to do, they'd do it. I had them singing. I wrote a
lot of the arrangements myself, you know. I would write what I'd call
"tight chords." I had those youngsters singing the type of chords you
hear on instruments. It was pretty good.

Youngsters today can't understand when we have these reunions.
They can't understand why these people come from all over the country
from coast to coast. All the way from Boston and the San Francisco Bay
area, up in Michigan, come back here for a reunion. All the Doyle "Ex's."
The last one we had was last year. Next one's next year. Anyhow, we were
sitting there and up in the choir were a bunch of these "Ex's." Some of
them with children, and some with grandchildren. They were up there
in the choir. Some of them started singing. I didn't know anything about
it. Somebody told me they were going to do it. But they had the same
sound like they were doing then back in the early fifties.

They were thither and yon. Some in Texas, some in Kerrville, some in
San Antonio.

ITASCO   To give you a little more about it, they performed at the
Schreiner Institute quite often and at the VA hospital in Kerrville. I just
want you to know how good he was.

Then, after that, he organized a band. He could blow on the horn, he
played the guitar, and he played the ukelele when he was a young man. I
had a cousin who wanted a job. Could he work with the band?

So we got this started, and then they gave us a man. Whenever he
looked for his teachers, you had to be of a wide variety—do a lot of
things. So he found somebody who could teach band and coach and
teach class. And the same thing he did in the home economics. She had
to teach home ec, and I had to teach a class. Things like that.

B.T.   You know, I had a criticism one time. A man came in to evaluate our school for thirty minutes and gave us a bad grade. He was from
the agency—from the Texas State Education Agency. He said, "You have
too many high school preparations. That's a long day. You've got too
many preparations, that's all. You can't have your accreditation."

Two years before he gave us the thumbs down, we had a week-long
evaluation by people from various institutions—other high schools, and

some colleges and universities. And the man who's over the Department of Education at Southwest Texas University, a teachers' college down at San Marcos—spent three days over here. When he left, he wrote me a letter asking me to outline our curriculum setup. He wanted to use the information in advising small isolated school districts on curriculums.

I said, "Say, man, you've got these kids over here that are doing well. And now you're telling me we can't have any accreditation? The reason why we can't have any accreditation is we have too many preparations?"

I said, "We have very few dropouts. We've got a football program here."

And the coach—well, the coach was a fellow from up the street who came down and coached these boys. I didn't have time to put into it, and these fellows had played high school football, and they were good football coaches. Now what more do you want a coach to do if he wins? It was good for the youngsters, kept them out of trouble, kept them in school. And it gave a manner of well-being, you know, to these young men who were out of school—veterans, you know, coming back after from the war. What was it later on people said? Use some community resources? Well, big deal. We started that. Our motto was to teach—the emphasis was on teaching.

ITASCO   One thing about it was the system was so good. And let's put this in. Tell that the other communities, not the black communities, started complaining. We had all kinds of extracurricular activities going on. That's how we could produce and get those children so up.

And there it begins. Come about quite a change. Some young people try to come home and see what they can do to help a little more. And that's how we got some more teachers—friendships.

And then he had another little system where he'd have children that had been here, born here, never been out of this community, and he asked one or two of the gentlemen about taking them to the park, Breckenridge Park in San Antonio. Every year, that would be the spring break recreation. All the schools. And we would supervise them.

And that went along, and then they had a rule that you couldn't take elementary children twenty-five miles. One of the principals, see, he was getting a lot of flack because he couldn't do that. But this was a special school. That principal couldn't do it, so he started complaining so that got stopped. But you know, you had a good time all the way through things. And 'course you could see how the other community would complain.

Then he'd put on a May Day. That was like what they have now—a field day. We put on we called them May Day. And we had the parents involved. They'd come and bring the baskets, and we'd have them wrapping the maypoles, something they'd never seen, you know. They'd wrap the maypole, and play softball, baseball, sack race, just everything.

Also we didn't have a competition in the UIL [University Interscholastic League]. We didn't have anybody to be put in with 'cause you're separated, you see. We didn't have any UIL. So we decided to just have competition among ourselves and let the children do their own entertainment. They would have spelling contests—who outspells—and math and speaking and singing. The winners got a pencil or a tablet or a ribbon. Wasn't much, just something to make them feel like they'd won something. Those were the ones we carried on. I think that's all. And then we would crown a queen and have a big party at night.

Every month on the last Friday—well, they knew if they'd been acting pretty good and everything was running smooth, that they were going to have a social. They'd get ready for that social. We didn't have live music then. They had jukeboxes. Guess what? They didn't come in slouching like they do nowadays. They would put on nice little shoes and dresses and things.

B.T.   Once they were in the building, if you left, you didn't come back. You were there until we closed. If they left, they couldn't come back.

ITASCO   Their parents were so proper—so cooperative. You know, a lot of times you can't do things like that.

However, when the integration started—oh, like everybody else they didn't know what was happening. We, as teachers, didn't want to think we were hindering them. We didn't talk, didn't say a word. Just whatever they wanted to do. They'd say, "Well, we want the best for our children, and they say integration is the best." They talked to me a lot out here at the house.

Well, that was a time when you were feeling bad. But otherwise we had all the cooperation we wanted. All the time, everything went. They still, you know . . .

B.T.   We got the limit down to ten miles, but not twenty-five. We wanted to go to San Antonio, the Alamo. So a friend of mine was a black secretary down there, so we started this interaction. They would come up here on the first Saturday in May when it wasn't a school day, and we would go down there two weeks later. We'd load up all the kids in buses and take them down there. Well, that went on for awhile, and then this thing came up. I don't know how the chilldren reacted. I should have reacted differently than I did. I should have asked them, "Say, why not?"

Ask me something instead of telling me something. They said, "How did you get those trips organized?"

What happened, of course, I would drive the school bus. Drive the band, drive the pep squad. I knew we had to involve a lot of parents into this thing, high school kids, involve a lot of parents in supervision. We had kids all the way from the bottom to the top. And we involved the teachers. I had to ask the teachers for their Saturdays, two Saturdays, and two weeks later I had to ask for their Saturdays. And then upperclass youngsters who proved themselves over the years. And what we would do, we had a workshop, just exactly how to handle these youngsters.

Do you know, I was kind of glad to get out of it in a way? 'Cause when we put that last kid off those old buses, back home, their parents waiting for them to get off, 'cause when you're taking them like that, it's a lot of responsibility. But it wasn't haphazard. Each were senior students that we had, girls mostly, because the boys were on the baseball team. Had a team with small children, but then we'd have a high school big boys' team— YMCA boys. The public school system in San Antonio didn't have baseball in high school. So the YMCA or some boys' club had baseball teams, and we'd play those teams. So most of these people were girls, seniors mostly, and they would be assigned a certain number of children just like in Boy Scouts with children in the water. You'd have the buddy system, and every once in a while we'd check. We always brought 'em back. It was planned. It wasn't an accident.

And that's one thing where I made a mistake. I should have told them that this thing is not nearly as haphazard, not nearly as dangerous as you might think. Because it was highly organized. And we'd give these youngsters credit for it in school, for leadership, and they'd check on those youngsters. Some groups used tags, but we didn't need tags with these girls. They'd keep their eyes on all these youngsters, or if anybody cut up or got out of line, that meant that next time we'd just have to think about that child.

And then we charged the youngsters an insurance fee. There was a company somewhere up North. It would insure the youngsters from the time they left home 'til they got home for twenty-five cents. I'd tell the parents the only thing, of course, that the child could go if they paid their twenty-five cents. I had everything on that sheet, and I made it out before we left town with the money for the insurance would be in the post office. So if something bad happened—well, you never can tell, but there would have been coverage. Quite a bit of coverage. It wasn't haphazard at all. So I don't know.

In education, my ideas are very intangible. A lot of people claim they can put their fingers on it. Just what is it whereby knowledge can be transferred from one person to another? What is this thing called motivation?

On this competency testing of teachers—you've heard about it? Well, it got down to that only those people who can answer certain questions on a teacher competency test are the ones who can teach, and those who can't are the ones who can't teach anymore. Now saying somebody has the business to do something just because the person answered some question is a poor way of doing with a person. For example, where my daughter teaches—not the one where she is now but there in Houston— they have a man with a Ph.D. teaching mathematics. What in the world he was doing in a junior high school I don't know. Youngsters didn't learn one thing from him. The youngsters were not motivated.

Some youngsters don't need teachers. All they need, when they come to school that first day, is that they are given a key to the library. You tell him where the library is and just get out of his way. They're bragging about this youngster? You're talking about somebody that doesn't even need teaching.

And there are some you have to nurture. What about those that need the teacher, that need somebody to open the door or point out into the wild blue yonder, and have them see something that really isn't there, but can be there if they can just see it? That's what I've got against teacher testing.

Now this is what I have to say about teachers. I'll tell you about the Judas goat. You've heard about the Judas goat? Well, some of these teachers are acting like they're Judas goats, acting when their tails hop through the little side door they're supposed to hop through, while allowing the pupils who follow to slide down the chute to be butchered. So it seems to me that teachers ought to go about it in a different way because, after all, they're kicking about something that they have children using all the time themselves. The rules of the game can change. They do change. Just like playing a game of football, playing a game of baseball, you're out there playing your opponent. And the opponent points the way and goes this way, and you have to react to it and not lose your head.

I know there's a lot of industry and big taxpayers and big employers of personnel that have been disappointed with some of the products that have been sent to them. These businesses, you know, they do pay taxes— school taxes—and they're not getting really what they wanted. There was a lot of pressure behind testing teachers. A whole lot of pressure. We're not perfect; I'll tell you that. And so the government reacted.

Maybe they got some of the most incompetent people out, but that was the very few teachers. But testing teachers is like motherhood, and you can't fight motherhood. It's painful, but you can't fight motherhood. There are certain things that you can't fight.

There's an old man in Texas here somewhere—minister—one of these I call them paupertricians. He went down to New Orleans and ran a meeting down there. He told the people down there that God was going to destroy New Orleans, so you get out. New Orleans was a sinful city, and God was going to destroy it. You know, some of those people got out, and some of those people came to stay right here in Kerrville. A lot of them came to Texas. Some to San Antonio, quite a few up there in Brownswood north of us, and some down by Victoria. They got out of New Orleans because this preacher said so.

So one old gentleman came here—he and his wife and grandchildren. So he used to come out here and garden the place out in back here. He'd be out here all the time, and he was telling me the reason why he came to be out here—because of that preacher.

So I told him it seemed to me if God wanted to destroy New Orleans, he could have done it a long time ago. Jean Lafitte used to walk up and down the street there, and prostitutes used to advertise in the newspapers. I said, "It looks to me if there's some sin in the French Quarter, why destroy Tulane University, one of the greatest medical research centers in the world? That sounds clumsy to me."

And I said, "Another thing, New Orleans is a town where you go up to the river instead of down to it. And it's been sitting there at the end of the biggest drainage system in the world almost." And I said, "If that hasn't happened, it never would. Those people back yonder just took the land away from the river and built it, and they lived there. So that sounds kind of funny that God is going to wait all this time to destroy that place." And I said, "It could less happen now than it used to be. Way back yonder they didn't have all those dams up the Missouri River and up the Tennessee River and up these other rivers that feed water into the Missouri." I was telling him about the Atchafalaya turnaround where they drained the Mississippi River where instead of it running into the Mississippi River, the Mississippi River runs into it. I said, "New Orleans is in better shape now than it's ever been."

I hate to see anybody take advantage of the naiveté of a people.

ITASCO   When I went over to Peterson, I went in the junior high. I was supposed to take the reading class, but there was a young lady just out of college, and she was being hired. She said, "Oh, I don't want to have special education," because that was really new. That was in 1966, and nobody knew what to do with it. Well, she asked me would I change?

I told her, "I don't know."

"Principal over there said so."

I guess I had to if I wanted my job. So that's what he had asked me. Finally he called me, and I told him the same thing.

He said, "Well, you all go home, have some lunch, come back and we'll see what we can find."

So anyway they decided to give me special ed. I was kind of nervous, too, and he didn't know what to do. He'd tell me, "The only thing I ask you to do, Mrs. Wilson, is keep them quiet."

Well, I went down there. See, we had just closed our school up. They had taken the high school in '63, and they took the whole school in '66.

Anyway, I went on. I got my class. We had a little room, very convenient. We had a stove and wash basin, and everything for that type of student.

Just keep them quiet?

I said, "You don't have any kind of literature or books? You haven't put out anything?"

"No, you just have to invent something."

Well, I sat there for about a week after that, and I thought, "I can't just do this 'cause they're going to run me out of here."

So I went to him, and I asked him if I could go back to our little black school and pick up first- and third-grade books for them—after I had kind of sorted them out.

And he said, "Anything you can do if you think that's going to help."

Well, I did that, and I started class, and we started getting along real fine. I found it interesting 'cause they were like immature beginners. It wasn't nearly as bad as I thought it would be. But that's where I really was kind of nervous because they were different children, and I always figured they might have a spell or something, you know, and I wouldn't know what to do.

Some of them get a fixation on you, and you'd have to watch. Well, I was much younger then. They come skedaddling by the desk, and they like to hug and kiss you so you get kind of nervous. All in all I found them just like beginners.

I stayed there in special ed until I retired in 1975. I took training. I went to Incarnate Word College and took special courses in it. Twelve weeks, I think it was to get my certificate. See, I already had my master's, and I had taught. I was experienced.

After I really got the knack of it, and the children started responding, I said, "They're just like all other children." They just had some peculiarities. One child could read real well but couldn't understand math. One could understand math, up to a certain point, I mean—how you could maybe in the second grade. They could add or subtract. And this one could spell a few words, and this one could read. But all of them couldn't do everything. This one boy who had math but never could get the letter *A*. He knew *B* but not *A*. You'd show him the *A*, and he'd just blank out.

I said, "When you say *ABC,* say that first." When you put it up there on the board, he never could understand it.

Now I'm going to brag awhile. In addition to special ed I coached dramatic presentation and prose reading under the UIC. My children won first and second place every time I coached dramatic presentation. And the same thing in prose reading. We always met in San Antonio, and we always won for the district.

I retired in '75. I started teaching over there in '66. My first job was in '31, but I didn't teach straight through. See, I had children in between there. I quit because I got married, and we were expecting our babies and everything.

B.T.   I'll tell you what. My father had become sick. When we got home from east Texas in '33, we were married that December before. We got home the last of May. My father was sick with cancer. And so all the brothers, three were in Waco there, and one was in Oklahoma. So my oldest brother was chairman of the board, and we had a meeting. Eeny, meeny, miney, mo. That's not four, but there were five of us. I was mo. I automatically pulled the short straw because I was the youngest. Somebody was going to have to stay home with Father and Mother, and they all looked at me. I looked around, and I didn't see anybody else, so that was that. And then my wife was expecting. Our son was born on the twentieth of October. She was out of school, I was out of school two years. It was '33. Father died in the fall of '34. Then in September of the next year, '35, I started teaching at San Angelo, Texas. The baby was just about two years old. She wasn't able to begin teaching again.

ITASCO   They didn't hire married women at that time. They did have a rule, didn't they? But the principal's wife was teaching there. However, they had been for twenty-five years. But they said they weren't hiring married teachers there. That's what they said.

B.T.   Sometimes women teachers married later in life. Some of them got a taste of being independent, and they wanted to hang on to that.

ITASCO   Sometimes they waited because they would have to support younger brothers and sisters or a mother. I had planned to do that myself, but my mother died young. Sometimes people would just live together because they weren't allowed to get married and teach.

B.T.   There's a big furor over prayer in schools. That's one of the big deals right now. But you brought up something there. The first schools in the New World were parochial schools, and the Catholics were here before we were, before any other denomination. In fact, the Catholics were more prolific than the public schools in America. So when public schools finally came along, nothing was brand new. They copied off Catholic schools.

Three main things I see that they copied off the Catholic schools was poverty—the oath of poverty. In the state of Texas now, I've been retired thirteen years. If I was teaching now, it would be the maximum teachers can make. I would be making over twice as much as when I retired. Over twice as much just in these thirteen years.

When I came to Kerrville in 1940, they had a garbage man up here. He took out the garbage—a colored fellow. They paid that garbage man a hundred twenty-five dollars a month, and they were paying his assistant a hundred dollars a month. And they paid me to run that school down there, paid me seventy dollars a month. It's still short of taking a tooth out.

ITASCO   What did I get? Forty dollars?

B.T.   Yes, forty-five dollars. Thing about it, that's just a little bit on this side of poverty—that oath of poverty.

The next thing that was copied off the Catholic schools was celibacy up until World War II. World War II is the thing that got rid of celibacy. When they took all the men and sent them into the service, then they let married women go into these schools.

So the third thing came out of the parochial school was prayer—the religious service. But the qualification of prayer in school is just not there. It's just something they copied off of parochial schools. They copied celibacy, copied poverty, and copied prayer. And so, two of them, one is pretty well gone. Celibacy is pretty well gone. As I said, World War II killed it. Poverty is gradually, gradually disappearing—the oath of poverty. But prayer, that's a biggie. And all it is is a political ploy. That's all it is.

I don't think much about driver education. I think it's a waste of money, waste of time. All this time these driver ed teachers—I didn't teach my children how to drive a car. See, when our children came along, at fourteen years old you could drive. You got a license at fourteen years old. What I did when my son got to be fourteen years old was I just stopped the car—we were on our way somewhere—I just stopped the car. I got out and told him move over. He moved over and drove the car

171

home. He sat up beside me from the time he was a little baby and had learned everything. He knew everything about driving a car.

My daughter was the same way. I was going to school at Our Lady of the Lake so sometimes I would take her to San Antonio to her music teacher. I'd leave her off, and go to school and then come back by and pick her up. One day we were coming through Comfort. She had just gotten to be fourteen. We stopped outside of Comfort. She said, "What's the matter, Daddy?"

I said, "Move over."

She got under the steering wheel and drove us on home. Less than a week after that she had her license. She went on and passed her test and everything. Got her license. You don't have to teach kids how to drive a car. What driver education is, it's trying to grind into these young drivers the correct way to manage having a car—the laws, judgment, all those types of things. That's what driver's ed is all about. But just as soon as these kids—I'd say ninety percent of them, ninety-five percent—get their license, they start breaking all the laws they find. And the reason why is because they sit up there and watch Daddy and Mamma break laws up until they started driving, too. The biggest teacher you have is the home. And their peers. But they learn most of their stuff off their own moms and dads.

That's why I said about whether public, tax-supported institutions ought to be the arm of some religion. Because even the religious people can't agree. I think I heard someone say there's over ten thousand different denominations in America, and that is all on the Christian side. Where will there be this common medium which doesn't ostracize somebody?

I personally—or you personally—take my religious beliefs, attitudes, very seriously. And of course, we could sit up here and disagree like I don't know what. And so I just don't think that belongs in school. When it first came out, I was appalled, and then I got to thinking. After all, the church has got a job to do. Let the church do the job.

I'll tell you the background of where it came from. I'll tell you what. If you're going to have prayer, go on back and start teaching school for nothing and go on back and not let women teach if they're married. I don't care—they're tax supported, baby, tax supported.

ITASCO   He's a deep thinker, and I'm a little lighter. That's what I think. Because, see, I started my classrooms every morning with the prayer.

B.T.   I did too!

ITASCO   Little singing and pledge allegiance to the flag. See, that's just—I still believe in that. But no compulsion, you know.

B.T.   Well, most of the people in the United States are Christians. But Christianity is a very late religion; it is, sure. Even Judaism. They had a religion in China a thousand years before Judaism started. That's right—one thousand years. So I just say keep it out of the public system. I don't want to agree with Madalyn O'Hair and a lot of people are against it. But the thing about it is they shouldn't have let her have that leverage.

ITASCO   Madalyn O'Hair—you know, the atheist.

B.T.   She's the one who filed suit up there in Baltimore that caused the decision. They shouldn't have let her have that leverage. Any time somebody has a point—somebody has to have a point at least—you can't go by euphoria or hysteria. You can't go by being hysterical about something. After all, you can control a whole lot of people with emotions. That poor old woman is right. I don't like her because of what she said, but she's got a point.

ITASCO   With his deep thinking, he can't. The preacher can't.

B.T.   I don't believe in emotionalizing.

Note

1. Thad Sitton and Milan C. Rowold, *Ringing the Children In : Texas County Schools* (College Station: Texas A & M University Press, 1987), 18–19.

CONCLUSION

The teachers in this book are full of contrasts, like the land and communities in which they worked. The same women who quietly surrendered their jobs for marriage contracts in the 1920s became by the 1950s the first generation who in large numbers combined lifelong professional careers outside the home with child-rearing and family life. These pioneers lived and worked in an environment they helped to alter even as they grew within it and demonstrated personal qualities that helped them succeed despite the constraints that defeated others of their generation.

ENVIRONMENTAL CONTEXT

In the United States and other English-speaking countries teaching has been an occupation particularly suited to women and dominated by them.[1] Although today's feminists may view yesterday's teachers as less significant in opening full-time careers to women than those who pioneered in male-dominated fields, such an interpretation risks perpetuating the notion that because teaching is "female" it is also inferior. As Susan B. Anthony said more than a century ago to a group of male teachers debating about why they lacked respect, "None of you quite comprehend the cause of the disrespect of which you complain. Do you not see that so long as society says a woman is incompetent to be a lawyer, a minister, or doctor, but has ample ability to be a teacher, that every man of you who chooses that profession tacitly acknowledge that he has no more brains than a woman . . . ? Would you really exalt your profession, exalt those who labor with you."[2]

A long history explains why teaching is viewed as "women's work." In colonial times, enterprising women established dame schools in their own homes, and schoolmarms brought literacy to children on the expanding

174

frontier. The teaching assignments of these professional women, however, were limited to young children at the early stages of learning. Until the 1920s males usually had responsibility for the "more important," "intellectually challenging" subjects and older scholars, and today men continue to dominate as principals and school administrators. Similarly, today's university professors are mostly men, including those in colleges and departments of education, some of which have never tenured a woman.[3]

It is clear that women teachers have experienced job discrimination just as have women in other professions. In fact, some might argue that the discrimination they experienced was more rife than for women in other fields since, in spite of their greater numbers, they were unable to enjoy the benefits of decent wages, career advancement, and job security equally with men. Moreover, women teachers were singled out for discriminatory practices not imposed on any other professionals. Only women teachers were forbidden by written contract from marrying in many communities. This was the most costly and humiliating intrusion into their private lives and continued until World War II, but there were many others. The length of one's skirt, the number of petticoats worn, and the gauge of one's stocking were regulated by a school teacher's employers.

Given the significant number of women teachers and the discriminatory restrictions that they endured that were not imposed on other working women, a nagging question arises about whether the prohibition against marriage and other personal restrictions probably could not have existed without at least the tacit collusion of a substantial proportion of the "oppressed."[4] If there were collusion against marriage by women teachers, however, then we must ask what benefits would have accrued to the participants through these practices.

In a world that offered almost no professional options to women—and few economic alternatives to being supported by a man—permitting only unmarried women to teach actually offered a woman who *chose* not to marry a safe haven. As Stella Miles Franklin quipped, "Any fool can get married, but it takes a devilishly clever woman to remain an old maid."[5] Once a teacher decided to remain single (or the decision was made for her), the stricture against marriage helped define her professional status, protected her job from dilettantes, and buttressed her intentions to remain independent and single. At the same time, society's need to provide a socially approved income for women who lacked men to finance them also was met in a way that fulfilled a useful function in the community.

In addition to economic advantages, single women and society may have found psychological advantages to desexualizing the role of teachers by prohibiting marriage and subsequent pregnancies. Single women and society had an interest in preserving teachers as "pure" and sexless.

Unmarried teachers may have been seen as sacrificing themselves for a higher calling, thereby elevating the status of their profession. As was the case for a Roman Catholic nun, societal rules that restricted a teacher's sexual behavior also helped to protect her from unwanted male attention. It was not until the arrival of the birth control pill and the sexual revolution in the 1960s that efforts to protect unmarried women in general (such as strict rules about dormitory living) and teachers in particular were relaxed.

The prohibition against marriage also may have reflected a Victorian need to protect children from viewing pregnancy in their teachers. (Presumably their mothers could be trusted to be sufficiently discrete in this regard!) Support for this idea is provided by the pre–World War II exception to the prohibition against marriage made for a teacher who had a "condition" that prevented her from becoming pregnant.[6] Even through the 1970s pregnant married teachers were forced to resign as soon as they began "to show." The older the students (and the more knowledgeable about the mechanics of sex), the earlier their pregnant teachers had to resign, as I heard from a principal during a job interview in the mid-1960s.

The rule against marriage is particularly repressive, however, in light of the generally accepted view that marriage for women is desirable. The idea that a woman could *prefer* to remain single has not caught the popular imagination in America. The well-known figure in nineteenth-century British literature of the genteel but destitute young woman who is forced into service as a governess as an alternative to starvation (at least until her wealthy male-rescuer could arrive) was transported to America as the local schoolmarm. For some women teaching may have been a necessary evil that helped solve unwanted financial exigencies, but other women saw teaching as an escape from marrying the local farmer, sharing his life in the fields, quite possibly dying young in childbirth, and certainly being worn out at forty. Catherine Beecher glorified teaching as a "respectable alternative to marriage" and "a profession offering influence and independence."[7] A woman who preferred working to being somebody's wife would consider a prohibition against mixing marriage and a career consistent with her interests.

The prohibition against marriage also may have served women who wanted a career for a few years and then marriage but not the two simultaneously. This group may not have existed prior to the development of a middle class in an industrialized society that could afford to think about the luxury of working or not, by choice, after an extended period of professional training. It would include women who wanted (or whose parents wanted for them) the security of professional skills in the event that their husbands' resources failed them for any reason.

The issue of whether some women preferred to reserve teaching for the unmarried cannot be resolved by the testimony of the interviewees. Readers must draw their own conclusions. Consistent with her proportion in the general population of women who became teachers, only one interviewee, Ethyl Scott, remained unmarried. Her history indicates that she was more successful in terms of climbing a career ladder than the other women, but she offers no opinions on teaching and matrimony.

Whatever its possible benefits to some, the prohibition against marriage did hamper many women teachers financially. Several interviewees remarked on the number of women teachers who married late or who married or lived with a man in secret, presumably to preserve their careers. Even married women who were able to teach during most of their adult lives often took a hiatus from teaching when their children were young. The degree to which their choice was unencumbered from social and spousal pressures is sometimes unclear. Then, too, in a world where men's protests were heard more clearly than women's, not having husbands to speak up about poor salaries, pensions, and working conditions lessened the possibility of change. Old maid schoolmarms did not spearhead teaching reform, and the erosion of the "oath of poverty" described by B.T. Wilson did not really begin until after World War II when greater numbers of women with husbands and men on the G.I. Bill entered teaching.

Other less pervasive intrusions into teachers' lives also may have been tacitly welcomed by some teachers, but that does not mean they were appropriate or embraced by the majority. At the very least, these petty restrictions provide examples of how teachers were infantilized by school administrators and the community. For example, Sibyl Sutherland recalls being criticized for breaking the rules imposed on teachers by principals for giving students permission to go to the bathroom. The incongruity of treating a woman who found a way to finance her entire college education during the depression and walked ten miles one way each day to obtain it as if she was incompetent to decide when and how children should go to the bathroom is obvious. The passage of time may have won teachers the right to marry at will, but more mundane decisions often remain outside their purview even today.

The restrictive aspects of a teaching career for women are only half the story, however. Despite the obvious handicaps prior to World War II for women who wanted to teach and be married, teaching's overall economic impact on women teachers has been positive. Their salaries and pensions were woefully inadequate—forcing Elizabeth Shelton, for one, to begin a second teaching career at age sixty-five—but women teachers fared better than women who lacked any profession at all. Almost all the interviewees regarded teaching as their only "decent" choice and being "washtub number two" as a far less attractive alternative than the classroom. A young widow like Elizabeth at least had a profession, however low-paying, to support herself and her children.

Women who were scarcely more than children themselves when they began teaching found a way to gain independence from their parental families, to support themselves, and, of paramount importance, to finance their own college educations and professional training. They also managed to maintain, and in some cases rise above, their parents' socio-economic success levels. This distinguishes them from others of their generation who came from backgrounds similar to theirs but who gave up their professional dreams because they did not foresee a way to finance their own college educations. The teachers may have mopped and dusted the library like Ethyl Scott or washed dishes for forty other students like Sibyl Sutherland, but they earned their own educations. They also continued to work on their degrees and careers even after marriage and children, as witnessed by Knowles Teel who boarded in San Antonio with her baby son so she could graduate with the first master's class in elementary education at Trinity College.

Today's college woman who is planning to enter a profession that traditionally was closed to women of the interviewees' era may find it difficult to understand how someone as capable as Elizabeth Shelton could give up her dream of being a lawyer. A few women of that generation *did* break through the barriers of prejudice and become attorneys and physicians. An even smaller number managed to combine their careers with marriage and a family. Their accomplishments are admirable, but so is the elegance of the compromise made by women teachers who took smaller risks, made smaller advances toward equal employment opportunities, and succeeded more often in combining career and family goals. Parents of young women like Gladys and Sibyl and Elizabeth gave them good, if not daring, advice to be teachers. For women of their generation who wanted both a career and a marriage with a future, teaching was an excellent choice.

Teaching afforded post–World War II women a realistic opportunity to combine lifelong careers with successful marriages and child-rearing. Thus, women who became teachers and remained in that career until retirement were as significant pioneers for women's rights as those who became business executives or wartime factory workers. They succeeded because at the beginning of their careers they enjoyed a supportive social milieu; in their middle years they took advantage of a need for teachers during World War II that permitted their return to their classrooms; and finally, once having exercised their right to teach as married women, they continued to do so. Because these women did not return to their homes once the war crisis had passed, they helped make full-time careers socially acceptable for wives and mothers. Just as today's working women help society accept women in less traditional jobs, teachers became role models for other women and provided daily proof to their students, male and female, that women can become capable professionals.

Practically speaking, combining a family and a career was difficult prior to World War II even for women who could succeed in overcoming the first hurdle—adequate professional training. The labor involved in raising a family and maintaining a home without modern appliances, easily prepared foods, and other life-style supports made it a physical hardship for women of average means to develop a second career outside the home. Teaching, with its shorter hours and extended vacation periods, afforded the best opportunity for career-minded married women to succeed both at home and in the workplace. This was particularly true, of course, once the prohibition against marriage was lifted during World War II when the shortage of teachers in the schoolroom prompted a lifting of old barriers.

Even when the prohibition against marriage was lifted, married women teachers, then as now, experienced some tension between the pull of the workplace and the lure of the home. Compared to other professions, however, such as medicine and law, the cultural norms accepted a career for women teachers. Even "emancipated" women are not free of their cultural context, although today this context tends to support married women's decisions to work outside the home, for usually one wage-earner alone can no longer maintain the middle-class life-style and upwardly mobile strivings expected of young American families.

Acknowledging that teaching offered women a greater degree of social support than other professions did is not to negate its limitations. Social support was (and perhaps still is) strong for women only when and where there were teacher shortages, such as in remote rural areas and during World War II. Even when social support was present, personal obstacles often intruded, especially parental, spousal, and financial impediments. Every teacher in this book faced and overcame at least one of these obstacles. Black teachers faced racial discrimination as well. All are among the "succeeders" of their generation.

The status of teaching in the American job hierarchy is another important issue uncovered by these oral histories. To those outside of education, and even to many in the field, teaching's identification as a "feminine" occupation has diminished its professional status. Recent writers on teaching, such as David Tyack, also describe women as scapegoats for the lack of professionalism in education.[8]

Although today the status of teaching may be unclear to many, the women in this book have a sure and certain image of what their profession meant to them, their families, and the people in their communities.

Frequent allusions are made to the high esteem in which teachers were held by themselves and others. Even more than a suitable career, teaching was a "calling" almost as sacred as the ministry is to others. With their shared religious-civic values[9] teachers believed they were helping to establish a millennial vision of America as, literally, God's country.

PERSONAL CHARACTERISTICS

The changed social environment contributed greatly to the conditions that finally allowed post–World War II teachers to become the first large group of women to combine a profession with a decent home life, but it was the efforts of individuals like those who have told their stories in this book that effected this change in the first place. A closer examination of these women's personal characteristics may provide clues as to why some succeeded.

The word *compromise* sometimes takes on a "second best" connotation that it may not deserve. For psychoanalysts it has a special meaning: a means to resolve conflicts within the self and conflicts with the environment.[10] The women of this generation who became teachers were successful because they were good compromisers. Rachael Luna is a prime example. As a young woman she wanted to have a career "on stage" and to be "in love," but she also knew that her environment mandated that love be consummated in marriage, home, and family. Teaching provided a compromise opportunity to match both her psychological needs to be "on stage" and "in love" with the social pressures for traditional marriage.

All the teachers in the book found teaching to be a good compromise between internal desires and external reality. Rachael and Elizabeth found self-expression and personal fulfillment through teaching when their first-choice careers were put aside; Knowles Teel and Gladys Meyers believed teaching was their true first choice. These seven women and one black man made realistic assessments of their personal, familial, and professional goals and weighed them against the societal constraints and opportunities of the time. They artfully balanced the conflicting elements of their internal and external worlds with the limited resources available to launch them on professional careers and therefore may be seen as highly successful individuals. Teachers of this generation, then, were successful because they integrated personal, familial, and social goals. As Susan B. Anthony said, everyone is enriched when compatibility between home and occupational goals is seen as a virtue.

All of these good compromisers have remained active into old age. Although they have retired from paid jobs, all have undertaken activities that engage their energies—poetry for Knowles; community service (what Rachael calls "doing these little freebie jobs") for Elizabeth, Gladys,

Itasco, and Rachael; working in the craft shop and doing the accounts at the Senior Citizens' Center for Scottie; playing with his jazz ensemble for B.T.; and reading for Sibyl.

As they learned to become good compromisers, the interviewees received guidance from three external sources. First, all had the active encouragement of at least one parent who supported their career choice: Sibyl, Gladys, and Scottie had mothers who wanted them to be self-sufficient; Elizabeth's father wanted her to be "a lady," and that meant being a teacher; Knowles, B.T. and Itasco, and Rachael had the support of both parents and also a teacher-mother as a role model. Second, all the married women had husbands who generally were supportive of their careers, even when community pressures dictated that the husband was supposed to be the sole breadwinner. Third, the interviewees were skillful in identifying with positive role models both within and outside their families: Rachael Luna and Gladys Meyers both recently attended funerals of the women they had boarded with as young, first-year teachers and spoke movingly to me about the significance these women had in their lives.

Several personal characteristics enabled these teachers to succeed. The trait of being reality-oriented dominated, as did the ability to extract positive elements from almost every situation and to emphasize them over negative aspects. Even those individuals who reported some unhappy periods in life, like Sibyl, tended to emphasize the good times. Nevertheless, the interviewees were realistic about the difficulties they faced and, like Elizabeth, were capable of openly acknowledging negative aspects of life. Partially because they were skillful at choosing realistic goals, they were equally adept at overcoming adversity. Failure was never mentioned as a possibility in any of the oral histories. Even a great personal loss, such as the closing of Doyle School, was turned into an opportunity to continue to serve others. Similarly, the interviewees took pride in their own accomplishments: they neither minimized their achievements nor spent much energy dreaming of what might have been; they knew they had made a contribution and were satisfied with it.

Humor can smooth over difficult times, and Scottie and Rachael had a knack for recreating a humorous situation, but the other teachers shared their ability to find the funny side of life.

These teachers could inspire and respond to help from other people and could make the most of the opportunities they were given. Turning difficult situations into periods of growth was a hallmark of Itasco and B.T. Wilson and others. Righteous anger over the inequitable and repressive rules imposed on teachers was heard most clearly in Rachael's and Elizabeth's words, but no one complied unquestioningly with situations they considered to be unjust.

A strong sense of the community and of their role and responsibility in it was another dominant theme in these narratives. For Gladys and Knowles this was formalized in social work responsibilities. Other teachers' care and concern for their students' well being was often demonstrated outside the classroom, including Elizabeth's and Sybil's helping motherless girls style their hair. Community awareness included a firm sense of what was "right" and "correct" behavior for women in general and for teachers in particular. Often the two were interconnected, even in small ways, such as Knowles's wanting to smell pretty for her students. The attachment of teachers to the community was perhaps stronger in rural areas than in any other localities.

Finally, whatever their first dreams may have been, they were transformed into an altruistic mission of service to others. Knowles's story of her development from a "mean" little girl to a teacher and poet traced the route taken by others as well. Although none of the teachers spoke directly of the spiritual quality attached to their profession, their words implied that they felt they had answered a higher calling. Time will tell whether their sense of mission is a legacy for future generations to share or an anachronism already passing out of memory.

Notes

1. Janina Trotman, "Job for the Girls: Family Ideology and the Employment of Women in Education," *Australian Journal of Education* 28, no. 2 (1984):132–44.

2. Elizabeth Cady Stanton, Susan B. Anthony, and Matilda Joclyn Gage, eds., *The History of Women's Suffrage*, vol. 1 (Rochester, N.Y.: Fowler and Wells, 1887), 514.

3. *Tufts University* [*Bulletin*] (Medford, Mass.: Tufts University, 1988), 125.

4. Sherna B. Gluck asked a similar question in *Rosie the Riveter Revisited: Women, War, and Social Change* (Boston: Twayne, 1987; p. 50) about the women who quietly returned to their homes once the crisis that permitted their entry into "men's" jobs was ended.

5. Julia Britton, *Miles Franklin and the Rainbow's End* (Adelaide, South Australia: The Stage Company, 1984), 1.

6. Personal observation, Edward H. Knight, M.D., New Orleans.

7. Kathryn Kis Sklar, *Catherine Beecher: A Study in American Domesticity* (New Haven, Conn.: Yale University Press, 1973), 97.

8. David Tyack, "An American Tradition: The Changing Role of Schooling and Teaching. Was There Ever a Golden Age in Teaching?," *Harvard Educational Review* 57, no. 2 (1987):171–74.

9. Tyack, "An American Tradition," 173.

10. Paul A. Deald, *Psychotherapy: A Dynamic Approach*, 2d ed. (New York: Basic Books, 1969), 53.

BIBLIOGRAPHY

Agre, G. P., and B. J. Finkelstein. "Feminism in School Reform: The Last Fifteen Years." *Teachers College Record* 80, no.2 (1978):307–15.

Anderson, N. D. "I Remember Springdale School." *Rural Educator* 8, no. 2 (1986):1–3.

Barker, B., and I. Muse. "One-Room Schools of Nebraska, Montana, South Dakota, California and Wyoming." *Research in Rural Education* 3, no. 2 (1986): 127–30.

Barker, R. R., and P. V. Gump. *Big School, Small School.* Stanford, Calif.: Stanford University Press, 1964.

Beecher, C. *The Evils Suffered by American Women and American Children: The Causes and the Remedy.* New York: Harper and Row, 1846.

Berkeley, K. C. "The Ladies Want to Bring about Reform in the Public Schools: Public Education and Women's Rights in the Post-Civil War South." *History of Education Quarterly* 24, no. 1 (1984):45–58.

Biklen, S. "Schoolteaching Professionalism and Gender." *Teacher Education Quarterly* 14, no. 2 (1987):17–24.

———. "Can Elementary Schoolteaching Be a Career? A Search for New Ways of Understanding Women's Work." *Issues in Education* 3, no. 3 (1985):215–31.

Binder, F. M. *The Age of the Common School, 1830–1865.* New York: Wiley, 1974.

Bralley, F. M. *Consolidation of Rural Schools.* Texas *State Department Bulletin No. 15* (1912):5.

Butler, N. M. *Across the Busy Years,* Vols. 1–2. New York: Charles Scribner's Sons, 1939.

Callahan, R. E. *Education and the Cult of Efficiency.* Chicago: University of Chicago Press, 1962.

Carney, M. *Country Life and the Country School.* Chicago: Row, Peterson, 1912.

Caro, R. *The Years of Lyndon Johnson: The Path to Power.* New York: Knopf, 1982.

Clifford, G. J. "Home and School in 19th Century America: Some Personal-Historical Reports from the United States." *History of Education Quarterly* 18, no. 1 (1978):3–34.

———"Saints, Sinners, and People: A Position Paper on the Historiography of American Education." *History of Education Quarterly* 15, no. 3 (1975):257–72.

Conway, J. *The Female Experience in 18th and 19th Century America: A Guide to the History of American Women.* New York: Garland, 1982.

Cremin, L. *The American Common School: An Historic Conception.* New York: Bureau of Publications, Teachers College, Columbia University, 1951.

Cuban, L. *How Teachers Taught: Constancy and Change in American Classrooms, 1890–1980.* New York: Longman, 1984.

Cubberly, E. P. *Rural Life and Education: A Study of the Rural School Problem as a Phase of the Rural-Life Problem.* Boston: Houghton Mifflin, 1914.

Donovan, Frances R. *The Schoolma'am.* New York: Frederick A. Stokes Co., 1938.

Eby, F. *The Development of Education in Texas.* New York: Macmillan, 1923.

———*Education in Texas: Source Materials.* Bulletin no. 1824. Austin: University of Texas, 1918.

Educational Policies Commission, *Research Memorandum on Education in the Depression.* Bulletin no. 28. New York: Social Science Research Council, 1937.

Etzioni, A., ed. *The Semi-Professions and Their Organization.* New York: Free Press, 1969.

Finkelstein, B. J. "Schooling and Schoolteachers: Selected Bibliography of Autobiographies in the Nineteenth Century." *History of Education Quarterly* 14, no. 2 (1974):293–301.

Fowler, S. B. *The Character of the Woman Teacher during Her Emergency as a Full-Time Professional in 19th Century America: Stereotypes vs. Personal Histories.* Boston: Boston University, 1985.

Fuller, W. E. *The Old Country School: The Story of Rural Education in the Middle West.* Chicago: University of Chicago Press, 1982.

Gershenberg, I. "The Negro and the Development of White Public Education in the South: Alabama, 1880–1930." *Journal of Negro Education* 39, no. 1 (1970):50–59.

Goodenow, R. K. and Arthur O. White, eds. *Education and the Rise of the New South.* Boston: G.K. Hall, 1982.

Graham, H. D. *The Uncertain Triumph: Federal Education-Policy in the Kennedy and Johnson Years.* Chapel Hill: University of North Carolina Press, 1984.

Hoffman, N. *Woman's "True" Profession, Voices from the History of Teaching.* New York: McGraw-Hill, 1981.

Jenson, J. "Not Only Ours but Others: The Quaker Teaching Daughters of the Mid-Atlantic, 1790–1850." *History of Education Quarterly* 24, no. 1 (1984):3–19.

Johnson, C. *The Country School in New England.* New York: D. Appleton, 1895.

———*Old Time Schools and School Books.* 1904, reprinted, New York: Dover, 1963.

Jordan, G. J. *Yesterday in the Texas Hill Country.* College Station: Texas A&M University Press, 1979.

Kaufman, P. W. *Women Teachers on the Frontier.* New Haven: Yale University Press, 1984.

Kirby, D. "Contributions of the Country Cousins." *Rural Educator* 6, no. 2 (1984–85):12–13.

Knight, E. W., ed. *A Documentary History of Education in the South.* 5 vols. Chapel Hill: University of North Carolina Press, 1949–53.

Laird, S. "Reforming 'Woman's True Profession.' A Case for 'Feminist Pedagogy' in Teacher Education?" *Harvard Educational Review* 58, no. 4 (1988):449–63.

Lortie, D. *Schoolteacher.* Chicago: University of Chicago Press, 1975.

Lightfoot, S. "The Lives of Teachers." In *Handbook of Teaching and Policy,* edited by L. Shulman and G. Sykes, 241–60. New York: Longman, 1983.

Link, W. A. *A Hard Country and a Lonely Place: Schooling, Society, and Reform in Rural Virginia 1870–1920.* Chapel Hill: University of North Carolina Press, 1986.

Martin, J. R. "Excluding Women from the Educational Realm." *Harvard Educational Review* 52, no. 2 (1982):133–48.

Mason, W., R. J. Dressel, and R. K. Bain. "Sex Roles and Career Orientations of Beginning Teachers." *Harvard Educational Review* 29, no. 4 (1959):370–83.

Mattingly, P. *The Classless Profession.* New York: New York University Press, 1975.

McPherson, G. *Small Town Teachers.* Cambridge: Harvard University Press, 1972.

Mullinax, Jane P. "The Schoolhouse Southern Style: One Year in a Country School." *Georgia Social Science Journal* 18, no. 1 (1987):1–7.

Nasaw, D. *Schooled to Order: A Social History of Public Schooling in the United States.* New York: Oxford University Press, 1979.

Nelson, M. "From the One-Room Schoolhouse to the Graded School: Teaching in Vermont, 1920–1950." *Frontiers* 7, no. 3 (1983):14–20.

Norton, Arthur O., ed. *The First State Normal School in America: The Journals of Cyrus Pierce and Mary Swift.* Cambridge: Harvard University Press, 1926.

Putnam, C. "Small Schools and Continuing Education." *Journal of Rural and Small Schools* 1, no. 1 (1986):17–18.

Ravitch, D. *The Great School Wars.* New York: Basic Books, 1974.

Roden, D. "From 'Old Miss' to New Professional: A Portrait of Women Educators under the American Occupation of Japan, 1945–1952." *History of Education Quarterly* 23, no. 4 (1983):469–89.

Ryan, Mary P. *Womanhood in America.* New York: Franklin Watts, 1975.

Sands, L. "Jesse Stuart: Lessons from the Kentucky Hills." *Journal of Rural and Small Schools* 1, no. 1 (1986): 13–14.

Schmuck, P. *Women Educators: Employees of Schools in Western Countries.* Albany: State University of New York Press, 1987.

"The School Mistress." *Harper's New Monthly Magazine,* September 1878, 607–11.

Schwager, S. "Educating Women in America." *Signs: Journal of Women in Culture and Society* 12, no. 2 (1987):333–72.

Shaw, A. M. "Common Sense Country Schools." *The World's Work* 8 (June 1904):4883–94.

Sher, Jonathan, P. and Rachel B. Tompkins. "The Myths of Rural School and District Consolidation, Part II." *Educational Forum* 40, no. 2 (1977):141.

Sitton, Thad, and Milam C. Rowold. *Ringing the Children In: Texas Country Schools.* College Station: Texas A&M University Press, 1987.

Sklar, Kathryn. *Catherine Beecher.* New Haven: Yale University Press, 1973.

Spenser, D. *Contemporary Women Teachers.* New York: Longman, 1986.

———"The Home and School Lives of Women Teachers." *Elementary School Journal* 84, no. 3 (1984):283–98.

Sterling, D. *Black Fore-mothers: Three Lives.* Old Westbury, N.Y.: The Feminist Press, 1979.

Sterling, P. *The Real Teachers.* New York: Random House, 1972.

Strober, M. H., and D. B. Tyack. *Sexual Asymmetry in Educational Employment: Male Managers and Female Teachers* (draft report). Palo Alto, Calif.: Stanford University Institute for Research on Educational Finance and Governance, February 1979.

Terrill, T. E., and J. Hirsch, eds. *Such As Us: Southern Voices of the Thirties.* Chapel Hill: University of North Carolina Press, 1978.

Texas Retired Teachers Association. *As We Remember.* Austin, Texas: TRTA, 1976.

Trotman, J. "Jobs for the Girls: Family Ideology and the Employment of Women in Education." *The Australian Journal of Education* 20, no. 2 (1984):132–44.

Tyack, D. *The One Best System.* Cambridge: Harvard University Press, 1974.

Tyack, D., and E. Hansot. *Managers of Virtue.* New York: Basic Books, 1982.

Tyack, D., R. Lowe, and E. Hansot. *Public Schools in Hard Times: The Great Depression and Recent Years.* Cambridge: Harvard University Press, 1984.

Wyatt-Brown, B. "Black Schooling during Reconstruction." In *The Web of Southern Social Relations: Women, Family, and Education,* edited by W. J. Fraser, R. Frank Saunders, and J.L. Wakelyn, 146–65. Athens: University of Georgia Press, 1985.

INDEX

ABOUT THE AUTHOR

Diane Thompson Manning is an associate professor in and former chair of the Department of Education at Tulane University and a research candidate at the New Orleans Psychoanalytic Institute. Like many of the teachers in this book, Manning became a teacher because her parents thought it was a good career for a woman. After graduating from Tufts University she became an English teacher in a rural school in her native Connecticut, earned advanced degrees in English and education, became a reading consultant and English-as-a-second-language teacher in an urban college laboratory school, and in 1970 obtained her Ph.D. in education from the University of Connecticut, where she was hired to direct a center to train teachers for urban schools. She later became an assistant professor of education at Tufts and a member of the Department of Behavioral Sciences at Harvard University's School of Public Health, where she earned her master's degree in public health in 1980.